TRANSITIONAL JUSTICE FROM BELOW

Although relatively new as a distinct field of study, transitional justice has become rapidly established as a vital field of enquiry. From vaguely exotic origins on the outer edges of political science, the study of 'justice' in times of transition has emerged as a central concern of scholarship and practical policy-making. A process of institutionalisation has confirmed this importance. The ICTY, the ICTR, the ICC, hybrid tribunals in Sierra Leone and East Timor and 'local' processes such as the Iraqi Higher Tribunal (IHT) have energised international law and international criminal justice scholarship. The South African TRC was for a time lauded as the model for dealing with the past and remains one of the most researched institutions in the world. It is one of approximately two dozen such institutions established in different transitional contexts over the past 20 years to assist conflicted societies to come to terms with a violent past. At the national level, international donors contribute huge sums of money to 'Rule of Law' programmes designed to transform national justice systems.

This collection seeks to offer something quite different to the mainstream of scholarship in this area, emphasising the need for bespoke solutions to different transitions rather than 'off-the-shelf' models. The collection is designed to offer a space for diversity, prompted by a series of perspectives 'from below' of societies beset by past violent conflict, which have sought to effect their transition to justice. In doing so the contributors have also sought to enrich discussion about the role of human rights in transition, the continuing usefulness of perspectives 'from above', and the still contested meanings of 'transition'.

Volume 14: Human Rights Law in Perspective

HUMAN RIGHTS LAW IN PERSPECTIVE

General Editor: Colin Harvey

The language of human rights figures prominently in legal and political debates at the national, regional and international levels. In the UK the Human Rights Act 1998 has generated considerable interest in the law of human rights. It will continue to provoke much debate in the legal community and the search for original insights and new materials will intensify.

The aim of this series is to provide a forum for scholarly reflection on all aspects of the law of human rights. The series will encourage work which engages with the theoretical, comparative and international dimensions of human rights law. The primary aim is to publish over time books which offer an insight into human rights law in its contextual setting. The objective is to promote an understanding of the nature and impact of human rights law. The series is inclusive, in the sense that all perspectives in legal scholarship are welcome. It will incorporate the work of new and established scholars.

Human Rights Law in Perspective is not confined to consideration of the UK. It will strive to reflect comparative, regional and international perspectives. Work which focuses on human rights law in other states will therefore be included in this series. The intention is to offer an inclusive intellectual home for significant scholarly contributions to human rights law.

Volume 1 Importing the Law in Post-Communist Transitions
Catherine Dupré

Volume 2 The Development of the Positive Obligations Under the European Convention on Human Rights by the European Court of Human Rights
Alastair Mowbray

Volume 3 Human Rights Brought Home: Socio-Legal Studies of Human Rights in the National Context
Edited by Simon Halliday and Patrick Schmidt

Volume 4 Corporations and Transnational Human Rights Litigation
Sarah Joseph

Volume 5 Human Rights in the Community: Rights as Agents for Change
Edited by Colin Harvey

Volume 6 Human Rights, Culture and the Rule of Law
Jessica Almqvist

Volume 7 Property and the Human Rights Act 1998
Tom Allen

Transitional Justice from Below

Grassroots Activism and the Struggle for Change

Edited by

KIERAN MCEVOY AND
LORNA MCGREGOR

·HART·
PUBLISHING

OXFORD AND PORTLAND, OREGON
2008

Published in North America (US and Canada) by
Hart Publishing
c/o International Specialized Book Services
920 NE 58th Avenue, Suite 300
Portland, OR 97213–3786
USA
Tel: +1 503 287 3093 or toll-free: (1) 800 944 6190
Fax: +1 503 280 8832
E-mail: orders@isbs.com
Website: www.isbs.com

Hart Publishing, 16C Worcester Place, OX1 2JW
Telephone: +44 (0)1865 517530 Fax: +44 (0)1865 510710
E-mail: mail@hartpub.co.uk
Website: http://www.hartpub.co.uk

British Library Cataloguing in Publication Data
Data Available

ISBN: 978-1-84113-821-3

Typeset by Columns Design Ltd, Reading
Printed and bound in Great Britain by
TJ International Ltd, Padstow, Cornwall

This book is dedicated to Órlaith Rachel McEvoy, a shiny wee button who brightened up the world during its preparation, and to Susan and Sam McGregor for all your love and support.

Series Editor's Preface

The field of transitional justice has emerged as a significant area of study and practical engagement. This edited book provides a distinctive contribution and offers a challenge to mainstream approaches. Mapping established metaphors of hierarchy, these scholars advance a 'from below' perspective. The aim is to create the space for marginalised voices to be heard and listened to, and therefore promote a more inclusive view of transitional processes. This collection is a timely and welcome addition to the Series.

Colin Harvey
Belfast
June 2008

Acknowledgements

This collection began life as series of increasingly animated conversations when we were both associated with the Human Rights Program (HRP) at Harvard Law School. We are both grateful for the encouragement offered by a number of key individuals on that program, in particular Henry Steiner, Peter Rosenblum and Jim Cavellero, as well as the support the HRP provided to Lorna McGregor in order to conduct her research in Ireland and her work as a Henigson Fellow in Sri Lanka. We are also very thankful to the contributors to the collection who have endured its long gestation with good grace and accepted our interminable commenting and re-commenting with professionalism and humour.

In Belfast Kieran McEvoy has also benefited from the encouragement of friends and colleagues in particular Kirsten McConnachie, Louise Mallinder, and Ron Dudai—all of whom took time out of their own busy research careers to offer comments and advice on various chapters in the book. John Morison, Shadd Maruna, Pete Shirlow, Jack Anderson and Gordon Anthony all gave good advice when the going got tough. This collection has also benefited from the input and example of those who actually *do* transitional justice from below, in particular Maggie Beirne, Brandon Hamber, Kate Turner, Mike Ritchie, Jim Auld, Harry Maguire, Debbie Watters, Harry Mika and Tom Winston. As ever, Lesley McEvoy combined a keen a critical eye with considerable forbearance.

Lorna McGregor would also like to thank Fionnuala Ni Aolain, Adrienne Reilly, Christine Bell, Colm Campbell, Carla Ferstman, Gabriela Echeverria, Alan Keenan, Ramani Muttettuwegama, Vasuki Nesiah, Kristen Sandvik, Annecoos Wiersema, Mark Ellis, Fiona Paterson, Mahmuda Ali, Moses Adriko, Angelina Namakula and Stephen Lamony who over the years have provided great help, support and the space for discussion and the exchange of ideas relating to the themes of this collection.

Finally we would like to thank Colin Harvey, our series editor, and Richard Hart, our publisher, for their encouragement and their enthusiasm for all things scholarly.

Kieran McEvoy and Lorna McGregor
January 2008

Table of Contents

The Contributors

The Editors

Kieran McEvoy (LLB, MSc, PhD) is a Professor of Law and Transitional Justice and Director of the Institute of Criminology and Criminal Justice, School of Law, Queens University Belfast. He has held a number of visiting positions at Cambridge, Fordham, London School of Economics, Berkeley and New York University, and was a Fulbright Distinguished Scholar at Harvard in 2001–02. He has published widely in academic journals. His books include *Resistance, Management and Release: Paramilitary Imprisonment in Northern Ireland* (Oxford University Press, 2001) (Clarendon Series in Criminology—winner of the 2002 British Society of Criminology book of the year award); *Crime, Community and Locale* (Ashgate, 2000, with D O'Mahony, R Geary and J Morison); and *Criminology, Conflict Resolution and Restorative Justice* (Palgrave, 2003, ed with T Newburn); *Judges Human Rights and Transition* (Oxford University Press, 2007, ed with J Morison and G Anthony); *Truth, Transition and Reconciliation: Dealing with the Past in Northern Ireland* (Willan Publishing, 2008); *Beyond the Wire: Ex-prisoners and Conflict Transformation in Northern Ireland* (Pluto, 2008, with P Shirlow). He is currently undertaking a comparative research project funded by the Arts and Humanities Research Council (with Brice Dickson and Louise Mallinder) examining amnesties in the process of conflict transformation in Uganda, South Africa, Argentina, Uruguay and Bosnia.

Lorna McGregor is the International Legal Advisor at REDRESS where she undertakes litigation, policy, research and law reform work aimed at improving access to justice for torture survivors. She is a member of the International Bar Association's Taskforce on Extraterritorial Jurisdiction and a tutor in international law at SOAS. Prior to joining REDRESS, Lorna was a Programme Lawyer at the International Bar Association where she led the outreach component of its International Criminal Court (ICC) Monitoring and Outreach Programme, working with lawyers in Sudan and Uganda to develop advocacy and litigation strategies to combat impunity for ICC crimes. She has previously worked for REDRESS as the State Immunity Project Coordinator and in Sri Lanka as the Coordinator of the Transitional Justice Working Group. Lorna holds an LLB (Hons) from Edinburgh Law School, an LLM from Harvard Law School, where she was a Kennedy Memorial Trust Scholar and a Henigson Fellow, and is a member of the New York State Bar.

The Contributors

James Cavallaro and Sebastián Albuja

James Cavallaro is a Clinical Professor of Law at Harvard Law School and the Clinical Director of the Harvard Human Rights Program. For a decade prior to coming to Harvard in 2002, Cavallaro directed the Brazil office of Human Rights Watch and founded and directed the Global Justice Center, a leading rights organisation in Brazil and Latin America. He has written more than a dozen human rights reports and books on rights abuse and practice, released by Human Rights Watch and the International Council on Human Rights Policy. His academic work has been published in the *Hastings Law Journal*, the *California Law Review*, the *British Journal of Criminology*, the *University of Chicago Journal of International Law* and the *Harvard Human Rights Journal*. He holds a BA from Harvard College and a JD from University of California, Berkeley (Boalt Hall).

His article is co-authored with Sebastián Albuja who holds a BA and a JD from Universidad San Francisco de Quito and is currently a PhD candidate at Northeastern University. In addition to his academic research, Albuja has acted as legal counsel on a pro bono basis in a petition for precautionary measures to the Inter-American Commission on Human Rights aimed at protecting two indigenous groups in Ecuador.

Catalina Diaz

Catalina Diaz is a Colombian lawyer with wide professional experience in human rights and international humanitarian law. She is currently an Associate with the Bogotá Office of the International Center for Transitional Justice and has previously done advocacy work and advised grassroots, victim groups and local NGOs on several issues related to the protection of their individual and collective fundamental rights. In 2005 she obtained a masters degree (LLM) from New York University, where she received a Global Public Service Law fellowship. With NYU support, Catalina then completed country comparative research on reparations in context of massive human rights violations.

Patricia Lundy and Mark McGovern

Patricia Lundy is a senior lecturer in Sociology at the University of Ulster, Jordanstown. She has researched and written on the subject of 'truth-telling', community and conflict transformation. She has undertaken comparative research in South Africa, Guatemala and Chile on truth recovery processes and is particularly interested in community initiatives and transitional justice. She was co-author in 2002 of *Ardoyne: the Untold Truth*, published by Beyond the Pale publications. In 2005 she undertook a survey of attitudes to truth recovery processes in the North of Ireland, which was the first of its kind to have been undertaken in a society emerging from conflict. She has published in *Sociology*, *Peace Review*, *Words and Silences*, *Action Research*, *Journal of Law and Society* and is co-author of *Community, 'Truth-telling' and Conflict Resolution* (Belfast, Community Relations Council, 2005). Her most recent research is a critical analysis of the Historical Enquiries Team (PSNI), which is due to be published 2008.

Mark McGovern is a Reader in the Department of Social and Psychological Sciences, Edge Hill College of HE, Ormskirk, Lancashire. He has written widely on politics in the North of Ireland and published articles in *Capital and Class*, *Political Geography* and *Terrorism and Political Violence*. He was co-editor of *Who are the People?*, a collection of essays on Ulster Unionism, for Pluto Press. Along with Dr Lundy he has conducted comparative research on post-conflict transition and truth-telling processes in South Africa, Chile, Guatemala and Sri Lanka. Following co-authorship of *Ardoyne: the Untold Truth* in 2002 and the publication of the report *Community, 'Truth-telling' and Conflict Resolution* in 2005, he undertook a survey of attitudes towards Truth Commissions as part of the 2004 'Northern Ireland Life and Times Survey'. He has been the author of articles on truth and post-conflict transition for *Sociology*, *Peace Review*, *Words and Silences* and *Action Research*.

Kirsten McConnachie and John Morison

Kirsten McConnachie is a researcher at the School of Law, Queens University Belfast. She holds an LLB from the University of Glasgow, an LLM with distinction from the University of Nottingham and is a member of the New York State Bar. She has published in a number of areas including political imprisonment, state crime, and transitional justice and is co-author of the forthcoming monograph (with K McEvoy and H Mika) *Reconstructing Transitional Justice: Transforming Cultures of Violence 'From Below'* (Cambridge University Press, 2008). She has conducted fieldwork on transitional justice in Rwanda, South Africa, Northern Ireland, Sierra Leone and Colombia.

John Morison (LLB, PhD, University of Wales) is Professor of Jurisprudence and former Head of School at Queen's University Belfast and one of the founders of the Institute of Governance, Public Policy and Social Research at QUB. He is active in a number of international research groups and is a member of the Board of the European Public Law Centre. In 2005, he was appointed to the Northern Ireland Judicial Appointments Commission. His research interests are in public law generally as well as legal theory. He has written widely on British constitutionalism. Major books include: *The Barrister's World and the Nature of Law* (Open University, 1992, with P Leith); *Reshaping Public Power: Northern Ireland and the British Constitutional Problem* (Sweet and Maxwell, 1995, with S Livingstone); *Crime, Community and Locale* (Ashgate, 2000, with R Geary, K McEvoy and D O'Mahony); and the co-edited essay collections: *Law, Society and Change* (Gower, 1990, with S Livingstone); *Tall Stories? Reading Law and Literature* (Dartmouth, 1996, with C Bell); and *Judges, Transition and Human Rights* (Oxford University Press, 2007, with K McEvoy and G Anthony).

Laura Piacentini

Laura Piancentini is a Reader in Criminology in the School of Law, University of Strathclyde. Laura's main interest and publication profile is in the area of penal policy in transition and how ideology is communicated, disseminated and received into societies in transition, both in Scotland and internationally. The present day Russian prison system is the main focus of her research, particularly how prisoners and prison officers embrace and interpret new policy and ideological agendas and the political motivations underpinning these imports. She is currently researching the geography of punishment and penal exile as it relates to Russian women prisoners with colleagues at Birmingham and Oxford Universities. Her book, *Surviving Russian prisons: Punishment, Economy and Politics in Transition* (Willan Publishing, 2004), was awarded the British Society of Criminology book of the year award in 2005.

Naomi Roht-Arriaza and Laura Arriaza

Naomi Roht-Arriaza is a Professor in Law at the University of California, Hastings College of Law, where she teaches in the areas of international human rights, torts, and domestic and global environmental law and policy. Roht-Arriaza has published extensively on transitional justice issues and is the author of *The Pinochet Effect: Transnational Justice in the Age of Human Rights* (2005) and *Impunity and Human Rights in International Law and Practice* (1995), and co-editor of *Transitional Justice in the Twenty First Century: Beyond Truth Versus Justice* (Cambridge University Press, 2006, with J Mariecurrena). She is an associate editor of the Yearbook on International Environmental Law and continues to write on accountability, both state and corporate, for human rights violations as well as on other human rights, international criminal law and global environmental issues. She serves on the boards of human rights and environmental groups. She holds a BA from UC Berkeley, following which she worked for eight years as an organiser, journalist and paralegal in immigration law before returning to Berkeley to complete a law degree at Boalt Hall (graduating first in her class) and a Masters at the Graduate School of Public Policy.

Her chapter is co-authored with her daughter, Laura Arriaza, who recently graduated in Political Science from Tufts University and who has conducted extensive fieldwork on post-conflict grassroots accountability and reconciliation processes in Guatemala.

Elizabeth Stanley

Elizabeth Stanley is a Senior Lecturer in Criminology at Victoria University of Wellington, New Zealand. She researches, writes and teaches on the topics of state crime, human rights and social justice, truth commissions and international tribunals. She has undertaken in-depth primary research in Chile, South Africa and Timor Leste. In 2004, she was given the Young Scholar Award by the Australian and New Zealand Society of Criminology for her writing on torture. She has published widely in academic journals including *Punishment and Society* and the *British Journal of Criminology.*

1

Transitional Justice From Below: An Agenda for Research, Policy and Praxis

KIERAN MCEVOY & LORNA MCGREGOR

I INTRODUCTION

ALTHOUGH RELATIVELY NEW as a distinct field of study, transitional justice would appear to be in rude good health. From vaguely exotic origins on the outer edges of the political scientific study of regimes in transition,[1] the styles of 'justice' in times of transition have emerged as core business in scholarship and practical policy-making.[2] A process of institutionalisation has confirmed this importance. The International Criminal Tribunal for the Former Yugoslavia (ICTY), the International Criminal Tribunal for Rwanda (ICTR), the International Criminal Court (ICC), hybrid tribunals in places like Sierra Leone and East Timor and even manifestly flawed 'local' processes such as the Iraqi Higher Tribunal (IHT) have collectively energised international law and international criminal justice scholarship.[3] The South African Truth and Reconciliation Commission was for a time lauded as the model for dealing with

[1] S Huntingdon, *The Third Wave: Democratization in the Late Twentieth Century* (Norman OK, University of Oklahoma Press, 1991).

[2] R Teitel, *Transitional Justice* (Oxford, Oxford University Press, 2000); UNSC, Report of the Secretary General to the Security Council, 'The Rule of Law and Transitional Justice in Conflict and Post Conflict Societies', (23 August 2004) UN Doc S/2004/616, available online at http://daccessdds.un.org/doc/UNDOC/GEN/N04/395/29/PDF/N0439529.pdf.

[3] A Cassese, *International Criminal Law* (Oxford, Oxford University Press, 2003); W Schabas, *An Introduction to the International Criminal Court* (Cambridge, Cambridge University Press, 2004); R Kerr, *The International Criminal Tribunal for the Former Yugoslavia: An Exercise in Law, Politics, and Diplomacy* (Oxford, Oxford University Press, 2004); D McGoldrich, P Rowe, and E Donnelly (eds), *The Permanent International Criminal Court* (Oxford, Hart Publishing, 2004); C Bassiouni, 'Post-Conflict Justice in Iraq: An Appraisal of the Iraq Special Tribunal' (2006) 38 *Cornell International Law Journal* 101.

the past and remains one of the most researched institutions in the world.[4] It is one of approximately two dozen such institutions established in different transitional contexts over the past 20 years to assist conflicted societies to come to terms with a violent past.[5] At the national level, international donors contribute huge sums of money to 'Rule of Law' programmes designed to transform national justice systems.[6] Amongst the academic community, the proliferation of scholarly monographs, articles, conferences, specialist journals and entrepreneurial consultancies encourages a confident swagger in the field.

This collection emerged as a result of a series of conversations initially between the editors and then more broadly amongst the contributors over several years. Transitional Justice is and should be a contested space. There are differences and debates on substance and shades of emphasis in this collection, and we regard that as a virtue. Indeed, one of the motivating factors for the collection was to emphasise the need for bespoke solutions to different transitions rather than 'off-the-shelf' models. For example, such is the international prominence of the South African Truth and Reconciliation model that it is occasionally difficult to move debates on truth recovery in other local contexts beyond the parameters that it unwittingly established.[7] This collection is designed to offer a space for that diversity.

Heterogeneity accepted, a number of themes permeated the original conversations and are now reflected in the chapters contained herein.

II THE 'FROM BELOW' PERSPECTIVE

First, the contributors share a broad interest in the outworkings of transitional justice 'on the ground' in the communities or organisations which have been directly affected by violent conflict. The editors and many

[4] A Boraine and J Levy, *The Healing of a Nation?* (Cape Town, Justice in Transition, 1995); A Boraine, *A Country Unmasked* (Oxford, Oxford University Press, 2000); D Tutu, *No Future Without Forgiveness* (New York, Doubleday, 1999); P Van Zyl, 'Dilemmas of Transitional Justice: The Case of South Africa's Truth and Reconciliation Commission' (1999) 52 *Journal of International Affairs* 647; C Villa-Vicencio, 'A Different Kind of Justice: The South African Truth and Reconciliation Commission' (1999) 1 *Contemporary Justice Review* 403; C Villa-Vicencio, *Looking Back, Reaching Forward: Reflections on the Truth and Reconciliation Commission of South Africa* (Capetown, University of Cape Town Press, 2000); R Wilson, *The Politics of Truth and Reconciliation in South Africa* (Cambridge, Cambridge University Press, 2001).

[5] P Hayner, *Unspeakable Truths—Facing the Challenge of Truth Commissions* (New York, Routledge, 2002); International Centre for Transitional Justice, 'Truth Seeking' (2007) available online at http://www.ictj.org/en/tj/138.html (visited 7 February 2007).

[6] R Brooks, 'The New Imperialism: Violence, Norms, and the "Rule Of Law"' (2003) 101 *Michigan Law Review* 2275.

[7] K McEvoy, *Truth Recovery, Transition and Reconciliation: Dealing with the Past in Northern Ireland* (Cullompten, Willan Publishing, 2008).

of the contributors have direct practical experience of working on grassroots projects in Northern Ireland, Sri Lanka, Colombia, East Timor, Guatemala, Brazil, Ecuador, and many other jurisdictions. While many would share, to varying degrees, the commonly expressed driving goals of transitional justice—such as combatting impunity for crimes under international law, those conversations revealed a shared disquiet that the voices of those most affected are not always heard or accorded adequate weight once the wheels of institutionalised international justice begin to turn. Indeed in some communities, such as Northern Ireland, Sri Lanka and Colombia, the absence of viable international justice mechanisms has resulted in much of the creative energy for transition actually coming 'from below'.[8] Often in such contexts national justice systems are themselves too aloof, corrupt, tainted, ineffective, overwhelmed or otherwise incapable of responding properly to the needs of transition. In such settings, it is frequently victims and survivor groups, community and civil society organisations, human rights non-governmental organisations, church bodies and others that have been the engines of change.

Secondly, the involvement in and affinity towards work which is ongoing in sites that are generally 'below' the gaze of formal institutions of transitional justice arises in part from a degree of wariness about the capacity of such institutions to actually deliver to such communities. The term 'from below' is increasingly used to denote a 'resistant' or 'mobilising' character to the actions of community, civil society and other non-state actors in their opposition to powerful hegemonic political, social or economic forces. Thus, for example, Brecher, Costello and Smyth, and also Falk talk of 'globalisation from below' in their discussions of grassroots resistance to neo-liberal capitalist encroachments on environmental justice, labour, developing world debt and related issues.[9] Inspired by the mobilising power of the internet to take resistance 'from the net to the street', these very diverse organisations and groupings self-describe in some instances as a viable social movement 'from below' defined by their

[8] C Campbell and F Ní Aoláinn, 'Local Meets Global: Transitional Justice in Northern Ireland' (2003) 26 *Fordham International Law Journal* 871; C Bell and J Keenan, 'Human Rights Nongovernmental Organizations and the Problems of Transition' (2004) 26 *Human Rights Quarterly* 330; F Haniffa, 'In the Pursuit of Democracy in Post Colonial Sri Lanka: Local Human Rights Approaches to Transitional Justice' (New York, ICTJ Monograph, 2006); R Uprimny, C Botero, E Restrepo and MP Saffron, *Justicia Transicional Sin Transición? Verdad, Justicia y Reparación para Colombia* (Bogota, Centro de Estudios de Derecho y Sociedad, 2006).

[9] J Brecher, T Costello and B Smyth, *Globalisation From Below: The Power of Solidarity* (Cambridge MA, Southend Press, 2000); R Falk, 'Globalization-from-Below: An Innovative Politics of Resistance' in R Sandbrook (ed), *Civilizing Globalization: A Survival Guide* (Albany NY, State University of New York Press, 2003)

common opposition to global capitalism.[10] In other instances, the concept has been framed within a specific legal context. Thus, for example, in his important critique of the imperialist tendencies of international law in general and human rights discourses in particular in the developing world, Rajagopal argues the need for movements 'from below' to be 'written back into' historical struggles for human rights and social justice.[11] The realisation of rights struggles, or indeed effective methods of dealing with the past in transitional contexts, is marked not simply by the deliberation of major legal institutions or landmark cases but by the individuals and groups involved in social and political struggles which placed them on the political agenda in the first place.[12]

Thirdly, and closely related, the themes running through this collection resonate strongly with efforts in history, political science and cultural studies by the advocates of 'subaltern studies' from the 1980s onwards.[13] Subaltern studies emerged from a weariness at the fixation within such disciplines upon societal elites in many traditional writings on South Asia, Africa, Latin America and elsewhere and a parallel desire to return a sense of agency to the dominated and the oppressed.[14] Of course one cannot ignore the dominant, not least because subalterns are always affected by their actions. However, as Ranajit Guaha has suggested, the subaltern studies project was designed to recapture a sense that the 'subalterns' had also acted in history 'on their own i.e. independently of the elites' and that their politics constituted 'an autonomous domain, for it neither originated from elite politics nor did its existence depend on the latter'.[15] Although some draw more explicitly than others from such a perspective, throughout these chapters one sees consistent efforts to explore the agentic practice

[10] A Escobar, 'Beyond The Third World: Imperial Globality, Global Coloniality And Anti-Globalisation Social Movements' (2004) 25 *Third World Quarterly* 207.

[11] B Rajagopal, *International Law from Below: Development, Social Movements and Third World Resistance* (Cambridge, Cambridge University Press, 2003).

[12] U Baxi, *The Future of Human Rights* (Oxford, Oxford University Press, 2002).

[13] The term 'subaltern' is drawn from the writings of Antonio Gramsci and refers to subordination on the basis of class, caste, gender, race, religion, language and culture and was used to denote the centrality of dominant\dominated relations in history: See V Chaturvedi (ed), *Mapping Subaltern Studies and the Postcolonial* (London, Verso, 2000).

[14] G Prakash, 'Subaltern Studies as Postcolonial Criticism' (1993) 99 *American Historical Review* 1475 at 1478. For an overview of the development of Subaltern Studies and its influence, see R O'Hanlon, 'Recovering the Subject Subaltern Studies and Histories of Resistance in Colonial South Asia' (1988) 22 *Modern Asian Studies* 189; F Mallon, 'The Promise and Dilemma of Subaltern Studies: Perspectives from Latin American History' (1993) 99 *American Historical Review* 1491; R Guha (ed), *A Subaltern Studies Reader, 1986–1995* (Minneapolis MN, University of Minnesota Press, 1995) and I Rodriguéz (ed), *The Latin American Subaltern Studies Reader* (Durham NC, Duke University Press, 2001).

[15] R Guha, 'On Some Aspects of the Histiography of Colonial India' (1982) I *Subaltern Studies* 3–4.

and potential of players other than the politicians, lawyers and policy-makers who normally dominate the cast of academic discussions of transitional justice.

The 'from below' perspective which runs through this collection includes both a critique of transitional justice 'from above' (in some cases more gentle than others) and an exploration of the praxis of grassroots actors who have taken on transitional responsibilities themselves. This 'actor-orientated' perspective[16] on transitional justice critically explores local efforts at truth recovery in Northern Ireland, houses of memory and body exhumation in Guatemala, and grassroots resistance efforts in Colombia to mobilise against a de facto impunity for right-wing paramilitary groups and parallel efforts to establish local methods of community truth-telling. In each of these contexts, such community and civil society efforts have emerged precisely because of the failings of the state in question to put in place sufficiently robust transitional mechanisms to meet the relevant needs for truth, closure, healing or some form of accountability on the ground.

III ENRICHING TRANSITIONAL JUSTICE 'FROM ABOVE'

Without exception, none of the papers adopts a simplistically rejectionist position towards the more traditional styles of transitional justice 'from above'. Indeed as Falk[17] has suggested, the 'from below' perspective is really a way of providing a different vantage point in order to 'see' more clearly interactions, accommodations and relationships with institutions and structures 'from above'. Such interactions will inevitably occur and do shape the lives of ordinary citizens. The collection is thus designed to encourage and challenge those who work in such institutions to improve *what* they do, to think more deeply about *why* they do it, and to explore ways in which those same institutions of transitional justice can broaden *ownership* and encourage the *participation* of those who have been most directly affected by conflict.

Thus, McEvoy calls upon lawyers in particular to develop a 'thicker' understanding of transitional justice, to think more reflectively about the consequences of legalistic discourses in such contexts and to be more imaginative in overcoming some of those consequences. McGregor suggests ways in which the traditional hegemon of international law can be broken down into a 'tiered' process which is sufficiently flexible to encompass the experience of local victims and communities. Similarly,

16 C Nyamu-Musembi, 'Towards and Actor Informed Perspective on Human Rights', IDS Working Paper 169 (Brighton, Institute of Development Studies, 2002).

17 Falk, 'Globalization-from-Below: An Innovative Politics of Resistance' (n 9 above).

McConnachie and Morison suggest ways in which democratic participation can be encouraged in even the most technical of transitional processes, such as the design of new constitutional templates, through outreach, education, story-telling and mobilisation by women's groups and other—all of which are generic measures which can broaden ownership and involvement in historically elites-driven processes. Piacentini addresses the important point that while 'from below' perspectives are normally assumed to operate outside the structures of the state, actually the ways in which transitional messages are translated and acted upon 'on the ground' within state institutions can have huge implications for the efficacy of the overall process, and that not all resistance is necessarily progressive. Using the transition in Russian prisons as an example, she argues that for some prison personnel top-down instructions on respecting the human rights of prisoners (largely driven by the need for international recognition) are viewed as 'Western' or 'European' rather than Russian, leaving some of those actually administering the programmes 'culturally adrift' and encouraged into a sense of defiance about the past record of the previous Soviet prison regimes. Finally, Cavallero and Albuja suggest that the direct involvement of grassroots organisations and social movements can broaden the gaze of what is in many ways the emblematic institution of transitional justice (the truth commission) to include economic crimes and corruption that have hitherto largely been absent from the deliberations.

IV THE CONTESTED MEANINGS OF TRANSITION

Transitional justice is by its nature a heavily politicised process. Inevitably, the forms of transitional justice developed speak practically and symbolically to precisely what kind of a transition (if any) is actually occurring.[18] Traditionally, transitional justice was understood to apply in the limited and linear time period of the transition from an authoritarian regime to democracy.[19] Yet, transitional justice processes are no longer understood to correlate to an exclusive 'moment' in time. Patricia Lundy and Mark McGovern challenge this orthodoxy by addressing a transition from conflict within an ostensible democracy—Northern Ireland. They argue that the framework within which transitional justice is addressed

> ignores the problem that human rights abuses may continue to take place in circumstances where, in theory at least, the norms of liberal democratic accountability prevail. It also therefore permits a radical critique of implicit

[18] See F Ní Aoláinn and C Campbell, 'The Paradox of Transition in Conflicted Democracies' (2005) 27 *Human Rights Quarterly* 172.

[19] See Huntingdon, *The Third Wave: Democratization in the Late Twentieth Century* (n 1 above).

liberal versions of transition that may otherwise struggle to deal with the subversion of the rule of law, under the guise of law itself, in ostensibly liberal democratic states.

Even in jurisdictions where governments have been all too happy to adapt the mantle, this has often been accompanied by efforts to manipulate the framework in ways that are best suited to their purpose. As McGregor, Stanley and Diaz discuss, governments have worked hard to make transitional justice initiatives part of the state's broader armoury of conflict management. In Uganda, as McGregor details, the president has switched intermittently between the offer of amnesty to members of the Lord's Resistance Army to prosecutions, following a successful referral of the situation of Northern Uganda to the International Criminal Court, which issued arrest warrants against five senior LRA figures. In effect, the president has sought to co-opt international criminal justice in an explicitly political fashion as the 'stick' while amnesties are offered as the carrot to pressurise the LRA to lay down their arms. In Timor Leste, while the Indonesians have clearly departed and a political transition is underway, Stanley argues that the 'top-down' transitional justice processes were used to embed impunity (particularly for Indonesian officials) while simultaneously providing the political cover that something had been done to attain justice. Indeed, she argues that Timor-Leste's government has in effect prioritised its relationship with its more powerful neighbour, Indonesia, at the expense of the rights of victims. Similarly, as Diaz explores, the Uribe government in Colombia sought to frame de facto impunity for their erstwhile allies and proxy agents amongst the right-wing paramilitaries (in return for their demobilisation) as a 'transitional justice' measure, while the conflict was (and is) ongoing. These manoeuvres provoked a titanic struggle between the government and its supporters, a highly sceptical international community and a well-mobilised NGO and civil society sector. As Diaz argues, at the very least, transitional justice gave such actors a framework within which to critique the understanding being propagated by the state.

V HUMAN RIGHTS AS A SITE OF STRUGGLE IN TRANSITIONAL JUSTICE

Another central issue which runs through many of the contributions is the ambivalent role which many transitional actors have with law in general and with human rights law in particular. Thus, as suggested above, McGregor and Diaz are broadly positive about the notion of international law as a check on the power of the state, in particular the prohibition of amnesties for crimes under international law and the 'right to reparations'.[20] As discussed, in both Uganda and Colombia, the deployment of explicitly *international* rights discourses was an important mobilising point for grassroots actors in seeking to either curtail state power or in trying to 'broaden the tent' of those who might benefit from transitional justice mechanisms to include traditionally marginalised groups such as women or children.

Activists in the transitional setting are perhaps the least likely to simply accept 'top-down' and legalistic limitations upon the interpretations of human rights discourses, particularly when these are promoted by the state in its own interest. Thus, McEvoy is critical of the strategic deployment of the 'human rights as trumps' argument in Northern Ireland and elsewhere. He argues that state justice organisations in these contexts—which are intuitively highly resistant to ceding any control or ownership over justice per se—have attempted to stifle the growth of community-based justice programmes and to prematurely foreclose important debates by playing the human rights card. He contends that there is potential for a thicker and potentially more powerful version of human rights discourse, when international standards are translated into usable language and embedded in the working practices of grassroots organisations which are actually *doing* transitional justice in the most difficult of communities.

Cavallero and Albuja are also highly critical of what they refer to as the 'dominant script' of transitional justice mechanisms such as truth commissions and their historic focus upon individual civil and political rights rather than issues of social justice, economic and social rights, and economic crimes and corruption. In Latin America, they point to the continued phenomenon of *caudillismo*, or support for authoritarian figures or 'strongmen', a trend which has continued well into the post-transitional period of the past two decades. However the 'Achilles heel' for such support is corruption. As Cavallero and Albuja argue, the real diminution in support in Chile for Pinochet was not necessarily the high-profile arrests and prosecution in Europe for human rights violations, but his arrest before his death on charges of tax fraud and the discovery of secret bank accounts containing millions of dollars. They contend that while community-based truth recovery mechanisms have historically struggled to address this broader canvas of past abuses, its political and moral significance is too important to continue to be overlooked by the better

[20] B Chigara, *Amnesty in International Law: The Legality Under International Law of National Amnesty Law* (London, Longman, 2002); P De Grieff (ed), *Handbook of Reparations* (Oxford, Oxford University Press, 2006); L Mallinder, *Amnesty, Human Rights and Transition: Bridging the Peace and Justice Divide* (Oxford, Hart Publishing, 2008)

resourced top-down institutional models. In a similar vein, Stanley criticises the failure of the Commission for Reception, Truth and Reconciliation (known by its Portuguese acronym, CAVR) for its focus upon individual acts of violence and state involvement and failure to address the continuing 'violence' of poverty—conditions which she argues persuasively 'perpetuate injustices and potentially create further conflict in the future'.

VI JUSTICE FROM BELOW 'WARTS AND ALL'

Finally, while there is an intuitive sympathy amongst many of the contributors to this collection for increased community ownership and participation in processes of justice in transition, this is not at the expense of a suspension of critical faculties. As McEvoy notes, many who have written in the field of informalism, community justice, community mediation or restorative justice are all too aware of the dangers of the community as a site of exclusionary practices or unequal power relationships.[21] Good practice only emerges in such sites through a cold-eyed and pragmatic assessment of risks and capacities and the development of strategies which buttress against those risks and build upon existing skills and abilities.

Across the contributions on bottom-up processes there are cautions against romanticising community intention or capacity. For example, Arriaza and Roht-Arriaza describe conflict between organisations in Guatemala over access to reparations and the ensuing politicisation of victims therein. Stanley also points out that community-based initiatives can merely replicate broader social inequalities. In Timor Leste, she discusses the Truth and Reconciliation Commission as a process 'inspired from the "bottom up"' but

> practised in ways that have re-iterated inequalities of power and economy at the local and regional levels. As a result, some groups experienced less 'truth' or 'justice' than others.

Focusing also on power relations, Lundy and McGovern ask, who are the 'locals' whose voices need to be heard and heeded? And how does a locally-empowering process overcome hierarchal differences (for example, of gender) within a local community that can otherwise preclude giving agency to the most marginalised? Again in Timor-Leste, Stanley notes that victims participated in the CAVR out of a sense of duty to the CAVR and

[21] A Crawford, *The Local Governance of Crime: Appeals to Community and Partnership* (Oxford, Oxford University Press, 1999); A Etzioni, *The Spirit of Community* (New York, Simon and Schuster, 1994); L Mulcahy, 'The Devil and the Deep Blue Sea? A Critique of the Ability of Community Mediation to Suppress and Facilitate Participation in Civil Life' (2000) 27 *Journal of Law and Society* 133; G Pavlich, *Governing Paradoxes of Restorative Justice* (London, Glasshouse Press, 2005).

the local community, often deferring to the panel or the *Chefe de Suco* (village head) or appearing reticent to speak. As both McGregor and Stanley point out, bottom-up variants of transitional justice which are not carefully managed or regulated may reify existing practices of 'silencing' the traditionally most disenfranchised.

Similarly, as is discussed above, capacity issues must be addressed. Thus for example, Cavallaro and Albuja's argue that community-based truth-seeking processes are unlikely to have the resources, skills or authority to investigate corruption and economic crimes. That reality suggests that in effect such transitional works should rightly be the task of a more 'top-down' institution. The role of the community processes in such contexts may be essentially as lobbyists, pressurising officials to overcome whatever technical impediments will no doubt obstruct the search for truth in this field.

None of this is to suggest that these difficulties provide a rationale for defeatism or default to the vicissitudes of elites-driven top-down processes of transition. Rather, it is to suggest that a candid acknowledge of the difficulties and challenges presented by 'bottom-up' engagement is a necessary first step in effective planning.

The mainstreaming, institutionalisation and significant resourcing of transitional justice in recent years make this an exciting area for research, policy and praxis. Much of the academic focus to date in the field has been dominated by the struggles of lawyers in seeking to come to terms with a comparatively 'new' body of international law. This collection points to a range of energetic scholarly and practical work which is happening beyond those struggles. While based mainly in law or criminology, the authors draw eclectically from a range of other disciplines including sociology, development studies, international relations and anthropology amongst others in making their case. Doubtlessly, this collection only scratches the surface of the ongoing work in these various fields concerning transitional justice from below. But it does hint that beneath that surface there is a hive of activity.

VII THE COLLECTION

In the first chapter, McEvoy explores the implications of the traditional dominance of transitional justice discourse by an overly legalistic and 'top-down' focused analysis. While acknowledging an obvious role for legal processes in responding to conflict and impunity for large-scale human rights violations, he argues that the centrality of the law often leads to generic, linear and overly simplistic templates for transitional justice, which fail to resonate and embed in the local context. Using three characteristics of the law which have resulted in its centrality: 'legalism as seduction'; the 'triumph of human rights'; and the tendency for transitional justice legal scholars and practitioners towards 'seeing like a state', he argues that transitional justice processes are often rendered 'thin' and under-inclusive. In advancing a 'thicker' understanding of transitional justice, McEvoy calls for 'legal humility' and greater fusion of human rights and development, and draws upon some of the insights provided by criminology to make transitional justice processes meaningful and empowering to local communities, victims and former combatants.

Following on from McEvoy's critique of overly legalist tendencies, McGregor discusses two constraining characteristics of transitional justice processes at the international and national levels. At the international level, McGregor explores the formalistic tendencies and 'remoteness' of international law from the communities most affected by the crimes they seek to address. McGregor highlights the adoption of blanket amnesties; the strategic or inadvertent control of the narrative of conflict through the portrayal of the state as a neutral 'third-party' in an 'inter-ethnic', 'religious' or 'political' conflict; the narrow focus on civil and political rights violations to the exclusion of social and economic rights and the structural impact of conflict; and the overlooking or simplification of the gender implications of conflict, as frequent characteristics of national policy solutions. Rather than propose informal and community-based initiatives as the solution, however, McGregor argues that international law offers a framework for transitional justice initiatives at all levels to ensure the rights of victims and traditionally disenfranchised groups. In this respect, she advances international law not as a static or sealed system, but as an evolving process increasingly developed and generated by actors other than the state.

Like McEvoy and Cavallaro and Albuja below, McConnachie and Morison align themselves with the critique of transitional justice leanings towards 'off-the-shelf' templates on 'how to emerge' from conflict. They focus on the centrality of constitution-making in post-conflict societies and underscore the tendency for constitutional texts to reflect 'somewhat formulaic and institutionalised approach[es] to the renegotiation of political power'. Drawing on governmentality literature, they then sketch out a more subtle understanding of power, which, they argue, could enhance the peace-building potential of constitutions through the facilitation of *participatory* processes of constitution making, *sharper articulation* of rights discourses and the *pursuit of democratic decision-making* which acknowledges the networked nature of social structures in the diffusion of a genuinely 'from below' perspective.

Lundy and McGovern identify a move away from the top-down 'one-size-fits-all' approach of transitional justice to an emphasis on popular participation and local agency at the policy level of the United Nations. Yet, they argue that evidence of this shift remains scarce in practice. On the basis of development literature, sociology and their own experience of a bottom-up truth-telling initiative in Northern Ireland—the Ardoyne Commemoration Project—they argue that a participatory approach to transitional justice is urgently needed in order to 'bed-down' and achieve sustainability for such processes in the longer-term. In line with many of the authors in this collection, Lundy and McGovern emphasise the key importance of learning from and incorporating an interdisciplinary approach to transitional justice in order to provide agency, depth and longevity to the processes adopted.

In the final thematic chapter, Cavallaro and Albuja again emphasise the 'dominant script' of transitional justice, this time through the lens of the truth commission. Contextualising the chapter in Latin America, Cavallaro and Albuja discuss the tendency for truth commissions to replicate the mandates of their predecessors, albeit applying to different societies, time periods and political events. As the first truth commissions focused on violations of civil and political rights, Cavallaro and Albuja argue that truth commissions have, in the main, simply reproduced these scripts without heeding the priorities of the communities most affected and the broader context from which these truth commissions have emerged. While maintaining the importance of civil and political rights, Cavallaro and Albuja document the wide-scale commission of economic crimes and corruption and the priority accorded to their eradication by grassroots actors in the Latin American context, as a key illustration of the disconnect between the mandates of generic truth commissions and their surroundings. Cavallaro and Albuja thus conclude that the inclusion of corruption and economic crimes in TRCs may be functional to de-legitimising authoritarian regimes and to democratic consolidation.

The first case study, by Laura Arriaza and Naomi Roht-Arriaza, offers a fresh and detailed perspective on transitional justice in Guatemala. While most accounts of transitional justice processes in Guatemala focus on the UN-sponsored Commission for Historical Clarification (CEH) and/or the Catholic Church-inspired Recovery of Historical Memory Project (REHMI), Arriaza and Roht-Arriaza's extensive fieldwork in Guatemala provides a deeper account and analysis of local houses of memory, community-sponsored psycho-social interventions and exhumations, and conflict resolution based on Mayan methods. As such, they argue that local-level mechanisms can reflect a country's diverse makeup and experience of conflict; provide crucial precursors or extensions to wider-scale national and international projects; involve community members; promote agency; and perhaps be less prone to large-scale patronage and corruption. In conclusion, Arriaza and Roht-Arriaza recommend greater attention to the systematic identification and support for local processes.

As a relatively recent site for transitional justice, Stanley analyses responses to conflict in Timor-Leste. On the basis of primary research,

Stanley critically examines the four main transitional justice mechanisms (the Ad Hoc Human Rights Court in Jakarta; the UN-sponsored 'Special Panels for Serious Crimes' in Dili; the 'Commission on Reception, Truth and Reconciliation' in Timor-Leste; and the 'Commission on Truth and Friendship') employed to deal with the violations of human rights committed during Indonesian occupation. Taken together, Stanley argues that economic and political agendas have been prioritised over the rights, needs and interests of individual and communities of victims. As a result, she highlights the persistent culture of impunity, 'othering' and exclusionary practices, and the consolidation of inequalities at global, regional and national levels.

In her chapter Diaz provides one of the few scholarly analyses in English of the attempts by the Colombian government to 'borrow from' the Transitional Justice lexicon. In particular she maps the ongoing demobilisation of right-wing paramilitaries. As a site of particular contestation, Diaz illustrates the way in which the Colombian government adapted transitional justice discourses by advocating demobilisation through reference to language such as 'healing', 'reconciliation' and 'restoration'. Reflecting the mobilisation against this initiative by local human rights NGOs, civil society, victims' groups and grassroots actors, Diaz characterises the projected transitional justice picture in Colombia as 'thin' and partial. Moving beyond the official framework, Diaz then explores the deeper debates on transitional justice among bottom-up actors, entailing notions of truth, the rights of victims and reparations, examining two particular 'from below' initiatives in Medellin and Eastern Antioqua, wherein some of the themes relating to the resistant capacity of a transitional justice 'from below' are highlighted.

Finally, Piacentini introduces the important corrective that a 'bottom-up' understanding of transitional justice processes should not automatically be assumed to be located outside the state system. Again, based on extensive fieldwork in the Russian prison system, Piancentini explores its transition from a brutal, repressive and overly populated regime, to one that adopts principles and practices which draw eclectically from human rights. In particular, she examines

> how a version of human rights discourse, inculcated as part of the supposed post-Soviet transition, has been interpreted and implemented 'on the ground' in the Russian prison system.

Based on her interviews with Russian prison personnel, Piancentini advances the 'from below' perspective as one which analyses the way in which human rights discourses are implemented, co-opted or resisted during a transition from totalitarian rule.

2

*Letting Go of Legalism: Developing a 'Thicker' Version of Transitional Justice**

KIERAN MCEVOY

I INTRODUCTION

TRANSITIONAL JUSTICE IS a field on an upward trajectory. In a relatively short period, it has come to dominate debates on the intersection between democratisation, human rights protections and state-reconstruction after conflict. As well as its historical associations with the post-war tribunals in Nuremberg and Tokyo, and the democratisation of previously authoritarian regimes in Latin America and the former Soviet Union, the term is now regularly deployed with regard to the Balkans, Rwanda, Sierra Leone, East Timor and elsewhere.[1] A flurry of scholarly activity in recent years suggests its growing political and scholarly importance.[2] A distinguishable transitional justice template has emerged involving possible prosecutorial styles of justice (sometimes with bespoke international, hybrid or local institutions), local mechanisms for truth

* This chapter was previously published in slightly amended form in (2007) 34 *Journal of Law and Society* 4. I am grateful to the editor for permission to re-publish here. I would also like to thank my co-editor Lorna McGregor as well as Kirsten McConnachie, Lesley McEvoy, Ron Dudai and Cath Collins for their detailed comments.

[1] The rising profile and broader gaze of transitional justice was confirmed by the publication of a report by the UN Secretary General in 2004, in which transitional justice is defined as: '*compris[ing] the full range of processes and mechanisms associated with a society's attempts to come to terms with a legacy of large-scale past abuses, in order to ensure accountability, serve justice and achieve reconciliation. These may include both judicial and non-judicial mechanisms, with differing levels of international involvement (or none at all) and individual prosecutions, reparations, truth-seeking, institutional reform, vetting and dismissals, or a combination thereof*'. See UNSC, Report of the Secretary-General to the Security Council, 'The Rule of Law and Transitional Justice in Conflict and Post Conflict Societies' (23 August 2004) S/2004/616. Available online at http://daccessdds.un.org/doc/UNDOC/GEN/N04/395/29/PDF/N0439529.pdf.

[2] The scholarly literature on the topic is discussed throughout the chapter.

recovery and a programme for criminal justice reform in previously conflicted societies. Transitional justice has emerged from its historically exceptionalist origins to become something which is normal, institutionalised and mainstreamed.[3]

This chapter will argue that a key trend is already apparent in this relatively new field—the dominance of legalism.[4] This scholarly emphasis is also prevalent in the policy and practice of transitional justice. For example, international donors are funding what Brooks has described as an 'explosion in promotion of the rule of law' in local criminal justice systems in transition.[5] International criminal justice appears increasingly to have been 'informally annexed' by international lawyers.[6] Focusing on both the local and international, this chapter will argue that transitional justice has become over dominated by a narrow, legalistic lens which impedes both scholarship and praxis. The dominance of legalism is seen in the outworking of a number of overlapping themes. These are grouped below as the notion of 'legalism as seduction', the much vaunted 'triumph of human rights', and the tendency for transitional justice legal scholars and practitioners towards 'seeing like a state'. The second part of the chapter suggests a range of practical and theoretical correctives to such tendencies. These are explored as *encouraging legal humility*, seeing *human rights as development* and finally developing a *criminology of transitional justice*. The chapter concludes that law's place as the core framework around which transitions from conflict are constructed is now assured. Such a context should encourage a more honest acknowledgement of the limitations of legalism and a greater willingness to give space to other actors and forms of knowledge.

It might be helpful at this stage to offer some background to the chapter by way of an honest declaration of interest and a short comment on terminology.

The chapter is drawn from a number of scholarly and practical experiences over the last decade. In Northern Ireland, these have included involvement with a range of practical peace-making projects. One such initiative involved efforts to supplant paramilitary punishment attacks with community restorative justice programmes. Partially staffed and led by

[3] R Teitel, 'Transitional Justice Genealogy' (2003) 16 *Harvard Human Rights Journal* 69.

[4] Of course, sociologists, psychologists, anthropologists, criminologists, political scientists and others are producing thoughtful and insightful scholarship about transitional justice (see e.g. the work of Claire Moon, Brandon Hamber, Richard Wilson, Laura Piacentini, Tim Kelman) as well as others cited below in this article. However, one suspects that few of these scholars would dispute that law is the dominant discourse.

[5] R Brooks, 'The New Imperialism: Violence, Norms, and the "Rule Of Law"' (2003) 101 *Michigan Law Review* 2275.

[6] P Roberts and N McMillan, 'For Criminology in International Criminal Justice' (2003) 1 *Journal of International Criminal Justice* 315.

former IRA and Loyalist combatants, these projects have faced considerable opposition from the state justice system and others concerning the 'ownership' of justice in the Northern Ireland transition.[7] In addition, my views have been shaped by involvement with a local human rights NGO (the Committee on the Administration of Justice, CAJ) and, more recently, a local truth recovery project (Healing Through Remembering).[8] Despite the fact that all these projects are heavily involved in transitional justice work at grassroots level, few define it as such. When pressed on this, transitional justice for many of those who actually *do* it on the ground in Northern Ireland appears to be viewed as something which 'belongs to' others—chiefly lawyers, policy-makers and state officials.[9] This sense of 'disconnect' amongst grassroots organisations was replicated in recent comparative fieldwork. In places like Sierra Leone and Rwanda in particular, transitional justice appeared, if anything, even more distant; something rooted firmly in the formal mechanisms and institutions of international criminal justice rather than in the communities most affected by conflict.[10] In short, this chapter is grounded in criminology and heavily influenced by the practice of these various grassroots projects and the political contexts in which they operate.

With regard to terminology, it might also be useful at this juncture to include a brief comment on the notion of a 'thicker' understanding of transitional justice. The distinction in the social sciences generally between 'thick' and 'thin' theories is often viewed as intellectual short-hand for juxtaposing complex, multi-layered and actor-orientated styles of scholarship with narrowly descriptive, uni-dimensional, instrumentalist or positivistic analysis.[11] Within legal scholarship, 'thin' writings on law tend to

[7] K McEvoy and H Mika, 'Restorative Justice and the Critique of Informalism in Northern Ireland' (2002) 43 *British Journal of Criminology* 534.

[8] K McEvoy, 'Beyond the Metaphor: Political Violence, Human Rights and "New" Peacemaking Criminology' (2003) 7 *Theoretical Criminology* 319; K McEvoy, *Truth, Transition and Reconciliation: Dealing with the Past in Northern Ireland* (Cullompten, Willan Publishing, 2008).

[9] For a classic discussion of this tension see Nils Christie, 'Conflicts As Property' (1977) 17 *British Journal of Criminology* 1. For a discussion on the nature of the Northern Ireland transition, see C Campbell, F Ní Aoláin and C Harvey, 'The Frontiers of Legal Analysis: Reframing the Transition in Northern Ireland' (2003) 66 *Modern Law Review* 317; C Campbell and F Ní Aoláin, 'Local Meets Global: Transitional Justice in Northern Ireland' (2003) 26 *Fordham Journal of International Law* 871.

[10] See K McEvoy, H Mika and K McConnachie, *Reconstructing Transitional Justice: Transforming Cultures of Violence 'From Below'* (Cambridge, Cambridge University Press, 2008).

[11] See generally C Geertz, *The Interpretation of Cultures* (New York, Basic Books, 1973); M Coppedge, 'Thickening Thin Concepts and Theories: Combining Large N and Small in Comparative Politics' (1999) 31 *Comparative Politics* 465; J Newman, 'Through Thick and Thin?: The Problem of the 'Social' in Societal Governance', Paper presented to the Contemporary Governance and the Question of the Social Conference, University of Alberta (June 004). Available online at http://www.open.ac.uk/socialsciences.

emphasise the formal or instrumental aspects of a legal system. They are inclined to assume the self-evident 'rightness' of the rule of law. While thin legal scholarship is not necessarily atheoretical—indeed it may be so highly theorised as to be largely disconnected from the real lives of those affected by the legal system[12]—it is broadly less likely to reflect critically on the actions, motivations, consequences, philosophical assumptions or power relations which inform legal actors and shape legal institutions. A thicker understanding of transitional justice is therefore intended to counteract at least some of these tendencies.

II TRANSITIONAL JUSTICE AND THE NOTION OF LEGALISM

In her classic 1963 account on the notion of legalism, Judith Shklar discussed the influence of legalism as a process which separates legal analysis from politics and from other social science disciplines.[13] She argued that many lawyers find it difficult to view any social or political process free from 'legal habits or beliefs' and that they distrust arguments based on expediency, the public interests or 'the social good'—believing that such terms are 'dangerous and too easily used as cloaks for arbitrary actions'.[14] Of course legal academics, particularly those who work on jurisdictions which have experienced violent political conflict, are well aware of the often precarious attachment to legal standards.[15] Much contemporary legal scholarship takes the intersection between law, politics and the social realm as a given.[16] From the legal realists of the 1930s, the critical legal studies of the 1970s, the pervasive influence of law and economics in the USA and the (arguable) dominance of socio-legal scholarship in the UK at least since the 1990s—the interdisciplinary, small 'p' political and anti-positivist analysis of law, legal institutions and legal

[12] For an excellent discussion of these various distinctions see R Peerenboom, *China's Long March to the Rule of Law* (Cambridge, Cambridge University Press, 2002).

[13] 'The urge to draw a clear line between law and non-law has led to the constructing of ever more refined and rigid systems of formal definition. This procedure has served to isolate law completely from the social context from which it exists. Law is endowed with its own discreet, integral history, its own science, and its own values, which are all treated as a single 'block' sealed off from general social history, from politics, from morality ... This procedure has served its own ends very well; it aims at preserving law from irrelevant considerations, but it has ended by fencing legal thinking off from contact with the rest of historical thought and experience': J Shklar, *Legalism* (Cambridge MA, Harvard University Press, 1963) 2.

[14] *Ibid* at 9.

[15] See, eg D Dyzenhaus, *Legality and Legitimacy* (Oxford, Oxford University Press, 1997). F Ní Aoláin and C Campbell, 'The Paradox of Transition in Conflicted Democracies' (2005) 27 *Human Rights Quarterly* 172.

[16] See generally M Loughlin, *Sword and Scales; An Examination of the Relationship Between Law and Politics* (Oxford, Hart Publishing, 2000).

actors has become a mainstay of most major law schools.[17] In such a context, the argument that transitional justice continues to be dominated by 'legalism' may seem somewhat anomalous.

In examining that apparent incongruity, I want to explore a number of overlapping variants of legalism within transitional justice discourses before suggesting how these might be addressed. Broadly, my argument is that a strongly positivistic trend of scholarship and practice persists in the legal understanding of transitional justice.[18] In part this may be understood as a by-product of the re-emergence and emboldening of international lawyers shaken free from the stasis of the cold war.[19] It is also a consequence of significant resourcing at the national and international level evidenced by the *institutionalisation* of transitional justice in major legal edifices such as the international tribunals for the former Yugoslavia and Rwanda, the International Criminal Court and the other local and hybrid models. It is also perhaps precisely because transitions from conflict shine a harsh light on the political and contingent nature of legality that legal formalism becomes the defensive default position for many lawyers working in this field.

A Legalism as Seduction

The pervasive influence of law in the social and political lives of 'stable' or 'settled' societies is well rehearsed.[20] What Bourdieu has discussed as 'the force of law' well captures the dominance of law in contemporary industrialised societies.[21] Bourdieu refers to the magnetic, almost mysterious 'pull' of law wherein large swathes of social, political and intellectual life are heavily influenced by the legal world or 'juridical field', as he refers to it. Law not only regulates behaviour, it shapes our political relations, our language, even the way we think.[22] In part, other spheres are amenable to law's influence because, as Clifford Geertz has argued, law represents a

[17] See generally S Roach Anleu, *Law and Social Change* (London, Sage, 2000); I Ward, *Introduction to Critical Legal Theory*, 2nd edn (London, Cavendish, 2004); F Cownie, *Legal Academics: Cultures and Identities* (Oxford, Hart Publishing, 2004).

[18] For a discussion of the philosophical underpinnings of this style of legal analysis, see M Kramer, *In Defense of Positivism: Law Without the Trimmings* (Oxford, Oxford University Press, 1999).

[19] M Koskenniemi, 'The Fate of Public International Law: Between Technique and Politics' (2007) 70 *Modern Law Review* 1.

[20] See, eg M Weber, *Economy and Society: An Outline of Interpretative Sociology* (Berkeley CA, University of California Press, 1978).

[21] See JR Terdiman, Translators Introduction to Pierre Bordieu's 'The Force of Law: Towards a Sociology of the Juridical Field' (1987) 38 *Hastings Law Journal* 805.

[22] P Ewick and S Silbey, *The Common Place of Law: Stories from Everyday Life* (Chicago, University of Chicago Press, 1998); J Conley and W O'Bar, *Just Words: Law, Language, and Power* (Chicago, University of Chicago Press, 2005).

way of conceptualising and articulating how we would like the social world to be. It encourages a notion of a rational and ordered place based on universal understandings; it enables people 'to imagine principled lives they can practicably lead'.[23]

For some, the socially privileged status of judges and lawyers, their monopoly on the delivery of legal services and the resultant sense of professional self-confidence all combine to encourage the dominance of legalism.[24] For others, the advancement of law as a particular subset of 'scientific knowledge', or what de Sousa Santos has termed 'creeping legalism', is bound up with the development of the modern capitalist state and in particular the need of the state to replicate other 'understandable' systems of thought beneath and beyond the state.[25] In more recent times, legal theorists discuss a new 'international legalism' wherein law's centrality to globalisation in general and international politics in particular has far outstripped its historic limitations associated with the notion of state sovereignty.[26]

For current purposes it is sufficient to note that the seductive qualities of legalistic analysis lend themselves particularly well to transitional contexts. Claims that the 'rule of law' speaks to values and working practices such as justice, objectivity, certainty, uniformity, universality, rationality, etc are particularly prized in times of profound social and political transition.[27] Often in such societies, it is either the absence of the rule of law or the distortion of forms of legality which is the defining characteristic of the previous regime.[28] Legal formations which emerge during a transition from conflict such as new constitutions, local, international or hybrid prosecutorial forums or even truth recovery mechanisms are inevitably infused with legalistic discourse. In such a context, law becomes an important practical and symbolic break with the past; an effort to *publicly* demonstrate a new found legitimacy and accountability.[29] In some such circumstances, the signing up to and implementing of international human rights

[23] C Geertz, *Local Knowledge: Further Essays in Interpretive Sociology* (New York, Basic Books, 1983) 234. See also S Roberts, 'After Government?: On Representing Law Without the State' (2005) 68 *Modern Law Review* 1.

[24] Eg T Halliday, *Beyond Monopoly: Lawyers, State Crises and Professional Empowerment* (Chicago, University of Chicago Press, 1987).

[25] B De Sousa Santos, *Towards A New Common Sense: Law, Science And Politics In The Paradigmatic Transition* (London, Routledge, 2002 (repr from 1995)) 55–61.

[26] See R Teitel, '"Humanity" Law: Rule of Law for the New Global Politics' (2002) *Cornell International Law Journal* 355 at 365. See also R Falk, *Human Rights Horizons: The Pursuit of Justice in a Globalizing World* (New York, Routledge, 2000).

[27] S Ratner, 'New Democracies: Old Atrocities' (1999) 87 *Georgetown Law Journal* 707.

[28] See R Teitel, *Transitional Justice* (Oxford, Oxford University Press, 2000); S Ellmann, *In a Time of Trouble: Law and Liberty in South Africa's State of Emergency* (Oxford, Oxford University Press, 1992).

[29] See, eg M Osiel, *Mass Atrocity, Collective Memory and the Law* (Somerset NJ, Transaction Publishers, 1999).

agreements are integral to seeking international respectability. A professed respect for the rule of law demonstrates a 'fitness of purpose' for countries to take a proper place amongst the community of nations, or even the recovery of a sense of national self-confidence and pride.[30]

As is discussed below, this description of legalism as 'seductive' is not to denigrate the importance of law and legal analysis in the process of transition. Rather, it is to suggest that legalism tends to foreclose questions from other complimentary disciplines and perspectives which transitional lawyers should be both *asking* and *asked*. It is perhaps understandable that many lawyers who practise international criminal law tend not to over-analyse fundamental existential questions such as 'What is transitional justice for?' or 'Who does it serve?' Similarly, although it is perhaps less excusable, many legal scholars of transitional justice appear to spend most energy in the formidable task of analysing the expanding case law and relevant international standards without addressing these larger questions. There is a comfort in staying within what organisational theorists refer to as a 'closed system' of thinking.[31] However, as I will suggest below, there are useful frameworks of analysis that can enrich and inform legal thinking and develop ways of avoiding some of the more negative consequences of laws seductive qualities.

B Legalism as the Triumph of Human Rights

As is discussed extensively elsewhere, human rights talk has become the new 'lingua franca' of global moral thought.[32] As Douzinas has argued, the 'triumph' of human rights has united

> left and right, the pulpit and the state, the ministers and the rebel, the developing world and the liberals of Hampstead and Manhattan.[33]

Human rights are attributed the capacity to deliver 'a set of values for a Godless age'.[34] In tandem with that rise in prominence, human rights discourses have been subject to increasingly rigorous critical scrutiny. At a philosophical level, some commentators such as Douzinas remain highly skeptical as to the intellectual rigour with which human rights advocates

30 See, eg L Piacentini, *Surviving Russian Prisons: Punishment, Economy and Politics in Transition* (Cullompten, Willan Publishing, 2004).

31 J Thompson, *Organizations in Action: Social Science Bases of Administrative Theory* (New Brunswick, Transaction Publisher, 2003).

32 M Ignatieff, *Human Rights and Politics and Idolatry* (Princeton NJ, Princeton University Press, 2001) 53.

33 C Douzinas, *The End of Human Rights* (Oxford, Hart Publishing, 2000) 1.

34 See generally F Klug, *Values for a Godless Age: The Story of the United Kingdom's New Bill of Rights* (London, Penguin Books, 2000).

press their claims.[35] More grounded critiques point to a universalist versus cultural relativism debate within human rights.[36] For some, there are perceived Western and imperialist tendencies in elements of human rights talk. Baxi has described this (in its crudest form) as the 'westoxification' critique, a view of the West as imposing standards of rights and justice which it has always violated in the developing world and amongst Islamic societies in particular.[37] Human rights institutions such as human rights commissions have also been criticised for their failure to properly document past abuses and some new human rights imbued constitutions have also been critiqued for their failure to address socio-economic rights in a meaningful fashion.[38] The pre-eminence of civil and political rights in particular is also viewed in some quarters as acquiescence in the neo-liberal economic order and an abandonment of some of the more traditional social justice concerns such as poverty and health.[39]

Some of these criticisms are framed as the logical result of the legalistic bent of contemporary human rights discourses. Thus, for example, Michael Ignatieff and David Kennedy have both criticised human rights talk as deliberately denying the quintessentially *political* nature of its argumentation and of obfuscating the reality of conflicting rights.[40] In some contexts, the realities of confusion, 'messiness' and tough choices that characterise the lives of many (including human rights activists themselves) are translated through rights discourses into the legalese of international standards, legal certainties and political objectivity.[41] This process 'thins out' the complexities of life in conflicted societies and positivises the norms that underpin such challenges in international conventions and tribunals, national constitutions and the domestic courts.[42] In the process, divorced from serious consideration of the wider political, social or cultural contexts which produced violence in the first place, the

[35] Douzinas, *The End of Human Rights* (n 33 above).

[36] C Norris, *Reclaiming Truth: Contribution to a Critique of Cultural Relativism* (Durham NC, Duke University Press, 1996).

[37] U Baxi *The Future of Human Rights* (Oxford, Oxford University Press, 2002) 111–12.

[38] See generally M Mandami (ed), *Beyond Rights Talk and Culture Talk* (New York, St Martin Press, 2000) and P Jones and K Stokke (eds), *Democratising Development: The Politics of Socio-economic Rights in South Africa* (Leiden, Brill, 2005).

[39] A Woodiwiss, *Making Human Rights Work Globally* (London, Glasshouse, 2003).

[40] Ignatieff, *Human Rights and Politics and Idolatry* (n 32 above) at 20; and D Kennedy, 'The International Human Rights Movement: Part of the Problem?' (2002) 15 *Harvard Human Rights Journal* 116.

[41] See, eg E Felner, *Human Rights Leaders In Conflict Zones: A Case Study of The Politics of 'Moral Entrepreneurs'* (Carr Centre for Human Rights Policy, Kennedy School of Government, Harvard University, 2004). Available online at http://www.ksg.harvard.edu/cchrp/pdf/Felner.2004.pdf .

[42] R Wilson, 'Is the Legalisation of Human Rights Really the Problem: Genocide in the Guatemalan Historical Clarification Commission' in S Meckled-García and B Çali (eds), *The Legalisation of Human Rights: Multi-Disciplinary Perspectives on Human Rights and Human Rights Law* (London, Routledge, 2006) 81.

potential power of human rights institutions to prevent future violence is correspondingly reduced.[43]

A further, related element of the pre-eminence of human rights discourses in transitional justice is a variant of what Stan Cohen has referred to as 'magical legalism'. Cohen uses the term in a very specific fashion to describe a technique of denial practised by governments which seek to 'prove' that an allegation of malfeasance cannot possibly be true because that action is illegal. A government will list the numerous domestic laws and precedents, ratifications of various international conventions, appeals and discipline procedures and, as Cohen argues,

> then comes the magic syllogism: torture is strictly forbidden in our country; we have ratified the Convention Against Torture: therefore what we are doing cannot be torture.[44]

The 'triumph' of human rights is turned on its head and becomes an additional weapon in the state's armoury, which is deployed to deny the very human rights abuses which the laws were intended to prevent. More broadly, the notion of magical legalism speaks directly to the disconnect between the 'real world' in some transitional societies and the plethora of 'law talk' which often characterises debates amongst the political elites. For example, Michael Taussig's treatment of 'law in a lawless land' concerning Colombia's contested 'transition' captures well the inverse relationship between Colombia's layers of laws upon laws, including ratifications of international human rights standards, and the lived reality of violence, corruption and impunity experienced by so many ordinary Colombians.[45]

In the Northern Ireland transition too, quintessentially political positions were masked in the technical legalese of 'human rights concerns' at various junctures by British government negotiators only to be summarily abandoned when the political winds shifted.[46] At one level, the fact that law

[43] *Ibid*.

[44] S Cohen, *States of Denial: Knowing About Atrocities and Suffering* (Cambridge, Polity Press, 2002) 108.

[45] M Taussig, *Law in a Lawless Land* (Chicago, University of Chicago Press, 2003). This disconnect is referred to in Colombia as 'Santanderismo'. Santander, known as the 'law giver', fought beside Simon Bolivar in the Colombian War of Independence and became President of the then New Granada in 1833. A quotation from him—'guns have given you independence, laws will give you freedom'—is inscribed over the entrance to Colombia's Supreme Court. I am indebted to Prof Rodrigo Uprimny, former Judge of the Colombian Constitutional Court for his impeccable guidance on the nuances of this aspect of Colombian legal and political culture.

[46] For example, one argument which was put forward by senior prison officials in Northern Ireland in the wake of the paramilitary cease-fires was that releases of politically motivated prisoners would discriminate against 'ordinary decent criminals'. The author and others spent considerable time contesting the legal validity of that position. Years later after all qualifying political prisoners had been released within two years of the Good Friday

and legal arenas become a key contested site in the inevitable struggle for political advantage of a transition is hardly noteworthy. What is arguably of more importance is that the triumph of human rights makes it a particularly powerful variant of magical legalism which can appear above the political fray. However, as Cohen has argued, the plausibility of that position is only possible if common sense is suspended. For some (particularly lawyers), the allure of complex legal argumentation makes such a suspension all to viable.

A final important criticism advanced in terms of the legalisation of human rights is that in some transitional societies human rights concerns become a byword for a retributive notion of justice. Often human rights standards are framed as the key bulwark against political calls for forgiveness and 'reconciliation'. For example, the post-communist transitions of Eastern Europe largely eschewed prosecutions in favour of releasing intelligence files and purging former 'collaborators' from public office. For some commentators, this absence of retributive justice has been described as a failure to live up to legal obligations, which could in turn sow the seeds of future violence.[47] Similarly, the possibility that *accountability* might be achieved through the operation of institutions such as truth and reconciliation commissions or local amnesties—and thus not trigger prosecutions by the International Criminal Court—produced considerable discomfort amongst some of the lawyers involved in drafting the Rome Statute.[48] In an environment where politically-constructed notions of 'pragmatism' and related offshoots such as reconciliation are often viewed as slippery bywords for impunity, 'human rights as retribution' provides an understandably comforting terra firma for many lawyers.

To recapitulate therefore, a crude characterisation of human rights in contemporary transitional justice discourses would suggest that human rights talk lends itself to a 'Western-centric' and top down focus; it self-presents (at least) as apolitical; it includes a capacity to disconnect from the real political and social world of transition through a process of

Agreement one senior official candidly acknowledged: 'You took all that human rights discussion far too seriously, of course it was just a negotiating position'. See K McEvoy, *Paramilitary Imprisonment in Northern Ireland* (Oxford, Oxford University Press, 2001) esp ch 11.

[47] J Borneman, *Settling Accounts: Violence, Justice and Accountability in Post-socialist Europe* (Princeton NJ, Princeton University Press, 1997). Richard Wilson makes a similar criticism concerning the de facto absence of retributive justice in the South African truth and reconciliation process. See R Wilson, *The Politics of Truth and Reconciliation in South Africa* (Cambridge, Cambridge University Press, 2001).

[48] See D Newman, 'The Rome Statute, Some Reservations Concerning Amnesties and a Distributive Problem' (2005) 20 *American University International Law Review* 293; W Schabas, *An Introduction to the International Criminal Court* (Cambridge, Cambridge University Press, 2004). Schabas does note, however (at 87), that 'it has been suggested that genuine but non-judicial efforts at accountability that fall short of criminal prosecution would have the practical effect of convincing the Prosecutor to set priorities elsewhere'.

'magical legalism'; and finally it suggests a predominant focus upon retribution as the primary mechanism to achieve accountability.

C Legalism and 'Seeing Like a State'

A final variant of legalism which is discernible in this field is a tendency towards an understanding of transitional justice that is both state-centric and 'top down'. The growth of transitional justice has seen an *institutionalisation* of transitional justice into expensive supra-state and 'state-like' structures.[49] For example, at the level above the state, the temporary ad hoc tribunals to deal with the crimes committed in Yugoslavia and Rwanda have now been in operation since 1993 and 1997 respectively.[50] The permanent International Criminal Court came into force in 2002 and began work in earnest in 2004.[51] At the national level, hybrid tribunals in locations such as Sierra Leone, East Timor and Cambodia have emerged which combine the efforts of local and international legal actors. Such developments have been matched by a plethora of other institutions that drive transitional justice at the national level, including truth and reconciliation commissions, reparations bodies, special trials of previous abusers and a range of other initiatives.[52]

In addition to these exceptional measures, huge energies have been invested in the state justice reconstruction programmes of the 'normal' criminal justice systems through 'rule of law' programmes designed to secure a fairer and more efficient delivery of justice.[53] The label of 'failed state' in places like Somalia or Liberia is often used as a catch-all phrase to describe Hobbesian violence and anarchy.[54] In effect, the absence of

[49] See R Kerr, *The International Criminal Tribunal for the Former Yugoslavia* (Oxford, Oxford University Press, 2004); LJ van den Herik, *The Contribution of the Rwanda Tribunal to the Development of International Law* (Leiden, Brill, 2005).

[50] Under pressure from the United Nations and elsewhere, the ICTY and the ICTR have attempted to speed up their legal processes through their respective completion strategies. In the most recent update on progress on the ICTY, the President of the Court, Fausto Pocar, confirmed that trials will continue into 2009 at least. The ICTR estimates that by the end of 2008 the trials of 65–70 persons will have been completed. See ICTY, *Assessment and Report of Judge Fausto Pocar, President of the International Criminal Tribunal for the Former Yugoslavia, Provided to the Security Council Pursuant to Paragraph 6 of Council Resolution 1534 (2004)* (29 May 2006) and ICTR, *Completion Strategy of the International Criminal Tribunal for Rwanda*. New York, (May 2006) UN doc S/2006/358.

[51] See generally Schabas, *An Introduction to the International Criminal Court* (n 48 above).

[52] See generally P Hayner, *Unspeakable Truths: Facing The Challenge Of Truth Commissions* (London, Routledge, 2002); P De Greif (ed), *A Handbook on Reparations* (Oxford, Oxford University Press, 2006).

[53] Brooks, 'The New Imperialism: Violence, Norms, and the "Rule Of Law"' (n 5 above).

[54] R Rotberg (ed), *State Failure and State Weakness in Time of Terror* (Washington DC, Brookings Institution, 2004).

functioning centralised state institutions becomes a byword for lawlessness. The converse is also true in some contexts. The reassertion of the authority of the state is often viewed as paramount in the transition from conflict, and respect for 'the rule of law' is frequently seen as the benchmark for such authority. Thus the reconstruction, or in some instances construction, of institutions designed to deliver justice is core transitional business.[55] Judicial and legal reform, the disbandment or reshaping of police forces associated with previous regime abuses, sporadic attention to often deplorable prison conditions, mainstreaming of human rights training throughout different agencies—these and other state-centred initiatives have become familiar and perfectly understandable elements of the transitional 'justice reconstruction' template. They are all evidence of an apparent faith in the capacity of state institutions to meet the aims associated with transitional justice.

At a conceptual level, the development of such institutions speaks to the tendency of a lawyer-dominated field towards what the anthropologist James C Scott has referred to as '*seeing like a state*'.[56] Scott's contention is that governments in particular which are seeking to achieve complicated and ambitious ends need to render them '*legible*' in order to *see* them properly, and thus inevitably deploy state-like institutions as the vehicles to achieve those ends. Such a perspective resonates in other disciplines. For some political scientists or international relations theorists, the state and state-like institutions may become practical and metaphorical mechanisms for making sense of complex situations,[57] rendering them *intelligible,* an idealised and orderly arrangement of 'a world of concepts rendered suitable for practice'.[58] For sociologists, particularly sociologists of institutions (such as Mary Douglas and others), states and state-like institutions are particularly prone to developing and reproducing their own rationality, their own reason for being, conferring and fixing a 'sameness' shaped by the shared thought, values and information within the institutions.[59] As Douglas has argued,

[55] See generally M Cherif Bassiouni (ed), *Post Conflict Justice* (New York, Transnational Press, 2002).

[56] JC Scott, *Seeing Like a State: How Certain Schemes to Improve the Human Condition Have Failed* (New Haven CT, Yale University Press, 1999).

[57] Eg J Bartelson, *The Critique of the State* (Cambridge, Cambridge University Press, 2001).

[58] P Steinberger, *The Idea of the State* (Cambridge, Cambridge University Press, 2004) 13.

[59] M Douglas, *How Institutions Think* (Syracuse NY, Syracuse University Press, 1986) 53. See also M Brinton and V Nee, *The New Institutionalism in Sociology* (New York, Russell Sage, 1998).

> the entrenchment of an institution is essentially an intellectual process as much as an economic and political one ... [E]very kind of institution needs a formula that founds its rightness in reason and in nature.[60]

Since lawyers, policy-makers and state officials often appear to think of justice as *belonging to* the institutions which make up a justice system and the people who staff it,[61] state-like models of justice are thus prone to replication.

The attention to 'stateliness' in societies in transition is, however, more than a conceptual replication of legalistic formations. Of course the achievement of a secure environment is the fundamental 'sine qua non' of post-conflict reconstruction.[62] Until recently (as is developed below), the provision of security in post-conflict societies was often viewed as synonymous with professionalising the security capacity of state agencies such as the police. Even in contexts where the state has perpetrated extreme violence, such as Colombia, 'strengthening' the state is frequently proposed as a key element to conflict resolution. More broadly however, as Fukuyama has argued, the reality is that in development work generally over the last decade there has been a much greater emphasis on the fact that 'institutions matter'.[63] The early zeal of post-Cold War economists who pressed for a smaller state and the 'will of the market' has given way to a much more overt acknowledgement of the centrality of developing functioning (and indeed democratic) political institutions, public administration that can deliver basic goods and services, and a legal framework which is sufficiently robust to encourage investment, trade and industry as well as more general public confidence in the state.[64] Institutional capacity enhancement is increasingly argued as the necessary precursor to liberalisation of the political and economic systems of transitional societies. Such institutionalisation typically requires a constitution, a constitutional court to interpret that constitution, a police force capable of enforcing the judgments of the court and a legal system to regulate the market economy.[65] Developing the state's institutional capacity to deliver justice is thus viewed as a core element in the process of re-building structures of

[60] Douglas, *How Institutions Think* (n 59 above) at 45

[61] Christie, 'Conflicts As Property' (n 9 above).

[62] J Stromseth, D Wippman and R Brooks, *Can Might Make Rights? Building the Rule of Law After Military Interventions* (Cambridge, Cambridge University Press, 2006) esp ch 5.

[63] F Fukuyama, *State Building: Governance and World Order in the 21st Century* (New York, Profile Books, 2004) 28.

[64] See, eg W Easterly, *The Elusive Quest For Growth: Economists' Adventures and Misadeventures in the Tropics* (Cambridge MA, MIT Press, 2001); N van de Walle, *African Economies and the Politics of Permanent Crisis 1979–1999* (Cambridge, Cambridge University Press, 2001); World Bank, *Reforming Public Institutions and Strengthening Governance* (Washington DC, World Bank, 2000).

[65] See R Paris, *At War's End: Rebuilding Peace After Civil Conflict* (Cambridge, Cambridge University Press, 2004) 205 and McConnachie and Morison in this collection.

governance more generally.[66] It is both a practical and symbolic necessity as well as a way of 'seeing' reconstruction.

The logic of developing state justice capacity at the national level, or 'state-like' institutions at the international level, to deal with international criminal justice would therefore seem unimpeachable. However, one of the reasons Scott suggests 'state-centric' grand schemes often fail spectacularly is that they oversimplify. They may fail to take sufficient account of local customs and practical knowledge and to engage properly with community and civil society structures. Such failures, often justified in the name of efficiency, professional expertise or simply 'getting the job done', may in turn lead to incompetence or maladministration and encourage grassroots resistance to such state-led initiatives.[67] Once such institutions are created, the capacity for self-justification and self-replication that Douglas identifies obscures the need for thicker forms of accountability or legitimacy towards those whom such institutions claim to serve.[68] In particular, when actors within such institutions develop a self image of serving higher goals such as 're-establishing the rule of law', the temptation to see victims or violence-affected communities as constituencies which must be managed, rather than citizens to whom they must be accountable, becomes all too real.

To summarise, there is a dialectic relationship between the dominance of legalism in much transitional justice discourse and the tendency to 'see' justice and justice delivery as quintessentially the business of state or 'state-like' institutions. Such a view is derived in part from an awareness of the complexities of the tasks being undertaken and the practical necessity for some form of institutional delivery mechanism in order to render such objectives legible. It is also a product of the self-replicating power of institutions and of the revitalisation of the state as the key vehicle for the delivery of justice and security over the past decade or more. However, there are real dangers that the concentration of the stewardship of transitional justice in such institutions mitigates against developing lines of ownership and accountability to the communities they were designed to serve. This tendency towards 'seeing like a state', together with the particular seductive qualities of law in transition and the dominance of the human rights framework are the key limitations associated with legalism, which hamper the theoretical understanding and practical work of contemporary transitional justice.

[66] D Brinkerhoff, 'Rebuilding Governance in Failed States and Post-Conflict Societies: Concepts and Cross Cutting Themes' (2005) 25 *Public Administration and Development* 3.

[67] Scott, *Seeing Like a State* (n 56 above).

[68] See generally D Beetham, *The Legitimation of Power* (London, Palgrave, 1991). For an excellent discussion on thicker forms of accountability at the community level see D Roche, *Accountability in Restorative Justice* (Oxford, Oxford University Press, 2003).

III TOWARDS A THICKER UNDERSTANDING OF TRANSITIONAL JUSTICE

As noted above, the origins of this article lie partially with an academic frustration at such legalistic dominance but also in the practical consequences of that phenomenon. The argument here is that these variants of legalism can cumulatively disconnect individuals and communities from any sense of sovereignty over transitional justice.[69] Legalism contributes directly to a process that Paul Gready has well captured as the distinction between 'distant justice' and justice which is actually 'embedded' in communities that have been directly effected by violence and conflict.[70] The need for praxis demands that one do more than simply delineate and critique the dominance of legalism and actually offer some normative and practical correctives. In this part of the chapter I shall attempt to suggest ways in which some of these limitations may be overcome.

Again it is important to bear in mind that what is being postulated here is not a rejectionist approach to the role of law within transitional justice. Notwithstanding the criticisms outlined above, it is obvious that, like institutions, law matters.[71] That said, what is being argued here is an attempt to 'thicken' the topic (for lawyers in particular) through the encouragement of legal humility, 'seeing' human rights as development and drawing upon some of the insights provided by criminology.

A The Encouragement of Legal Humility

Lawyers, like other professionals, have rarely been associated with a lack of self-regard.[72] The combination of the intellectual and technical demands of law, a traditionally elevated social status, the importance of the subject-matter, the relatively closed social and professional worlds of lawyers, the peculiarities of legal education and models of professional self-governance and a range of other factors, can contribute to a sense of elitism and arrogance in the legal profession.[73] As was noted above, law's

[69] For a useful overview of the relationship between sovereignty and law see M Loughlin, *Sword and Scales* (n 16 above) esp ch 9.

[70] P Gready, 'Reconceptualising Transitional Justice: Embedded and Distanced Justice' (2005) 5 *Conflict, Security and Development* 2.

[71] For a provocative discussion on this issue see J Griffith, 'Is Law Important?' (1979) 54 *New York University Law Review* 342.

[72] See M Larson, 'On the Matter of Experts and Professionals, or How is It Possible to Leave Nothing Unsaid' in R Torstendal and M Burrage (eds), *The Formation of Professionals: Knowledge, State and Strategy* (London, Sage, 1990).

[73] See generally T Johnson, *Professions and Power* (London, Macmillan Publishers, 1972); K MacDonald, *The Sociology of the Professions* (London, Sage, 1995); J Morison and P Leith, *The Barristers World and the Nature of Law* (Milton Keynes, Open University Press,

generic seductive qualities are all the more pronounced in times of transition and thus the privileging of legal knowledge and the work of legal professionals becomes manifest. Such innate tendencies in the law profession, allied to the imperialist tendencies associated with even well-meaning international involvement in transitional contexts,[74] make the case for greater legal humility in such sites all the more pressing.

At an operational level, as was noted above, common sense dictates that lawyers will be embroiled in the day-to-day work of transitional justice. The drafting of new constitutions, the establishment of prosecutorial or truth recovery mechanisms, the re-shaping of criminal justice systems, the release of political prisoners or the design of amnesties—these and other processes and products associated with transition are of course 'creatures of law'. However, there are ways in which lawyers can do their work in transitional contexts and yet be more honest about the limitations of legalism.[75]

For example, an international or local tribunal or a truth commission is self-evidently but one element of a broader transitional process and it should be constantly articulated as such both in public utterances and in the working practices of the legal professionals involved. The 'overselling' of the capacity of major legal institutions to deliver forgiveness, reconciliation or other features associated with post-conflict nation-building may well encourage unrealisable public expectations and ultimately an unfair assessment that such institutions have 'failed'.[76] In addition, the tendency of international lawyers to eulogise the glory and majesty of international law being 'brought to' previously war-torn regions often renders them oblivious to the strong evidence of a disconnect between such imperious aims and their perception in the communities affected by such violence. In Sierra Leone, for example, despite considerable evidence of ambivalent and

1995); R Abel, *English Lawyers: Between Market and State* (Oxford, Oxford University Press, 2003); F Kay, 'Professionalism and Exclusionary Practices: Shifting the Terrain Of Privilege and Professional Monopoly' (2004) 11(1) and (2) *International Journal of the Legal Profession* 11; K McEvoy and R Rebouche, 'Mobilising the Professions : Lawyers, Politics and the Collective Legal Conscience' in J Morison, K McEvoy and G Anthony (eds), *Judges, Human Rights and Transition* (Oxford, Oxford University Press, 2007).

[74] See generally M Ignatieff, *Empire Lite: Nation Building in Bosnia, Kosovo and Iraq* (London, Vantage, 2003); R Paris, *At War's End: Rebuilding Peace After Civil Conflict* (n 65 above); R Caplan, *International Governance of War-Torn Territories: Rule and Reconstruction* (Oxford, Oxford University Press, 2005).

[75] For example, as one prominent human rights lawyer who was intimately involved in the processes of early release of prisoners in South Africa and later in Northern Ireland told the author, 'of course the law is important, but at the end of the day you have to remember that this is a political and not a legal process': Interview Brian Curran. See K McEvoy, 'Prisoner Release and Conflict Resolution: International Lessons for Northern Ireland' (1998) 8 *International Criminal Justice Review* 33 for further discussion.

[76] See Wilson, 'Is the Legalisation of Human Rights Really the Problem' (n 42 above); C Moon, 'Prelapsarian State: Forgiveness and Reconciliation in Transitional Justice' (2004) 17 *International Journal for the Semiotics of Law* 185.

complex attitudes amongst ordinary Sierra Leoneans towards the Special Court, international lawyers have shown little reticence in speaking in grandiose terms 'on their behalf'.[77] In addition, the special tribunal was created as a result of an agreement between the UN and the local government. That agreement led to the indictment of senior members from three of the factions in the war, including militia leader Sam Hinga Norman (who was Deputy Minister of Defence and the principal political rival to the incumbent president), but no key government actors such as the President (who, as Minister for Defence during the war, was Hinga's boss) or Vice President—omissions which have undermined some of the more grandiose claims with regard to the Court.[78] Similarly in Iraq, the Iraqi High Tribunal which was established to try Saddam Hussein was originally framed by some as 'justice for the Iraqi people' but that position has been significantly undermined by the actual conduct of the trial and macabre farce of his execution.[79] Lawyers would do well in such contexts to keep their discussions and analysis more measured and grounded in local realities.

Similarly, in the ubiquitous delivery of 'rule of law' and human rights related training and education in transitional justice settings, a more honest acknowledgement of the contingent, partial and political history of such discourses is much more likely to resonate with those who have lived

[77] Extracts from the opening statement by American Prosecutor David Crane at the trial of former CDF militia leader Samuel Hinga Norman are illustrative. 'One this solemn occasion, mankind is once again assembled before an international tribunal to begin the sober and steady climb upwards towards the towering summit of justice ... The rule of law marches out of the camps to the downtrodden onward under the banner of never again and no more ... The light of this new day today and the many tomorrows ahead are a beginning of the end of the life of that beast of impunity, which howls in frustration and shrinks from the bright and shining light spectre of the law. The jackals whimper in their cages certain of their impending demise. The Law has returned to Sierra Leone and it stands with all Sierra Leoneans against those who seek their destruction': 3 June 2004, Trials of Samuel Hinga Norman, Moinana Fofana, Allieu Kondewa, Case No SCSL-030140I. For a review of public opinion on these and other cases see E Sawyer and T Kelsall, 'Truth Vs Justice: Popular Views on the Truth and Reconciliation Commission and the Special Court of Sierra Leone' (2007) 7 *Online Journal of Peace and Conflict Resolution* 36.

[78] See T Kelsall, 'Politics, Anti-politics, International Justice: Language and Power in the Special Court for Sierra Leone' (2006) 32 *Review of International Studies* 587.

[79] Although the tribunal was staffed by the Iraqi judiciary, it was heavily influenced by the US Department of Justice Regime Crimes Liaison Office, which was involved in selecting and training the judges, drafting the relevant statute and assisting the tribunal throughout its deliberations. For an interesting debate on the format of the tribunal see C Doebbler and M Scharf, 'Will Saddam Hussein get a Fair Trial?' (2005–2006) 37 *Case Western Reserve Journal of International Law* 21–40. See Amnesty International (30 December 2006) 'Amnesty International Deplores Execution of Saddam Hussein', which describes the trial as 'a deeply flawed process' and as 'being seen by many as little more than victors' justice'. AI Index: MDE 14/043/2006 at http://www.amnesty.org.

through conflict.[80] Indeed, I would contend that such a critical and contextual approach to the 'law in action rather than the law in books' is more likely to assist in the embedding of such frameworks in transitional contexts (precisely because it appears real, grounded and even 'flawed') rather than a positivistic reiteration of international standards in the 'law, is the law, is law' style adopted by some more traditional lawyers. The historical fallibility of 'the rule of law' is not necessarily a fundamental weakness in education or training. Rather, I would argue that it is an entry point for an engaged discussion about the importance of the ideal as the bedrock for a transforming society.[81]

Legal institutions associated with transitional justice can and should operate most effectively if they run in conjunction with properly managed, effective and accountable local or indigenous processes, which comply with basic international human rights standards. Indeed, the UN has in recent years acknowledged the notion that the rule of law in transitional contexts should embrace precisely such a willingness to ally international norms with 'respect for local ownership, values and traditions.[82] With such a mindset, lawyers could ideally establish the broad legal parameters within which aspects of the transition should be framed, but the 'filling in' of the transitional process on the ground should as much as possible be left to local political, community and civil society structures. Peace-making circles in South Africa and community-based restorative justice programmes in Northern Ireland are evidence that properly resourced and managed local community structures are capable of engagement in and direction of transitional justice processes. Again to paraphrase Nils Christie, a more humble approach to transitional justice thus requires a 'ceding of ownership' by the legal professionals involved towards such structures.[83]

[80] For useful critical discussion see T Carothers, 'The Rule of Law Revival' (1998) 77 *Foreign Affairs* 95; D Sharp, 'Prosecutions, Development, and Justice: The Trial of Hissein Habré' (2003) 16 *Harvard Human Rights Law Review* 147.

[81] See Stromseth, Wippman and Brooks, *Can Might Make Rights?* (n 62 above) esp ch 8. Certainly the author's own experience in doing human rights training and education with ex-combatants in Northern Ireland would strongly suggest that such a style of delivery is more readily received and arguably much more likely to be genuinely internalised into the actual practice of the participants than a more traditional doctrinal exposition of the relevant international standards. For a discussion on different styles of human rights education and training see F Tibbits, 'Understanding What We Do: Emerging Models for Human Rights Education' (2002) 48 *International Review of Education* 159. For an interesting approach which compares legal, educational and civil society styles of delivery in seeking to harness both the 'normative and enforcing capacity of law and the persuasive potential of education' see L McEvoy and L Lundy, 'In the Small Places: Education and Human Rights Culture in Conflict Affected Societies' in J Morison, K McEvoy and G Anthony (eds), *Judges, Human Rights and Transition* (Oxford, Oxford University Press, 2007).

[82] Report of the Secretary-General to the UN Security Council (n 1 above) at 17.

[83] Christie, 'Conflicts As Property' (n 9 above).

B Human Rights as Development

The reluctance of lawyers to relinquish control in many contexts, but in particular in transitional societies, is often expressed explicitly in terms of the human rights framework. It is as though a top-down and state-centric ownership over human rights were the *sole* guarantor of the rights of those involved in the process of transition. I would argue, however, that there is an alternative perspective on rights discourses which offers a potentially more fruitful pathway to embedding rights discourses in communities affected by violence.

Many of the critiques of human rights discourses outlined above are drawn from the sociological, anthropological and socio-legal writings on the subject. In seeking to address these various criticisms in transitional settings, debates on human rights within the development literature have also become increasingly relevant.[84] Such a pull is perhaps inevitable. In conducting research on transitional justice in settings such as Sierra Leone for example, one cannot but be struck by the stark juxtaposition of the gleaming edifices of international justice such as the Special Court and the bleak poverty in which they are physically situated.[85] The literature on human rights and development is rich, and doing justice to its complexity is well beyond the confines of this chapter. However, what resonates in particular for current purposes is the notion, increasingly prevalent in development circles, that human rights can provide a practical and normative basis for grassroots justice work in communities which have been affected by conflict and violence. If, as Sen has argued, we regard 'development' as essentially the expansion of human freedoms[86]—freedoms which are embodied in the relevant international instruments on traditional civil and political rights as well as those which focus upon economic, social and cultural rights (access to health care, education, shelter, work and food)—then the relationship between rights and development is a symbiotic one. Development is required to expand those human freedoms; it is necessary to make rights *realisable*.

[84] See eg J Häusermann, *A Human Rights Approach To Development* (London, Rights and Humanity 1998); P Uvin, *Human Rights and Development* (London, Rights and Humanity, 2004); P Alston and M Robinson (eds), *Human Rights and Development: Towards Mutual Reinforcement* (Oxford, Oxford University Press, 2005); P Gready and J Ensor, *Reinventing Development?: Translating Rights-based Approaches from Theory into Practice* (London, Zed Books, 2005); B Andreassen and S Marks (eds), *Development as a Human Right: Legal, Political, and Economic Dimensions* (Cambridge MA, Harvard University Press, 2007).

[85] See also J Cockayne, 'The Fraying Shoestring: Rethinking Hybrid War Crimes Tribunals' (2005) 28 *Fordham International Law Journal* 616.

[86] A Sen, *Development as Freedom* (Oxford, Oxford University Press, 2001).

This explicit linkage between human rights and development has moved centre-stage in the language, at least, of a range of international institutions in the past decade or so. A major shake-up occurred at the United Nations following the pitiful response to the unfolding tragedy in Rwanda.[87] All of the agencies of the UN involved in development and humanitarian relief have increasingly placed human rights to the fore in discussing their work.[88] In 1998, the World Bank, while acknowledging that it has historically been 'less forthcoming about articulating its role in promoting human rights within the countries in which it operates', declared its core belief that 'creating the conditions for the attainment of human rights is a central and irreducible goal of development'.[89] Similarly, a range of important national donors such as the United Kingdom's Department for International Development have described strategies for reaching international development targets as 'realising human rights for poor people'.[90] In addition, many of the major international humanitarian agencies such as Oxfam, Save the Children, CARE and others have mainstreamed human rights across their policy and delivery programmes.[91]

Many of the documents and publications produced by these international institutions and agencies are replete with frameworks, benchmarks and practical mechanisms designed to guide both these agencies themselves and their local 'partners' in embedding rights discourses in their work.[92] The emphasis has shifted from a welfare-based approach to people 'because they have needs' to one which provides assistance 'because they have rights', ie entitlements which give rise to legal obligations on the part of others including the state, donors and aid agencies themselves.[93] Thus, mission statements, strategic objectives, evaluation reports and the like

[87] T Howland, 'Mirage, Magic or Mixed Bag? The United Nations High Commissioner for Human Rights Field Operation in Rwanda' (1999) 21 *Human Rights Quarterly* 1.

[88] See 'Renewing the United Nations: A Programme for Reform', UN Doc A/51/950 (July 1997).

[89] World Bank, 'Development and Human Rights: The Role of the World Bank' (Washington DC, World Bank, 1998). Available online at http://www.worldbank.org/html/extdr/rights/hrtext.pdf .

[90] Department for International Development, *Realising Human Rights for Poor People: Strategies for Achieving International Development Targets* (London, DFID, 2000).

[91] See, eg Oxfam GB, *Development and Rights* (London, Oxfam, 1998); Save the Children, *Child Rights Programming: Child Rights-Based Approach To Programmes Summary* (London, Save the Children, 2003); CARE International, *Principles into Practice: Learning from Innovative Rights Based Programmes* (London, Care International, 2005).

[92] See, eg M Picard, *Measurement and Methodological Challenges to Care International's Rights Based Programming*, Paper submitted to the EDIAIS Conference, University of Machester (24–25 November 2003). Available online at http://www.enterprise-impact.org.uk/pdf/Picard.pdf ; R Eyben, C Ferguson and L Groves, 'How Can Donors Become More Accountable To Poor People?' in L Groves and R Hinton (eds), *Inclusive Aid: Power and Relationships in International Development* (London, Earthscan, 2004).

[93] See Institute of Development Studies, *The Rise of Rights: Rights-Based Approaches to International Development* (Surrey, Institute of Development Studies, 2003).

often now address familiar development themes—such as accountability, transparency, non-discrimination legitimacy, partnership, empowerment and so on—explicitly by reference to international human rights standards. Human rights are emerging as the key benchmarks against which to measure not just the effectiveness or 'outputs' of development but its practical and epistemological starting point, the breadth of its gaze and the process through which it is planned and delivered. As well as the international actors involved in development work, one also sees increased articulation of environmental justice, participation, information, ownership over natural resources and so forth expressed as 'rights' by indigenous development groups on the ground.

Of course the outworking of such a relatively new fusion of discourses is inevitably contested. For some commentators, the adoption of 'human rights talk' is viewed cynically as the 'Emperor's new clothes': fashionable buzzwords which dress up familiar imperialist and other flaws in the same old development work.[94] Uneven power relationships, cultures of dependency, chronic mismanagement and other fault-lines in relations between international donors and local agencies persist.[95] Organisations at all levels continue to be involved in unedifying competition for 'a market share in money and misery'.[96] Some international and local actors inappropriately stretch the language of rights to such an extent that the legal integrity of the rights discourse begins to fray.[97] Of course controversy persists over the application of human rights discourses to non-state actors and who precisely can and cannot be held accountable by such standards.[98] These and many other features underline inevitable tensions between rights and development.

Such perfectly reasonable caveats aside, human rights discourses in the hands of suitably skilled grassroots organisations still offer a compelling corrective to legalistic understandings of the field. Imbuing rights discourses with what Nyamu-Musembi has referred to as 'an actor-orientated perspective on human rights'—a perspective she describes as exploring how legal principles play out in terms of their concrete effects in social

[94] See Uvin, *Human Rights and Development* (n 84 above) for a review of this debate.

[95] See, eg M Maren, *The Road to Hell: The Ravaging Effects of Foreign Aid and International Charity* (New York, Free Press, 2002); W Easterly, *The White Man's Burden: Why the West's Efforts to Aid the Rest Have Done So Much Ill and So Little Good* (Oxford, Oxford University Press, 2002).

[96] Ignatieff, *Empire Lite* (n 74 above) at 98.

[97] For example, the utilisation by Oxfam of the 'right to be heard' or the frequent exhortation in some community and educational publications of the right of elders or teachers to 'respect' would undoubtedly make even the most relaxed of lawyers wince a little as they searched for a relevant international standard. See Institute of Development Studies, *The Rise of Rights* (n 93 above).

[98] See P Alston (ed), *Non-State Actors and Human Rights* (Oxford, Oxford University Press, 2005).

settings from the viewpoint of traditionally subordinated actors[99]—creates the space to challenge power differentials and underpin the *resistant* potential of rights discourses for such individuals and communities. Rajagopal, while sharing some of the critiques advanced earlier concerning human rights, also notes how human rights has emerged as an organising framework for variants of 'third world resistance' which span a host of popular movements including peasant, urban, ecological feminist and others—well beyond the historically lawyer-driven 'human rights movement'.[100] In post-conflict societies in particular, properly resourced and translated grassroots rights talk and action has the capacity to inspire, to mobilise, and to restore a sense of agency to the powerless.[101]

By way of example, I have written elsewhere about the embedding of human rights discourses in the work of the community-based restorative justice programmes in Northern Ireland. In those projects international standards were adapted, translated into locally understandable language and became the benchmarks for the delivery of services in these conflict-affected communities.[102] It is precisely because of the politically fraught context in which these programmes have operated, as John Braithwaite has argued, that this jurisdiction has seen perhaps the most mature debate on restorative justice standards anywhere the world.[103] While the state has arguably sought to use the human rights framework in order to *control* these projects, the debate has been constantly nuanced and indeed 'thickened' by the practical experiences of community-based practitioners (many of them ex-combatants) and the people in local communities with whom they are working rather than by lawyers or state officials.[104] In such contexts human rights do not offer pat answers to complex problems. Provided that the integrity of the discourse is maintained, they do provide a disciplined framework for what Habermas has described as the potential

[99] C Nyamu-Musembi, 'Towards an Actor-Orientated Perspective on Human Rights' (Surrey, Institute of Development Studies, Working Paper 169, 2002).

[100] B Rajagopal, *International Law from Below: Development, Social Movements and Third World Resistance* (Oxford, Oxford University Press, 2004) esp ch 7.

[101] A Cornwall and C Nyamu-Musembi, 'Putting the 'Rights-Based Approach' to Development into Perspective' (2004) 25 *Third World Quarterly* 1415.

[102] K McEvoy and A Eriksson, 'Restorative Justice in Transition: Ownership, Leadership and 'Bottom Up' Human Rights' in D Sullivan and L Tift (eds), *Handbook of Restorative Justice* (London, Routledge, 2006).

[103] J Braitwaite, 'Setting Standards for Restorative Justice' (2002) 42 *British Journal of Criminology* 563.

[104] For example, protocols which are designed to regulate the relationship between these community programmes and the criminal justice system, are insistent about the involvement in the police and prosecution service 'in order to ensure that rights are protected'. The retort from some of the community programmes has been framed in terms of the 'rights' of victims to determine the level and nature of the involvement of state agencies in addressing *their* harms. See K McEvoy and A Eriksson, 'Justice, Community and the State in Transition in Northern Ireland' in J Shapland (ed), *Justice, Community and Civil Society: A Contested Terrain* (Cullompten, Willan Publishing, 2008).

for 'communicative action'[105]—a space where a dialogue about competing rights claims can occur, where power relationships can be named, and where the needs of the state (even when expressed in human rights terms) do not necessarily trump the needs of individuals and communities most affected by violence.

C Developing a Criminological Understanding of Transitional Justice

The final theme I would suggest for transcending some of the legalistic traits associated with transitional justice that are explored above is an approach which draws from criminology in particular. Posner and Vermeule have argued that transitional justice is much more like ordinary justice than many of its advocates would acknowledge.[106] Certainly I would agree that criminological understandings historically derived from 'normal' societies are of relevance. Criminology has been famously described by David Downes as a 'rendezvous discipline'. It is a subject where other disciplines meet and its liveliness (at its best) is precisely because it is located on the busy crossroads of sociology, psychology, law and philosophy. By virtue of its interdisciplinarity, and the rigour of its better scholarship, I would argue that criminology brings a number of attributes to the table which can assist in developing a 'thicker' understanding of transitional justice. In particular criminology provides a helpful framework in asking practical questions about judging whether transitional justice *works* as well as more philosophical questions as to who and what it is *for*. A fully theorised criminology of transition is beyond the scope of the current chapter, but a number of pointers are useful for illustrative purposes.

The most obvious place to begin is with the notion of crime itself. Transitional justice has emerged in large part as a result of attempts to deal with the crimes of past regimes. Criminology has obviously a long tradition in seeking to better understand the aetiology of crime and the ways in which crime is a socially and politically constructed phenomenon. Over the last decade in particular these analytical traditions have been deployed in conflict and post-conflict settings in exploring the most serious of 'political' crimes, including genocide.[107]

[105] J Habermas, *The Theory of Communicative Action: Reason and the Rationalization of Society* (Boston MA, Beacon Press, 1981) vol 1, 8.

[106] E Posner and A Vermeule, 'Transitional Justice As Ordinary Justice' (2004) 117 *Harvard Law Review* 761.

[107] See, eg S Cohen, 'Crime and Politics: Spot the Difference' (1996) 47 *British Journal of Sociology* 1; R Jamieson, 'Genocide and the Social Production of Immorality' (1998) 3 *Theoretical Criminology* 131; J Hagan, W Rymond-Richmond and P Parker, 'The Criminology of Genocide: The Death and Rape of Darfur' (2005) 43 *Criminology* 525. For a

Of course criminologists are not just interested in crime, they are also interested in justice. Thus, criminological writing on transitions has focused on issues such as the delivery of justice and security by national criminal justice systems, the efficacy of local and international policing, the particular durability of informal styles of justice delivery and a host of other theoretical and practical concerns about the relevance and utility of the discipline in understanding and seeking to resolve conflict.[108] Given the emphasis on state-centricity in transitional contexts discussed above, perhaps of central relevance for this chapter is the criminological approach to the state.

With regard to the state and justice ownership and delivery, criminologists have developed quite an advanced theoretical position.[109] Indeed, the fragmentation of the state in the delivery of aspects of justice, security, policing, punishment and so forth is now largely taken as a given by most contemporary criminologists. As Garland and Sparks argue, criminologists of all stripes have for some time been thinking well 'beyond the state' in their analysis of crime and justice.[110] In particular, for those who have been influenced by the writings of Foucault on governmentality, the 'hollowed out state' is now no longer perceived as the sole provider of such services, but rather as a partner doing business with a range of other actors. The state is recast, to use Nikolas Rose's phrase, as 'exercising only limited powers of its own, steering and regulating rather than rowing and providing'.[111]

For example, in policing, intelligence and security work there is now a considerable ceding of authority and resources *above and beyond* the nation state. Authority is ceded to 'outside' major powers such as the United States. American police agencies have a long history of involvement in anti-drugs strategies in Latin America and more recently have become

discussion of the broader relationship between crime and transition see, eg B Dixon and E Van der Spuy (eds), *Justice Gained? Crime and Crime Control in South Africa's Transition* (Cape Town, Cape Town University Press, 2004) 193–226; RT Naylor, *Wages of Crime: Black Markets, Illegal Finance and the Underworld Economy*, revised edn (Cornell, Cornell University Press, 2004).

108 Eg, see D Bayley, *Developing Democratic Policing Abroad* (Oxford, Oxford University Press, 2006); A. Snodgrass Godoy, *Popular Injustice: Violence, Community, and Law in Latin America* (Stanford, Stanford University Press, 2006); A Wardak, 'Building a Post-war Justice System in Afghanistan' (2004) 41 *Crime, Law & Social Change* 319; K McEvoy and T Newburn (eds), *Criminology, Conflict Resolution and Restorative Justice* (London, Palgrave, 2003); V Ruggiero, 'Criminalizing War: Criminology as Ceasefire' (2005) 14 *Social & Legal Studies* 239.

109 See especially I Loader and N Walker, *Civilizing Security* (Cambridge, Cambridge University Press, 2007).

110 D Garland and R Sparksm, 'Criminology, Social Theory and the Challenge of Our Times' in D Garland and R Sparks (eds), *Criminology and Social Theory* (Oxford, Oxford University Press, 2000) 5.

111 N Rose, 'Government and Control' in D Garland and R Sparks (eds), *Criminology and Social Theory* (Oxford, Oxford University Press, 2000) 186.

highly active in anti-terrorist policing in a wide range of countries. Authority also moves to supra-state policing structures such as Interpol and Europol or to the rapidly expanding supra-national private sector entities involved in the provision of security in both 'settled' and transitional contexts.[112] In addition, the development in many jurisdictions of justice provision *along-side* the state, through private prisons, private security and private immigration services, has seen the state become a contracting and regulating party which sets parameters within which non-state corporate actors are supposed to deliver a required service for an agreed fee.[113] Finally, many industrialised countries have been divesting justice responsibilities *below* the state to local community, voluntary and civil society organisations involved in crime prevention, restorative justice, ex-offender management and reintegration, youth justice and other activities.[114] In effect, the idealised state with its monolithic ownership over justice functions which is 'imagined' in many of the state-centric transitional justice discourses and evidenced in the massive expenditure on 'rule of law programmes' does not exist in much of the developed world.[115]

The difficulties of holding accountable these various private sector actors which operate above and alongside the state are well rehearsed in the criminological literature on transitional settings such as South Africa and Iraq.[116] However, what is of particular interest is the ways in which this 'imagined state' is perhaps most prescient with regard to the apparent difficulty of delegating *downwards* justice functions to local community and civil society structures in times of transition. As was discussed above with regard to Northern Ireland, the debate concerning community-based restorative justice has provoked quite a heated political tussle. In South Africa, despite the intuitive sympathy of many in the ANC, particularly in the early days of the transition, there has been an at times uneasy

[112] See, eg J Sheptycki, *Issues in Transnational Policing* (London, Routledge, 2000); C O'Reilly and G Ellison, 'Eye Spy Private High': Re-Conceptualizing High Policing Theory' (2006) 46 *British Journal of Criminology* 641.

[113] See, eg C Logan, *Private Prisons: Pros and Cons* (New York, Oxford University Press, 1990); I Loader, 'Thinking Normatively About Private Security' (1997) 24 *Journal of Law and Society* 377; G Lahav, 'Immigration And The State: The Devolution And Privatisation Of Immigration Control' (1998) 24 (EU) *Journal Of Ethnic And Migration Studies* 675.

[114] See, eg A Crawford, *The Local Governance of Crime: Appeals to Community and Partnership* (Oxford, Oxford University Press, 1999); G Bazemore and M Schiff, *Restorative Community Justice: Repairing Harm and Transforming Communities* (Cincinatti OH, Anderson Publishing Co, 2001); G Hughes, *The Politics of Crime and Community* (London, Palgrave, 2006).

[115] There is an interesting parallel here with the symbolic importance of the police and other justice functions in the historical forging of a 'national identity' of a number of European nations in the 19th Century. See, eg C Elmsley, *Gendarmes and the State in 19th Century Europe* (Oxford, Oxford University Press, 2000).

[116] B Baker, 'Living With Non-State Policing In South Africa: The Issues And Dilemmas' (2002) 40 *Journal of Modern African Studies* 29; R Jamieson and K McEvoy, 'State Crime By Proxy And Juridical Othering' (2005) 45 *British Journal of Criminology* 504.

relationship between the formal justice system and community-based justice and peace-making initiatives.[117] Similarly, in the context of Rwanda, some of the legalistic criticisms levelled at the admittedly imperfect system of Gacaca (the adaptation of local indigenous traditions by the national government to process lower-level perpetrators of genocide) have been entirely disproportionate given the scale of the outrages that were being dealt with and the limited alternatives on offer.[118] Indeed, arguably one of the most compelling criticisms of the Gacaca system is precisely the high level of state ownership and control over the process and the concurrent lack of community autonomy.[119]

Contemporary criminology is in no way immune to the dangers of vigilantism, exclusionary communitarianism, reification of unequal gender or other power relationships and the related potential failings in ceding justice ownership to local communities. In fact, as Goldsmith has suggested, those dangers are undoubtedly significantly enhanced in transitional settings with weak or flawed states and an abundance of Kalashnikovs.[120] I have argued elsewhere that it is criminology which provides the least dewy-eyed and the most critically informed appreciation of the difficulties of 'doing' justice in such community settings.[121] However, what distinguishes modern criminology from much legal scholarship on the topic, both in settled and transitional justice settings, is that it appears more willing to *try* to take on the challenges of informal or community justice. Unlike many lawyers whose default position is the tried and failed methods of legal formalism, more considered criminology by and large does not set expectations from state justice that cannot be delivered.[122]

It is this pronounced weariness in the capacity of traditional state institutions to actually *deliver* justice that underpins much of the practical

[117] See Roche, *Accountability in Restorative Justice* (n 68 above).

[118] For measured reviews of some of these criticisms see E Daly, 'Between Punitive And Reconstructive Justice: The Gacaca Courts In Rwanda' (2002) 34 *New York University Journal of International Law and Politics* 355; M Drumbl, 'Restorative Justice and Collective Responsibility: Lessons For and From the Rwandan Genocide' (2002) 5 *Contemporary Justice Review* 5–22. W Schabas, 'Genocide Trials and Gacaca Courts' (2005) 3 *Journal of International Criminal Justice* 879.

[119] L Waldorf, 'Rwanda's Failing Experiment in Restorative Justice' in D Sullivan and L Tift (eds), *Handbook of Restorative Justice* (London, Routledge, 2006).

[120] A Goldsmith, 'Policing Weak States: Citizen Safety and State Responsibility' (2005) 13 *Policing and Society* 3.

[121] See, eg M Cain, 'Beyond Informal Justice' (1985) *Contemporary Crisis* 335; R Matthews (ed), *Informal Justice* (London, Sage, 1988); McEvoy and Mika, 'Restorative Justice and the Critique of Informalism in Northern Ireland' (n 7 above).

[122] For classic accounts of the socio-legal scholarship in this field see R Abel (ed), *The Politics of Informal Justice*: vol 1 The American Experience, vol 2 Comparative Studies (New York, Academic Press, 1982); and S Merry and N Milner (eds), *The Possibility of Popular Justice* (Ann Arbor, University of Michigan Press, 1993).

contribution of criminology to the transitional justice debate. Amongst the key themes that a first-year undergraduate criminology student is required to unpick is what is referred to as the 'attrition rate' in criminal statistics. This refers to the number of crimes actually committed and the number which ultimately result in a successful prosecution. The figure for the United Kingdom, which is fairly typical of most advanced industrial societies, is that approximately three to four per cent of crimes result in a successful prosecution.[123] This disparity, which the Home Office itself refers to as the 'justice gap', occurs in a context where expenditure on criminal justice in England and Wales will top £22.7 billion in 2007–08, or 2.5 per cent of Gross Domestic Product.[124] In short, it is little wonder that many criminologists pose the fundamental question whether the traditional state-centred justice system is actually 'fit for purpose'. This is precisely why so much criminological emphasis in recent years has been focused upon an ever-greater technical refinement of 'what works' in criminal justice practice.[125] It also explains the rapid development of restorative justice initiatives in particular as governments, policy communities and academics increasingly appear to have concluded that much traditional criminal justice practice 'wasn't working' and wasn't providing value for money.[126]

Such a critical approach to the practical effectiveness of state justice has potentially profound implications for transitional justice at the national level. As noted above, national criminal justice systems in transition have received significant investment through numerous 'rule of law programmes' designed to improve criminal justice systems previously characterised by brutality, inefficiency and corruption.[127] The *need* for better policing, an impartial judiciary, better prisons and so forth in such contexts is indisputable. However, the reality from the experience of the developed world suggests that even in the unlikely event that such justice systems could eventually be 'raised' to the performance levels of their Western counterparts, they would still most likely fall far short of the mark. This note of realism needs to be injected into these programmes. There is little point in promoting an ideal of state justice that does not work in the better resourced context of the developed world where 'rule of law' norms have

[123] See R Garside, *Crime, Persistent Offenders and the Justice Gap* (London, The Crime and Society Foundation, 2004).

[124] E Solomon, C Eades, R Garside and M Rutherford, *Ten Years of Criminal Justice Under Labour: An Independent Audit* (London, Centre for Crime and Justice Studies, 2007) 10.

[125] See, eg S Farrell, *Rethinking What Works with Offenders: Probation, Social Context and Desistance from Crime* (Cullompten, Willan Publishing, 2004); D Bayley, *What Works in Policing?* (New York, Oxford University Press, 1998).

[126] G Johnstone, *Restorative Justice: Ideas, Values, Debates* (Cullompten, Willan Publishing, 2002).

[127] Brooks, 'The New Imperialism' (n 5 above).

(arguably) had much longer to become embedded in the political and social fabric. At the very least such programmes need to be alive to the possibility of justice capacity existing elsewhere and be willing to deploy resources to 'skill up' potential civil society, community or even private sector partners. They need to be willing to try to transform centralising and monopolising organisational cultures in state agencies, and to put in place structures to ensure that partnership arrangements are properly regulated. Such relationships, referred to by Clifford Shearing and his colleagues as 'nodal forms of governance',[128] will inevitably be required for more effective justice delivery. 'Seeing' like a state in such contexts may well result in failure and disillusionment.

The final significant criminological contributions are to ask: *Who* and *what* is transitional justice for?[129] Such questions are particularly pertinent to the international tribunals because they appear to have the least well-developed answers.[130] Typically, the legalistic responses to such questions are framed in terms of 'bringing justice to victims' or 'holding offenders accountable'.[131] There appears to be little cognisance here of the complex array of victims' needs beyond the *punishment* of perpetrators. These needs are well rehearsed not only in criminology, victimology and restorative justice but also in the transitional literature itself that has emerged from the experiences of truth recovery, memorialisation and other strategies for dealing with the past.[132] Although victim/witness protection, counselling and other protective measures have been put in place by the various tribunals, suspicions that an instrumentalist attitude applies towards victims as primarily a means to achieve a successful prosecution persist.[133]

Similarly, the unashamed emphasis in international criminal justice is upon retribution as a means of holding senior perpetrators, planners or

[128] See L Johnston and C Shearing, *Governing Security: Explorations of Policing and Justice* (London, Sage, 2002); J Wood and C Shearing, *Imagining Security* (Cullompten, Willan Publishing, 2007).

[129] These questions will be more fully developed elsewhere. See McEvoy, Mika and McConnachie, *Reconstructing Transitional Justice* (n 10 above).

[130] Roberts and McMillan, 'For Criminology in International Criminal Justice' (n 6 above); M Drumbl, 'Toward a Criminology of International Crime' (2003) 19 *Ohio State Journal On Dispute Resolution* 263.

[131] See P Akhavan, 'Beyond Impunity: Can International Criminal Justice Prevent Future Atrocities?' (2001) 95 *American Journal Of International Law* 7.

[132] See J Goodey, *Victims and Victimology: Research, Policy and Practice* (London, Longman, 2005); H Strang, *Repair or Revenge: Victims and Restorative Justice* (Oxford, Oxford University Press, 2003); B Hamber, D Nageng and G O'Malley, 'Telling it like it is ... Survivors' perceptions of the Truth and Reconciliation Commission' (2000) 26 *Psychology in Society* 18.

[133] See S Garkawe, 'The Victim Related Provisions of the Statute of the International Court: A Victimological Analysis' (2001) 8 *International Review of Victimology* 269–89; B Nowrojee, *Your Justice is Too Slow: Will the ICTR Fail Rwanda's Rape Victims?* (Geneva, United Nations Research Institute for Social Development, 2005).

instigators accountable for previous atrocities.[134] Punishment is linked casually with the assertion that it will serve as a deterrent to other would-be perpetrators of genocide or other gross violations.[135] Again, this logic takes little apparent account of the criminological literature which asks serious questions of deterrence theory generally, never mind in the particular social, political or cultural circumstances which lead to genocide.[136] Such a focus also fails to capture the much richer notions of deliberative accountability developed within restorative justice circles[137] or indeed the ways in which a focus on *individual* responsibility fails take proper account of the complex *collective* factors which contribute to violence.[138] In declaring a relatively small number of individuals officially guilty, we also run the risk of creating many more 'false innocents'.[139]

In broad terms there is a rich potential for a criminological contribution to transitional justice at the theoretical and practical level. Criminology, or at least good criminology, has a sophisticated theory of the state and other actors involved in justice work. Its practical bent provides a framework for the assessment of capacity, measurability, efficacy and value for money in each of these contexts. Its philosophical and moral curiosity asks the right questions about who and what transitional justice is actually for. Finally, its interdisciplinary origins afford it breadth and depth. And, given that law is one of the disciplines which has been key to the intellectual development of the subject, it is a discipline that is (mostly) less than 'awed' by the seductive certainties of legal analysis.

[134] The phrase used in Art 1 of the Statute for the Special Court in Sierra Leone is that the court has '*the power to prosecute persons who bear the greatest responsibility for serious violations of international humanitarian law and Sierra Leonean law*'. Available online at http://www.sc-sl.org/scsl-statute.html.

[135] Interestingly, the Rome Statute, which governs the International Criminal Court, has virtually nothing to say about the purpose of sentencing other than the rather vague formulation in the preamble that the ending of impunity for serious international crimes will 'contribute to the prevention of such crimes'. As Schabas points out, it suggests that the question about purpose is so obvious 'as to require no comment or direction': Schabas, *An Introduction to the International Criminal Court* (n 48 above) at 163.

[136] For example, the review of the deterrence literature conducted by Von Hirsh et al concluded that 'the studies reviewed did not provide any basis for inferring that increased severity of sentence had any deterrent effect' and was inconclusive as to whether certainty of punishment was any more effective: A Von Hirsch, A Bottoms, E Burney and PO Wiklstrom, *Criminal Deterrence and Sentence Severity* (Oxford, Hart Publishing, 1999).

[137] Roche, *Accountability in Restorative Justice* (n 68 above).

[138] As Lubin has argued, 'getting people to murder and torment their neighbours is not hard; in some ways, it turns out to be ridiculously easy': D Luban, 'Interventions and Civilization: Some Unhappy Lessons of the Kosovo War' in P De Greiff and C Cronin (eds), *Global Justice and Transnational Politics* (Cambridge MA, MIT Press, 2002) 107.

[139] H Steinert, 'Fin De Siècle Criminology' (1997) 1 *Theoretical Criminology* 111.

IV CONCLUSION

Although as Bell et al have argued, transitional justice discourses are themselves still 'in transition',[140] the centrality of 'the rule of law' is now firmly entrenched as a central pillar in the broader architecture of transition from conflict.[141] Perceived initially as a sub-discipline of international law, transitional justice arguably cloistered a peculiarly durable variant of legalism, precisely because the area was so self-evidently political. In re-reading some of the texts on legal developments in the field,[142] one gets the impression that lawyers are struggling against the obvious contingency of political expediency, are rightly wary of 'pragmatic' deals being struck with outgoing regimes and are holding firm to the safe ground of international human rights standards. In such a context the need for staying firmly fixed on legal principles was self-evident.

However, the transitions from authoritarian rule of the 1970s with their blanket amnesties and crude efforts to obliterate the past are much less legally or politically viable.[143] In Latin America in particular, many of the most obnoxious of these accommodations have been steadily whittled away by the Inter-American Court or national courts seemingly becoming more confident that democracy has taken a firm hold. More broadly, there is now a solid bedrock of international criminal law. There are binding international standards and a range of case law across the transitional field in the most contentious of areas, including what is permissible in local amnesty laws. The myriad of tribunals and International Criminal Court are all operational. A sophisticated body of knowledge exists about how truth recovery should and should not be effected.

'Letting go' of legalism does not require abandoning these advances. Rather it entails building upon them. It suggests a more honest acknowledgment of the limitations of legal thinking and practice that aren't properly grounded in the 'real world' in which law operates in places like Rwanda, Colombia, or Sierra Leone.[144] It contemplates a greater willingness to give space to actors other than the state or 'state-like' institutions in justice provision. It means being open to the insights of disciplines and forms of knowledge other than law in better understanding the meaning of

[140] *Ibid* at 306.

[141] See G O'Donnell, 'Why the Rule of Law Matters' (2004) 15 *Journal of Democracy* 32.

[142] See, eg A Cassesse, *International Criminal Law* (Oxford, Oxford University Press, 2002) and W Schabas, *The UN International Criminal Tribunals: The Former Yugoslava, Rwanda and Sierra Leone* (Cambridge, Cambridge University Press, 2006).

[143] L Mallinder, 'Can Amnesties and International Justice be Reconciled ?' (2007) 1 *International Journal of Transitional Justice* 208.

[144] See R Mani, *Beyond Retribution: Seeking Justice in the Shadow of War* (Cambridge, Polity Press, 2002).

justice in a transition. A thicker variant of transitional justice will be also better equipped to actually *deliver* to those who have been most affected by conflict.

3

International Law as a 'Tiered Process': Transitional Justice at the Local, National and International Level

LORNA MCGREGOR*

I INTRODUCTION

IN HER GENEALOGY of transitional justice, Teitel highlights the central presence of the law. She locates the first phase of the transitional justice discourse within the post-World War II time period, epitomised by the Nuremberg trials. As such, she characterises transitional justice as 'interstate cooperation, war crimes trials, and sanctions'.[1] In the second phase, marked by the truth commissions of Latin America and South Africa in the late 1980s and early 1990s, Teitel asserts that

> the transitional dilemmas at stake in Phase II were framed in terms more comprehensive than simply confronting or holding accountable the predecessor regime, and included questions about how to heal an entire society and incorporate diverse rule-of-law values, such as peace and reconciliation, that had previously been treated as largely external to the transitional justice project.[2]

* The author would like to thank Kieran McEvoy, Gabriela Echeverria, Kristin Sandvik and Annecoos Wiersema for their extensive and useful comments on earlier drafts as well as the International Bar Association for whom the author used to work as an ICC Programme Lawyer. The chapter does not necessarily reflect the views of any organisation mentioned above and all errors, of course, remain the author's own.

[1] R Teitel, 'Transitional Justice Genealogy' (2003) 16 *Harvard Human Rights Journal* 69 at 70.

[2] *Ibid* at 77.

In recent years, transitional justice has presented something of a paradox. On the one hand, demands for transitional justice have become normalised, shifting from the exceptional to the routine.[3] On the other, at both the formal and informal level, the centrality of legal processes has generated a sense of 'transitional justice fatigue'.[4] Thus, in spite, or perhaps because of, the establishment of the International Criminal Court (ICC), major actors within the international community appear less enthusiastic towards supporting mechanisms which have become emblematic of transitional justice, such as the ad hoc international criminal tribunals. On a parallel level, the dominance of legal models has led to increasing demands for a more prominent role and recognition to be given to existing and developing informal and community-led initiatives. This chapter seeks to address this paradox by exploring the ways in which developments in international law which emphasise the rights of traditionally disenfranchised groups, participation and ownership may offer a framework within which transitional justice processes at the international, national and local level can operate.

Part II of this chapter outlines the hegemonic origins of international law, its formalistic tendencies and institutional base, in addition to the criticism that international justice mechanisms often seem remote from the communities most affected by the crimes they seek to address. While acknowledging these features, this section argues that analysis of the role of international law must go further than simply critiquing its shortcomings and limitations. As international law is not a static or sealed system, certain developments, particularly those generated by actors other than the state, highlight a role for international law in responding to conflict.

Part III of this chapter first addresses the ways in which national policy solutions to dealing with conflict often close the space in which to develop multiple responses to conflict, particularly through the grant of blanket amnesties. As a related matter, the chapter addresses the tendency of transitional justice models resulting from national policy decisions to exclude or distort the experience of traditionally disenfranchised groups. By strategically or inadvertently controlling the narrative of conflict, national policy decisions often attempt to portray the state as a neutral 'third-party' in an 'inter-ethnic', 'religious' or 'political' conflict. They focus narrowly on civil and political rights violations to the exclusion of social and economic rights and the structural impact of conflict. Furthermore, they overlook or simplify the gender implications of conflict. The

[3] *Ibid* at 85 (describing '*Fin de Siècle Transitional Justice*' as discourse 'ever-present in politics').

[4] LA Dickinson, 'The Promise of Hybrid Courts' (2003) 97 *American Journal of International Law* 295 at 308 (attributing 'tribunal fatigue' as the reason for the establishment of hybrid courts).

chapter then considers the positive contribution of community and localised approaches as an alternative means to dealing with conflict, and contrasts the extensive critique of formal transitional justice processes with the tendency to eulogise informal and community-based initiatives (by virtue of their locality) without assessing their impact on the rights of traditionally marginalised groups.

In considering options for transitional justice, the choice between indigenous processes and formal justice mechanisms should not be viewed as mutually exclusive. Rather, the challenge for both is to ensure the rights of victims and traditionally marginalised groups. In the final section, the chapter explores a number of illustrative ways in which international law has played a significant role in solidifying the rights of marginalised groups including the limitations placed on blanket amnesties and the development of principles which place a specific emphasis on the rights of victims in addition to outreach, ownership and participation.

II BEYOND THE INTERNATIONAL LAW HEGEMON

The hegemonic, Euro-centric origins of international law are well documented. Mohammed Bedjaoui, a former president of the International Court of Justice, stated that

> [t]his classic international law thus consisted of a set of rules with a geographical basis (it was European Law), a religious-ethical inspiration (it was a Christian law), an economic motivation (it was a mercantilist law) and political aims (it was an imperialist law).[5]

The foundations of international law and its ability to develop thereof reflect a recurring project of international scholars. For example, Anghie provides an examination of the emergence and development of international law during the 19th century as a positivist and ostensibly scientific discipline which attached the mutually reinforcing conceptions of sovereignty and society to exclude and oppress non-European states through the requirement of 'civilisation'.[6] While acknowledging the number of developments in international law since the 19th century, Anghie argues that the

[5] Cited in D Otto, 'Subalternanity and International Law: The Problem of Global Community and the Incommensurability of Difference' in E Darian Smith and P Fitzpatrick (eds), *Laws of the Postcolonial* (Ann Arbor MI, University of Michigan Press, 1999) 145 at 148

[6] A Anghie, 'Finding the Peripheries: Sovereignty and Colonialism in Nineteenth-Century International Law' (1999) 40 *Harvard International Law Journal* 1 at 75.

core structure remains fundamentally unchanged.[7] Against this background, the shortcomings and limitations of legal processes within the transitional context have been addressed at a number of junctures within this collection.[8]

In addition, the process by which an international justice model is established can have as much of a determinative impact on its eventual 'success' as its substantive outcomes. As Drumbl argues, 'sensitivity to the local contours the effectiveness of international justice initiatives'.[9] Challenges to the legitimacy of a process may be based on claims of a democratic deficit, a right to self-determination[10] and a lack of 'buy-in'.[11] Legitimacy is a complex notion and cannot simply be demarcated by an international and local divide.[12] As Ibhawo points out,

> dominant groups or classes may hold, or at least be open to, different perceptions and interpretations that are helpful for their struggle for control for justice and improvements for themselves. This type of internal struggle for control over cultural resources and symbols can be said to underline the contemporary discourse on cultural legitimacy of human rights.[13]

In this respect, 'perceptions of ... validity and legitimacy may differ significantly among different groups within a given society'.[14] Nevertheless, the introduction of internationalised institutions often lends itself to resistance by local opinion leaders and influential groups by portraying the initiatives as outside interventions. In essence, internationalised bodies have to work even harder to overcome internal points of resistance.

When created by virtue of a supra-national policy, the lack of opportunity for stakeholders and interest-based groups to contribute, shape and participate in the formation and implementation of the process can often undercut receptivity to the mechanism within the communities in which it seeks to operate. If seen as a 'top-down' imposition, the experience of the international criminal tribunals for the Former Yugoslavia (ICTY) and Rwanda (ICTR) indicates that the body may be seen as less relevant to the needs and interests of the communities most affected. This can result in

[7] *Ibid.*

[8] See chs 2, 6 and 7 of this collection.

[9] MA Drumbl, 'Rights, Culture, and Crime: The Role of Rule of Law for the Women of Afghanistan' (2004) 42 *Columbia Journal of Transnational Law* 349 at 363.

[10] L McGregor, 'Beyond the Time and Space of Peace Talks: Re-Appropriating the Peace Process in Sri Lanka' (2006) 11 *International Journal of Peace Studies* 39 at 41–2.

[11] Dickinson, 'The Promise of Hybrid Courts' (n 4 above) at 301.

[12] See D Beetham, *The Legitimation of Power* (London, MacMillan, 1991) (discussing the 'multi-dimensional' and complex character of notions of legitimacy).

[13] B Ibhawo, 'Between Culture and Constitution: Evaluating the Cultural Legitimacy of Human Rights in the African State' (2000) 22 *Human Rights Quarterly* 838 at 850.

[14] *Ibid* at 842.

what Drumbl terms 'the externalization of justice'.[15] As international justice mechanisms usually reflect highly formalised and quite often, legalistic, processes, they can seem remote, inaccessible and unfamiliar and may even create an institutional bias towards victims and survivors with formal education.[16] Indeed, as noted in the Annual Report of the ICTY,

> the Tribunal is unlike any other Court. National courts exist within each state's criminal justice system and an institutional framework that supports the conduct of criminal proceedings. Within the international community, there are no such mechanisms to ensure the dissemination and interpretation of the work of the Tribunal. The gap thus created between justice and its beneficiaries—victims of the conflict—is exacerbated by the Tribunal's physical location far from the Former Yugoslavia.[17]

International human rights principles are particularly vulnerable to characterisation as external or Euro-centric impositions if not accompanied by outreach and participation. In his discussion of the ad hoc international criminal tribunals, Drumbl characterises transitional justice initiatives as a form of 'unidirectionalism' which,

> [i]nstead of building accountability and restoration from the bottom-up through involvement of indigenous laws, customs, personalities, politics, and practices, international criminal law interventions tend to drop from the top-down.[18]

The lessons learned from recent transitional justice mechanisms, such as the UN Mission in Kosovo (UNMIK), underscore the importance of 'engagement with the local populace' in order to avoid disillusionment, cynicism, and disengagement with the underlying principles of the process, namely human rights and the rule of law.[19] In Marshall and Inglis' evaluation of UNMIK's attempts to implement a human rights policy in Kosovo, they attribute many of the shortcomings and challenges to the intervention to the failure to develop 'real connections and genuine working relationships ... with prominent Kosovo human rights groups' in addition to a trivialisation of, 'the local community and the importance of its sense of ownership and input'.[20]

[15] Drumbl, 'Rights, Culture, and Crime' (n 9 above) 352; MA Drumbl, 'Collective Violence and Individual Punishment: The Criminality of Mass Atrocity' (2005) 99 *North Western University Law Review* 539 at 602.

[16] See N Roht-Arriaza, 'Reparation Decisions and Dilemmas' (2004) 27 *Hastings International & Comparative Law Review* 157 at 169.

[17] Security Council, 'Report of the International Tribunal for the Prosecution of Persons Responsible for Serious Violations of International Humanitarian Law Committed in the Territory of the Former Yugoslavia Since 1991' (25 August 1999) S/1999/846 at para 147.

[18] Drumbl, 'Collective Violence and Individual Punishment' (n 15 above) at 596.

[19] D Marshall and S Inglis, 'Human Rights in Transition: The Disempowerment of Human Rights-Based Justice in the United Nations Mission in Kosovo' (2003) 16 *Harvard Human Rights Journal* 95 at 97.

[20] *Ibid* at 140.

However, acknowledging the hegemonic nature of international law does not mean that it must be rejected completely. To only focus on the shortcomings of international law suggests a sealed and static system incapable of developing and contributing to the transitional context. It also fails to recognise the omnipresence of legal processes which will continue to result in hegemonic structures unless engaged with and shaped. In this respect, I would argue that international law is a process marked by contradictions and imperfections, the frictions of which enable its development and evolution. Most evidently and simply, international human rights law is predicated on the challenge to the traditional Westphalian conception of international law as an exclusively state-centric model. Moreover, Nader points out that the

> last twenty years of historical and comparative research into law and colonialism or law and globalization has had a major intellectual impact, with a central achievement being the enlarged and innovative perspective of law ... The unlearning of fundamental assumptions and conceptual frameworks has not fully worked itself out, but ... the contradictions are clearer and the fight is on as the field of inquiry continues to expand.[21]

Schiff Berman also argues that

> given that any state policy decision is inevitably the result of a contest among various bureaucratic power centers, all of which are themselves influenced by outside pressure groups, lobbyists, NGOs, and the like, a more complex understanding of international law would need to explore ways in which international legal norms empower specific interests both within and without the state policy-making apparatus and provide arguments and leverage that they might not otherwise have had.[22]

In this respect, actors other than states increasingly have a catalytic effect in demanding and shaping the evolution of international law to ensure the rights and protection of traditionally marginalised groups. Non-governmental organisations (NGOs) have played a particularly key role in the 'development, interpretation, judicial application, and enforcement' of international law.[23] NGOs contributed significantly to the adoption of the Set of Principles on Impunity[24] and the Basic Principles on the Right to a Remedy and Reparation, discussed below, and were centrally involved in

[21] L Nader, 'Anthropological and Historical Foundations: A Wide-Angle on Dispute Management' (2002) 10 *Williamette Journal of International Law & Dispute Resolution* 37 at 41–2.

[22] P Schiff Berman, 'Book Review Essay: Seeing Beyond the Limits of International Law' (2006) 84 *Texas Law Review* 1265 at 1280. See also Piacentini's chapter in this collection.

[23] See S Charnovitz, 'Nongovernmental Organizations and International Law' (2006) 100 *American Journal of International Law* 348 at 352.

[24] UNHRC, 'Promotion and Protection of Human Rights—Impunity: Report of the Independent Expert to Update the Set of Principles to Combat Impunity' (18 February 20[illegible] UN Doc E/CN.4/2005/102 at para 3.

the development of the Rome Statute and the subsequent establishment of the ICC. The contribution of NGOs was diverse, intricate and complex and the impact thereof is difficult to assess empirically. However, the combination of a visible presence at the Preparatory Commissions and the Rome Conference; the provision of information, legal expertise and expert analysis; coordination and organisation; and the employment of lobbying strategies meant that NGOs played a key role in the development of the Rome Statute,[25] particularly in ensuring provision for issues such as victims' rights, participation and reparation.

In addition, NGOs increasingly submit amicus curiae briefs to assist courts in their interpretation of international law and have employed innovative legal strategies to ensure that accountability is satisfied. For example, in Northern Ireland, victims' families have used the individual complaints mechanism before the European Court of Human Rights (EctHR) to push for the investigation of human rights violations where no political will existed internally.[26] Ni Aolain frames the importance of these cases as a representation of the 'enormous accountability gap for the State',[27] the result of which has led to the government of the United Kingdom's presentation of a 'package of measures' to the Committee of Ministers at the Council of Europe responsible for the implementation of ECtHR decisions.[28] Similarly, the initiation of criminal and civil proceedings by private parties is common to many expressions of universal jurisdiction. As Orentlicher points out,

> proceedings in Spanish courts against various military officials associated with crimes committed during Argentina's 'dirty war' were instituted by private

[25] Z Pearson, 'Non-Governmental Organisations and the International Criminal Court: Changing Landscapes of International Law' (2006) 39 *Cornell International Law Journal* 243.

[26] For example, see *Jordan v United Kingdom*, 24746/94 [2001] ECHR 327 (4 May 2001); *McKerr v United Kingdom*, 28883/95 [2001] ECHR 329 (4 May 2001); *Kelly and Others v United Kingdom*, 30054/96 [2001] ECHR 328 (4 May 2001); *Shanaghan v United Kingdom*, 37715/97 [2001] ECHR 330 (4 May 2001) (finding that the British state had violated Art 2 of the European Convention on Human Rights on the right to life in its failure to carry out an effective and thorough investigation into deaths allegedly committed by state agents during the conflict).

[27] F Ni Aolain, 'Truth Telling, Accountability, and the Right to Life in Northern Ireland' (2002) 5 *European Human Rights Law Review* 572 at 588.

[28] K McEvoy, *Truth, Transition and Reconciliation: Dealing with the Past in Northern Ireland* (Cullompton, Willan Publishing, 2008) 122 (citing the measures as including the 'establishment of the Police Ombudsman's Office; arrangements allowing for the 'calling in' of other police forces to investigate deaths; the establishment of the Serious Crimes Review Team ... the option for families to judicially review decisions not to prosecute; new practices relating to the verdicts of coroners' juries at inquests and developments regarding disclosure at inquests; legal aid for inquests; measures to give effect to recommendations following reviews of the coroner's system and the Inquiries Act'.)

> parties. Individual victims and human rights organizations were also the engine behind criminal proceedings against former Chadian leader Hissène Habré in Senegal.[29]

In a similar vein, Otto provides an approach to imagining the 'reshaping of the international community and its democratic potential'[30] by exposing 'the distortions of European hegemony' which renders it

> possible to recognize alternative democratic discourses at the edges of modernity and to imagine options for radical resistance within modernity.[31]

Otto argues that international law,

> as a 'prominent conversation' in international relations, could play a powerful role in ... transformation. Although law is one of the disciplinary techniques of global governmentality, it is a site where the limits of the readability of narratives of difference, community, and democracy are constantly contested. It provides one form for representing the incommensurability of difference within the global polity.[32]

From this perspective, international law need not be viewed only as a statist institution but as a vehicle which, because of its constant internal and external struggle and evolution, may result in social transformation and change.

III NATIONAL AND LOCAL RESPONSES TO CONFLICT

Against the discussion of international law above, this section explores other potentially complimentary normative frameworks within which traditionally disenfranchised groups can assert—and shape—their rights. I first consider the ways in which state-centric policies on dealing with the effects of conflict have often projected an exclusive mechanism which forecloses all other possibilities. I then explore both the positive contribution of community-based responses and their potential to suffer from similar hegemonic tendencies if the rights of traditionally disenfranchised groups are not integrated.

[29] DF Orentlicher, 'The Future of Universal Jurisdiction in the New Architecture of Transitional Justice' in S Macedo (ed), *Universal Jurisdiction: National Courts and the Prosecution of Serious Crimes under International Law* (Philadelphia PA, University of Pennsylvania Press, 2004) 214 at 230. See also DF Orentlicher, 'Whose Justice? Reconciling Universal Jurisdiction with Democratic Principles' (2004) 92 *Georgia Law Journal* 1057 at 1072.

[30] Otto, 'Subalternanity and International Law' (n 5 above) at 170.

[31] Otto, 'Subalternanity and International Law' (n 5 above) at 171.

[32] Otto, 'Subalternanity and International Law' (n 5 above) at 174.

A The Challenges of State-Centred Policies

A dominant characteristic of the transitional justice landscape has been the tendency of states to adopt national policies which seek to 'close the books' on human rights violations associated with a violent conflict.[33] Such prescription has most often reduced to a failure to deal with the past in any significant way and to the marginalisation of victims' and other key stakeholders' rights, needs and interests. As discussed below, one of the favoured ways in which to achieve this objective has been to provide for blanket amnesties. In addition, states often advocate 'reconciliation'—an intangible and uncertain term—which seemingly offers a positive move away from conflict but very often provides a cover for governments to do nothing to redress the violations and crimes which have taken place.[34]

(i) The Impact of Amnesties on the Rights of Victims

The first wave of transitional justice models in the late 1980s and early 1990s precipitated the normalisation of transitional justice as a discourse. Framed as 'national political solutions',[35] these models were designed to demarcate the authoritarian past from the newly democratic present. In this respect, the options identified and implemented emanated from centralised decision-making processes at the national level, often providing for a blanket amnesty. By Cassel's count, in 11 Latin American states,

> new civilian leaders have chosen or been compelled, sooner or later, either to decree an amnesty for serious human rights violations, or to accept one previously decreed by outgoing military rulers.[36]

[33] J Elster, *Closing the Books: Transitional Justice in History* (Cambridge, Cambridge University Press, 2004).

[34] For an analysis of the use of reconciliation within the transitional justice rubric, see L McEvoy, K McEvoy and K McConnachie, 'Reconciliation as a "Dirty Word": Conflict, Community Relations and Education in Northern Ireland' (2006) 60 *Journal of International Affairs* 81; L McGregor, 'Reconciliation: Where is the Law?' in S Veitch (ed), *Law and the Politics of Reconciliation* (Aldershot, Ashgate, 2006) 111–28 and L McGregor, 'Reconciliation: I Know It When I See It' (2006) 9 *Contemporary Justice Review* 155.

[35] Teitel, 'Transitional Justice Genealogy' (n 1 above) at 84.

[36] D Cassel, 'Accountability for International Crime and Serious Violations of Fundamental Human Rights: Lessons from the Americas: Guidelines for International Response to Amnesties for Atrocities' (1996) 59 *Law & Contemporary Problems* 197 at 201. See CS Nino, 'The Duty to Punish Past Abuses of Human Rights Put into Context: The Case of Argentina' (1991) 100 *Yale Law Journal* 2619 and DF Orentlicher, 'Settling Accounts: The Duty to Prosecute Human Rights Violations of a Prior Regime' (1991) 100 *Yale Law Journal* 2537 (debating whether a duty to prosecute exists under international law).

Despite calls for accountability by victims and human rights' groups, proponents of these 'insurance policies'[37] argued in favour of a *realpolitik* approach within which certain political trade-offs became necessary in order to secure the transition by appeasing ousted leaders and their military forces.[38] Thus, for example, in response to a constitutional challenge to the truth-for-amnesty formula in South Africa[39] on the basis that,

> the applicants have a clear right to insist that such wrongdoers should properly be prosecuted and punished, that they should be ordered by the ordinary courts of the land to pay adequate civil compensation to the victims or dependants of the victims and further to require the state to make good to such victims or dependants the serious losses which they have suffered in consequence of the criminal and delictual acts of the employees of the state[40]

the Constitutional Court focused on the priorities identified by the negotiators to the peace process, holding that,

> but for a mechanism providing for amnesty, the 'historic bridge' itself might never have been erected ... It was for this reason that those who negotiated the Constitution made a deliberate choice, preferring understanding over vengeance, reparation over retaliation, ubuntu over victimisation.[41]

The Court continued to hold that where,

> the erstwhile adversaries of such a conflict inhabit the same sovereign territory. They have to live with each other and work with each other and the *state concerned is best equipped to determine what measures may be most conducive for the facilitation of such reconciliation and reconstruction*[42] (emphasis added).

Accordingly, during the first wave of transitional justice models, the rights of victims did not feature as a priority or determinate in debates on how to deal with the past. Rather, the state was vested with the power to decide

[37] Cassel, 'Accountability for International Crime and Serious Violations of Fundamental Human Rights (n 36 above) at 200.

[38] See Nino, 'The Duty to Punish Past Abuses of Human Rights Put into Context' (n 36 above). See also K Asmal, MP, 'International Law and Practice: Dealing With the Past in the South African Experience' (2000) 15 *American University International Law Review* 1211 at 1216 (commenting on the Pinochet litigation: 'where, as in Chile ... a state declines to prosecute past despots as a result of democratic, conscious, public decision widely seen as fundamental to the implementation of democracy, I doubt that other states are, or ought to be, free to take up the task'.).

[39] Promotion of National Unity and Reconciliation Act, 1995 (No 34 of 1995). Section 20(7)(a) of the Act foreclosed the possibility of bringing a criminal or civil case against any individual who had been granted amnesty.

[40] *Azanian People's Organization (AZAPO) and others v President of the Republic of South Africa and others* CCT 17/96 at para 8 (1996 (4) SA 671 (CC)).

[41] *Ibid* at para 19 (citing the cases of Chile, Argentina and El Salvador as justification for amnesty despite the underlying human rights violations).

[42] *AZAPO v President of the Republic of South Africa* (n 40 above) at para 31.

how best to ensure the peaceful move from an authoritarian regime to a form of democracy. As such, amnesties were routinely used as the pivotal legal means by which to 'close the book' on the past.

(ii) Excluding the Experience of Disenfranchised Groups

One of the most striking failings of a number of transitional justice models resulting from national policy decisions has been the 'silencing' or distortion of the experience of traditionally disenfranchised groups. Drumbl argues that truth processes can

> through a process of accretion over time ... create an overarching historical narrative that can displace pre-existing narratives that may have normalized or legitimized the violence.[43]

However, much turns on the authors involved. The complexity of conflict may result, either inadvertently or strategically, in an elevation of certain objectives, histories, narratives or violations and the marginalisation of others. Indeed, Sarat asserts that

> [a]cts of commemoration are the very stuff of politics; in and through our political processes we decide who or what should be remembered or memorialized and in what ways.[44]

As discussed above, amnesties reflect one way in which states have often sought to avoid addressing the impact of conflict. Linked to this discussion is the potential risk that governments attempt to portray the state as a neutral 'third-party' in an 'inter-ethnic', 'religious' or 'political' conflict. Thus, transitional justice initiatives can narrow to inter-communal conflict rather than address any structural underpinnings. As Ni Aaloin points out,

> [t]he star role in this modern morality play is given to the state. The state's first soliloquy should be the acknowledgment that it has not been a neutral or passive actor in the experience and management of societal conflict.[45]

Thus, in a number of transitional justice settings, the narrative projected by the state often reflects a distancing from its responsibility in the conflict. Such projection is what Cohen terms as 'denial':

[43] Drumbl, 'Collective Violence and Individual Punishment' (n 15 above) at 594.

[44] A Sarat, 'When Memory Speaks: Remembrance and Revenge in *Unforgiven*' in M Minow (ed), *Breaking the Cycles of Hatred: Memory, Law and Repair* (Princeton NJ/Oxford, Princeton University Press, 2002) 241.

[45] F Ni Aolain, *The Politics of Force, Conflict Management and State Violence in Northern Ireland* (Belfast, The Blackstaff Press, 2000) 12. See also E Stanley's chapter in this collection.

> [A]nother move is to attribute responsibility to forces ... that supposedly have nothing to do with the government and are beyond its control ... the violence is 'endemic'—communal violence, civil war, war-lords, barons, tribal rivalry, ethnic tensions.[46]

In Northern Ireland, for example, the portrayal of the British state as the neutral 'third' party in a religious and/or political conflict between Catholics and Protestants or Unionists and Republicans, has proved one of the most contentious issues in the ongoing transitional justice debate.[47] In particular, the use of public inquiries has been seen as a way in which to control the narrative of the conflict. In her discussion of earlier public inquiries in Northern Ireland, Hegarty states that

> those conducting inquiries were aware of the dangers of the competing narratives of the events and were keen to minimize the opportunities for the opposing narrative to be heard. The opposing narrative was that of those who opposed the State. That it was seen as propaganda demonstrates the attitude of the State and those appointed to by it to investigate its actions. For them, human rights violations were a political battleground and the refutation of the claims of those who had been subject to those violations was a key aim.[48]

Similarly, Roht-Arriaza argues that the consequent impact of the South African transitional justice policy was to shift

> the focus from the complicity and benefits of apartheid to whites as a group to the misdeeds of a smaller group of security force operatives, easily characterized as 'bad apples'.[49]

In Sri Lanka, the position of the Minister for Reconciliation, sponsored by the World Back Triple R (Reconstruction, Rehabilitation and Reconciliation) Programme diverts attention from the responsibility of the dominant political actors to reconciliation between communities in order to transcend the 'tendency for each community to dwell exclusively on its own sufferings'.[50] In Algeria, a referendum was held to decide on whether the Algerian president could 'take "any steps necessary" to advance his vision of reconciliation, while effectively criminalizing public opposition'.[51]

[46] S Cohen, *States of Denial: Knowing About Atrocities and Suffering* (Cambridge, Polity Press, 2002) 109.

[47] CAIN (Conflict Archive on the Internet), Key Events: Bloody Sunday—Chronology, obtainable online from <http://can.ulst.ac.uk/events/bsunday/chron.htm.

[48] A Hegarty, 'Dealing With the Past: The Government of Memory: Public Inquiries and the Limits of Justice in Northern Ireland' (2003) 26 *Fordham International Law Journal* 1148 at 1161.

[49] Roht-Arriaza, 'Reparation Decisions and Dilemmas' (n 16 above) at 178–9.

[50] Government of Sri Lanka, Ministry for Reconciliation, 'A Vision for Sri Lanka' (19 December 2003).

[51] International Center for Transitional Justice (ICTJ), 'Algerian Charter Risks Reinforcing Impunity and Undermining Reconciliation', Press Release, 26 September 2005.

In addition, transitional justice processes have often concentrated on violations of civil and political rights. The focus on 'seeking accountability regarding a narrow range of human rights violations such as extra-judicial killings, forced disappearances and torture' is what Nesiah and Keenan refer to as the 'dominant human rights framework'.[52] In some instances, processes have even been selective therein. For example, in Chile, a truth process was instituted to examine killings and disappearances by the security forces,

> leaving aside the vastly larger number of those who were tortured while in detention and survived, and those who were forced into exile.[53]

Structural violations or the underpinnings of conflict have often not been addressed within macro-level processes.[54] In South Africa, crimes under international law formed the focus of the Truth and Reconciliation Commission's inquiry, but the

> legal pillars of apartheid: forced removals, pass laws, residential segregation and other forms of racial discrimination and detention without trial,

were not addressed.[55]

Thus, the way in which the transitional justice model is framed very often results in a narrow, under-inclusive portrayal of the experiences of conflict. At the national level, the mandate of the transitional justice model employed may strategically avoid the accountability of the state by characterising the conflict in ways such as 'inter-ethnic' or religious. The structural underpinnings of conflict may be intentionally or inadvertently omitted from the transitional justice account through the adoption of the 'dominant script'—what Cavallaro and Albuja refer to as a standardised approach to dealing with conflict based on an aggregation of comparative experience rather than a model rooted in the context in which it applies.[56]

B Localised Processes and the Dangers of Eulogisation

Local and community initiatives have and continue to play a 'public accountability' role in response to national policy determinations in

[52] V Nesiah and A Keenan, 'Human Rights and Sacred Cows: Framing Violence, Disappearing Struggles' in N Gordon (ed), *From the Margins of Globalization: Critical Perspectives on Human Rights* (Landam MD, Lexington Books, 2004) (discussing the human rights framework in Sri Lanka).

[53] Roht-Arriaza, 'Reparation Decisions and Dilemmas' (n 16 above) at 178.

[54] UNSC, Report of the Secretary-General to the Security Council, 'The Rule of Law and Transitional Justice in Conflict and Post-Conflict Societies' (23 August 2004) UN Doc S/2004/616 at para 4.

[55] Roht-Arriaza, 'Reparation Decisions and Dilemmas' (n 16 above) at 178–9.

[56] J Cavallaro and S Albuja, ch 5 in this collection.

transitional justice. As Panizza points out in her discussion of the role of the Mothers of Plazo de Mayo in Argentina,

> [t]heir action effectively put into question the dividing line between the personal and the political: their grief as mothers became the first intensely private issue to reconstitute a public space hitherto closed by the government.[57]

Beyond responding and shaping formal processes, a number of indigenous processes have been developed to directly address the impact of conflict. The *gacaca* proceedings in Rwanda, and the Recovery of Historical Memory (REHMI), which the Catholic Church in Guatemala established to document 55,000 cases of human rights violations against indigenous communities, probably reflect the most well-known.[58] One of the most recent examples of a 'bottom-up' response took place in the United States. The residents of the community of Greensboro established a Truth and Reconciliation Commission to examine the 'context, causes, sequences and consequences' of the killing of five demonstrators at a public rally against the Ku Klux Klan in 1979[59]; the final report and accompanying DVDs of the hearings have just been published. Sri Lanka also provides a number of examples: a civil society organisation, Kalape Ape, located in the Gampaha district, developed strategies to advocate for redress for families of the 'disappeared', including pushing for the implementation of the recommendations of the official commissions of inquiry and individual prosecutions.[60] It also held commemoration ceremonies and built a monument to the 'disappeared'.[61] In the border villages of Sri Lanka, another civil society organisation, Movement for Inter Racial Justice and Equality, established the Citizen's Commission on Border Villages. The Commission held public hearings to record the impact of the conflict on a community already affected by severe poverty.[62] However, as discussed by Arriaza and Roht-Arriaza in this collection, the lack of inquiry, research and mapping of localised processes inevitably means that many more have been established without substantial publicity.

[57] F Panizza, 'Human Rights in the Processes of Transition and Consolidation of Democracy in Latin America' (1995) XLIII *Political Studies* 168 at 169.

[58] R Mani, *Beyond Retribution: Seeking Justice in the Shadows of War* (Cambridge, Polity Press, 2002) 116. See L Arriaza and N Roht-Arriaza's chapter in this collection.

[59] Greensboro Truth and Reconciliation Commission Report, Executive Summary (May 25 2006) 2. See also P Lundy and M McGovern's chapter in this collection.

[60] Three regional and one island-wide commission of inquiry have investigated and issued recommendations on allegations of tens of thousands of 'disappearances' by security forces.

[61] For a more comprehensive discussion on this transitional justice strategy, as well as the Citizen's Commission on Border Villages discussed below and other local transitional justice initiatives, see F Haniffa, 'In the Pursuit of Democracy in Post Colonial Sri Lanka: Local Human Rights Approaches to Transitional Justice' (Law and Society Trust (Sri Lanka), 2006).

[62] *Ibid.*

In general, localised processes can flesh out and make meaningful centralised processes that may be unable to deal with the complexity of conflict comprehensively. As Braithwaite notes, 'human rights meta-narratives that come from above can be made concretely meaningful by local standards that have contextual relevance'. Citing Habermas, he argues that,

> [t]his concrete experience can then generate democratic impulses that can inform the reframing of top-down human rights discourse,

thus moulding centralised transitional justice processes and making them more relevant and publicly accountable.[63]

Yet, while community-based initiatives fill a necessary gap, the diversity and contradictions inherent in local approaches do not lend themselves easily to regulation and systematisation. Although the organic nature of local initiatives reflects a strength, it may also entail obvious limitations and challenges. In particular, difficulties may arise when these processes do not align with universal principles of human rights. In this respect, informal approaches must not be eulogised unquestioningly or deemed impenetrable by virtue of their locality; rather they must be guided by the same human rights standards as inform formal processes.

A local or indigenous process may also exclude victims or traditionally marginalised groups in the same way as formal mechanisms. In particular, the power of the initiators or the facilitators will very often control and constrict the agenda of the process. What may appear as an 'organic' response may actually reflect an internal power manifestation by community leaders or prominent and professionalised civil society organisations. As a result, the priorities and narrative produced may suffer from the same shortcomings as macro models. It may also have the effect of silencing traditionally disenfranchised groups, whose agenda, interests and needs may contrast to the projected informal response. As Drumbl argues,

> it may further disempower and victimize other, more marginalized, constituencies. For these marginalized constituencies, such as women of Afghanistan, the local may have limited meaning as a mechanism of justice and may in fact serve as a conduit for further violence.[64]

Moreover, as Mani notes,

[63] J Braithwaite, 'Setting Standards for Restorative Justice' (2002) 42 *British Journal of Criminology* 563 at 563.

[64] Drumbl, 'Rights, Culture, and Crime (n 9 above) at 353–4. See E Stanley's chapter in this collection (discussing the bottom-up Commission of Reception, Reconciliation and Truth in Timor-Leste's consolidation of 'inequalities at personal, social and structural levels', particularly to victims.)

> [i]t may lead them to substitute formal mechanisms backed by official commitment and resources with informal, inexpensive and politically convenient ones.[65]

For example, the *gacaca* process in Rwanda was lauded for 'using community as the base for justice and reconciliation' and aiming to,

> reinstate a collective social and judicial voice in communities deeply divided and traumatized by the atrocities of the past.[66]

Yet, the *gacaca* courts did not arise as an organic response to the genocide but as a policy implemented by the Rwandan government.[67] As such, some commentators, such as Phil Clark, caution against romanticising *gacaca* as its formalisation means that it differs significantly from its traditional form. Rather, he portrays *gacaca* as an evolving system constituting,

> a hybrid of traditional elements and features; the result of a crucial political compromise among Rwandan policy-makers and an attempt to respond to the specific needs of the post-genocide environment.[68]

He thus terms *gacaca* not as

> *indigenous,* which connotes a native enterprise, occurring 'naturally' and inevitably accepted by the local population [but] *endogenous*: initiated and synthesised within Rwandan society but—because of the complicated nature of that synthesis, and how markedly current gacaca differs from the original practice that partly inspired it—viewed by much of the population as a new, and perhaps confusing or even disagreeable, entity.[69]

Gacaca proceedings have received criticism for a perceived biased focus on Hutu atrocities[70] and the failure to incorporate due process and human rights standards.[71] Moreover, the *gacaca* system has been challenged for its exclusion of sexual violence[72] as well as the lack of provision for

[65] Mani, *Beyond Retribution: Seeking Justice in the Shadows of War* (n 58 above) at 118.

[66] SL Wells, 'Gender, Violence and Prospects for Justice at the Gacaca Courts in Rwanda' (2005) 14 *Southern California Review of Law & Women's Studies* 167 at 177.

[67] *Ibid* at 169–76 (for a discussion of the reinvention of a 'system of traditional community courts' and the laws enacted thereof).

[68] P Clark, 'Hybridity, Holism and "Traditional" Justice: The Case of the Gacaca Courts in Post-Genocide Rwanda' (Spring 2007) 39(4) *George Washington International Law Review*. Clark also offers a more positive account of the role of *gacaca* in promoting 'social outcomes' such as reconciliation.

[69] *Ibid.*

[70] Wells, 'Gender, Violence and Prospects for Justice at the Gacaca Courts in Rwanda' (n 66 above) at 179. Clark, in 'Hybridity, Holism and "Traditional" Justice' (n 68 above) notes, however, that although women were previously 'excluded from being judges or providing testimony at gacaca ... in the modernised institution women play a key role both as leaders and general participants'.

[71] For a legal critique of *gacaca*, see J Fierens, '*Gacaca* Courts: Between Fantasy and Reality' (2005) 3 *Journal of International Criminal Justice* 896.

[72] Wells, 'Gender, Violence and Prospects for Justice at the Gacaca Courts in Rwanda' (n 66 above) at 187.

reparations for victims, 'to offset the light sentences for genocidaires'.[73] Structural constraints to participation also persist, as the lengthy proceedings mean that individuals may not be able to participate due to the accompanying loss of income.[74] Thus, the *gacaca* experience highlights that informal processes may perpetuate the same structural deficiencies as top-down models but may be more difficult to hold publicly accountable through the cover of cultural relativism.

The current debate on the ICC in Uganda also provides an interesting example of the complexity of such debates. Local, national and international organisations have challenged the initiation of investigations and the subsequent issuance of arrest warrants in Uganda for a number of reasons, including the timeliness of the ICC's involvement within an ongoing conflict; the perceived one-sidedness of the investigations; and the perceived inability of the ICC to enforce the warrants of arrest against the leaders of the Lord's Resistance Army.[75] Operational challenges aside, the ICC is also part of a much more complex debate over the mechanisms most appropriate to respond to the conflict in Uganda. At the centre of this discussion, lies the relationship of the ICC as an international justice mechanism to a domestic amnesty process and traditional justice mechanisms.

Unlike many of the amnesties that emanated from the Latin American region in the late 1980s, the blanket amnesty process in Uganda is presented as an indigenous attempt to end 20 years of conflict. The Refugee Law Project argues that

> [t]he initiative for creating an amnesty came from within this region, spearheaded by the religious and cultural leaders, and was a clear rejection of a failed military approach to ending the war. The fact that the Amnesty Law was in keeping with wishes of the victims of conflict, rather than by perpetrators trying to negotiate their own safety, is a crucial aspect of Amnesty.[76]

Despite the grounding of the justification for the amnesty in victims' rights rhetoric, advocacy for the amnesty process has still taken place within the leadership of particular communities. Moreover, the President of Uganda has offered amnesty interchangeably with the threat of ICC prosecution as part of a political debate on prospects for peace.[77] Alongside support for the amnesty process, calls have also been made to make use of the

[73] L Waldorf, 'Mass Justice for Mass Atrocity: Rethinking Local Justice as Transitional Justice' (2006) 79 *Temple Law Review* 1 at 56.

[74] Clark, 'Hybridity, Holism and "Traditional" Justice (n 68 above).

[75] International Bar Association (IBA), 'First Outreach Report' (June 2006) 13–21.

[76] Refugee Law Project, 'Whose Justice? Perceptions of Uganda's Amnesty Act 2000: The Potential for Conflict Resolution and Long-Term Reconciliation' (February 2005) 6.

[77] 'IBA's Human Rights Institute Says Ugandan Government Must Meet Its Obligations under the Rome Statute', Press Release, 13 July 2006.

traditional justice system, despite questions over whether it has the capacity to deal with large-scale crimes under international law; its particularity to the Acholi region of Uganda; and questions over the availability of gender-sensitive procedures given its traditionally patriarchical structure.[78]

While the ICC Prosecutor has recognised the contribution of indigenous processes, very little work has been undertaken to examine possibilities to overcome the current limitations to these processes. When pitted against an institution which may not be functioning optimally, it becomes easier to aggregate and generalise the needs and interests of a particular society. In a similar fashion to the problems arising with formal mechanisms, such amalgamation risks the marginalisation of the most vulnerable groups, such as women, children, victims and minorities.

IV INTERNATIONAL LAW AND RE-SHAPING THE TRANSITIONAL HEGEMON

This section considers the ways in which international law can challenge controlling narratives of states and work alongside localised approaches to dealing with the impact of conflict. In particular, it focuses on the restriction on amnesty as an option for dealing with crimes under international law; the prioritisation of victims' rights and reparation; and attempts to make formal processes more inclusive and participatory.

A Prioritising Victims' Rights Above Amnesties

Since the first wave of transitional justice models, international law—and Latin American jurisprudence, in particular—has intervened to limit the scope of permissible transitional justice initiatives which impinge upon the rights of marginalised groups such as victims. The line of Inter-American jurisprudence has been particularly instructive on the invalidity of amnesties for crimes under international law. Initially, the Inter-American Commission made the distinction between amnesties decreed by 'the appropriate democratic institutions ... with the participation of all representative sectors', from self-amnesties, which it determined enjoyed, 'no juridical validity'.[79] However, the Commission later found that even amnesties that enjoyed democratic support could not displace the right of victims and society as a whole to the truth. In 1992, for example, the

[78] For further discussion, see IBA, 'First Outreach Report' (n 75 above) at 16.
[79] *Annual Report of the Inter-American Commission on Human Rights*, 1985–86 at ch

Inter-American Commission heard three cases on the amnesties in Argentina, El Salvador and Uruguay. The amnesties differed in nature—from the El Salvadorian blanket amnesty, which prohibited any investigations, prosecutions or compensation, to the Argentinian amnesty, which sat alongside a handful of prosecutions and a truth commission.[80] Yet, in each case, the Inter-American Commission found that the amnesty violated

> the state obligation—part of its duty to 'ensure' human rights under article 1(1)—to investigate violations. Second, at least in states that permit victims to participate in criminal proceedings, the amnesties violated the state duty under article 8(1) to afford victims a fair trial. Third, the amnesties violated rights of victims and survivors to adequate compensation, required both by article 1(1) and by the right to judicial protection under article 25.[81]

In the *Barrios Altos* case, the Inter-American Court on Human Rights held that international law prohibits amnesties because, 'they violate non-derogable rights recognised by international human rights law'.[82] Like the Commission, the Court grounded its reasoning in the rights of victims, noting that

> [s]elf-amnesties laws lead to the defenselessness of victims and perpetuate impunity ... This type of law precludes the identification of the individuals who are responsible for human rights violations, because it obstructs the investigation and access to justice and prevents the victims and their next of kin from knowing the truth and receiving the correspondent reparation.[83]

In his concurring opinion, Judge Trindade, made clear that while an amnesty may be given legal expression at the domestic level, if it conflicts with the 'superior' rights of the right to truth and the right to justice, it will not be recognised within 'the ambit of International Human Rights Law'.[84]

Similarly, the United Nations' Human Rights Committee has found that

> [a]mnesties are generally incompatible with the duty of States to investigate such acts; to guarantee freedom from such acts within their jurisdiction; and to ensure that they do not occur in the future. States may not deprive individuals of the

[80] For a full discussion of these amnesties, see Cassel, 'Accountability for International Crime and Serious Violations of Fundamental Human Rights' (n 36 above) at 211–12.

[81] Cassel, 'Accountability for International Crime and Serious Violations of Fundamental Human Rights' (n 36 above) at 212 (discussing *Masacre Las Hojas v El Salvador*, Case No 10.287, 24 September 1992; *Consuelo Herrera v Argentina*, Case No 10.147, 2 October 1992; and *Leonardo de los Santos Mendoza v Uruguay*, Case No 10.029, 2 October 1992).

[82] *Barrios Altos* Case: *Chumbipuma Aguirre et al v Peru*, Inter-American Court of Human Rights (March 14 2001) at para 41.

[83] *Ibid* at para 43.

[84] *Barrios Altos* Case (n 82 above), Concurring Opinion of Judge AA Cançado Trindade, at para 6.

> right to an effective remedy, including compensation and such full rehabilitation as may be possible.[85]

Moreover, in a recent report on the rule of law, the Secretary-General noted, 'a growing shift away from a tolerance for impunity and amnesty',[86] within the international community and recommended the rejection of

> any endorsement of amnesty for genocide, war crimes, or crimes against humanity including those related to ethnic, gender and sexually based international crimes,[87]

in 'negotiations, peace agreements and Security Council mandates'. Article 24 of the UN Set of Principles on Impunity also provides that, '[e]ven when intended to establish conditions conducive to a peace agreement or to foster national reconciliation', amnesties cannot displace the state's obligation to investigate and prosecute serious crimes under international law; the jurisdiction of an 'international, internationalized or national' tribunal to prosecute the accused; and victims' right to reparation.[88]

Under this clarified international landscape, some national courts are beginning to revisit prior amnesty policies. For example, the Argentinian Supreme Court recently found the amnesty laws adopted in the 1980s—the Ley de Punto Final and the Ley de Obediencia Debida[89]—unconstitutional and incompatible with the requirements of international law.[90] Coupled with

[85] UNHRC, *General Comment No 20* (10 March 1992) at para 15. The Human Rights Committee later reaffirmed this position in the individual communication of *Rodríguez v Uruguay*, UN Doc CCPR/C/51/D/322/1988 (9 August 1994) at paras 11–12. See also Final Report of the Peruvian Comisión de La Verdad y Reconcilación (released 28 August 2003).

[86] Secretary-General's Report to the UN Security Council (n 54 above) at para 40.

[87] Secretary-General's Report to the UN Security Council (n 54 above) at para 64(c).

[88] UNHRC, 'Promotion and Protection of Human Rights—Impunity: Report of the Independent Expert to Update the Set of Principles to Combat Impunity: Addendum' (18 February 2005) UN Doc E/CN.4/2005/102.Add.1 8 Art 24 (a)–(b). See also, *Prosecutor v Kallon*, Case No SCSL-2004–15-AR72(E) (2004), Special Court at Sierra Leone (finding that the amnesty resulting from the Lome Peace Accords, 'ineffective in removing the universal jurisdiction to prosecute persons accused of such crimes that other states have by reason of the nature of the crimes. It is also ineffective in depriving an international court such as the Special Court of jurisdiction' at para 88).

[89] Law No 23.492, published in the Boletin Oficial on 29 December 1986; Law No 23.521, published in the Boletin Oficial on 9 June 1987.

[90] *Simon, Julio Hector y otros s/privacion ilegitima de la libertad*, Argentinian Supreme Court, causa No 17.768 (14 June 2005) S.1767.XXXVIII (these laws were repealed by Congress in 2003). For a further discussion of this case, see CAE Bakker, 'A Full Stop to Amnesty in Argentina: The Simon Case' (2005) 3(4) *Journal of International Criminal Justice* 1106.

> the emergence of a new generation of military leaders in Chile and the assumption of the Chilean presidency by Ricardo Lagos, who was known to be in strong sympathy with the victims of the Pinochet dictatorship,[91]

the decision of the UK House of Lords to deny General Pinochet immunity as a former head of state[92] is cited as contributing to the line of cases which have now been brought before Chilean courts in an attempt to have those responsible for crimes under international law, such as torture and 'disappearances,' held to account, and domestic amnesty laws annulled.[93] The most recent illustration is a decision of the Supreme Court of Chile denying Pinochet immunity in a case involving allegations of torture and other crimes of international law committed between 1974 and 1977 in the Villa Grimaldi Prison.[94] As a result, the intervention and consolidation of international law underscores that national policies on transitional justice can no longer 'close the books' on the past at the expense of the rights of victims.

B Recognising Rights of Traditionally Disenfranchised Groups

The recent adoption of the Basic Principles on the Right to a Remedy and Reparation by the General Assembly of the United Nations provides a codification of the right to a remedy and reparation under international law and identifies a range of means required to give effect to these principles. The right of individuals to reparation for violations of international human rights and humanitarian law was also recently reaffirmed in *The Wall* case before the International Court of Justice.[95] Along with the updated Set of Principles on Impunity, these two developments underscore the fundamental importance of the right of victims and survivors of crimes under international law to a remedy and reparation under international law.

As such, the rights of traditionally disenfranchised groups are given prominence by way of international law. For example, the inclusion of

[91] RA Falk, 'Assessing the Pinochet Litigation: Whither Universal Jurisdiction?' in Macedo, *Universal Jurisdiction: National Courts and the Prosecution of Serious Crimes under International Law* (n 29 above) 97 at 101.

[92] *R v Bow Street Metropolitan Stipendiary Magistrate and Others, ex parte Pinochet Ugarte (No 3)* [2000] 1 AC 147; [1999] 2 WLR 827.

[93] For example, see the Chile Supreme Court case in *Miguel Angel Sandoval Rodriguez* (17 November 2004) (finding that the 1978 amnesty decree covering human rights crimes committed between 1973 and 1978 did not apply.) For a full discussion of these developments, see R Evans, 'Pinochet in London—Pinochet in Chile: International and Domestic Politics in Human Rights Policy' (2006) 28 *Human Rights Quarterly* 207–44.

[94] 'Court Lifts Pinochet Immunity', BBC News Online (9 September 2006) (visited 21 September 2006).

[95] *Legal Consequences of the Construction of a Wall in the Occupied Palestinian Territory* (Advisory Opinion), ICJ (9 July 2004) at paras 151–2.

gender-based crimes has only recently been integrated into transitional justice processes,[96] largely precipitated by the decisions of the ICTY in *Prosecutor v Kunarac*,[97] *Prosecutor v Kvocka*[98] and the ICTR in *Akayesu*.[99] At the same time, however, the inclusion of a gender-perspective into transitional justice processes is often narrowly defined by rape and crimes of sexual violence and indicates the remaining challenges for international law. In the context of Rwanda, Wells argues that,

> [t]oo often, Rwandan women are conceptualized as a singular, homogenous category. Such a narrow view obscures their roles and experiences as other than rape victims.[100]

Kumi Samuel argues that as civil and political rights violations are often committed predominantly against men, 'the impact of conflict on women is often overlooked or minimised'. In particular, she points out that very few processes include,

> reference to structural or systemic abuse and violation of rights—rights that were more in the realm of a socio-economic and cultural framework that would have encompassed internal and external displacement, war related trauma, the emergence of female-headed household, war related disability and so on.[101]

She concludes,

> while some attention has been paid to situations in which women are direct victims, very little attention has been paid to crimes against women as 'indirect' victims of conflict. For example, the consequences of the loss of family members, through death or disappearance, mental and psychosocial trauma and stress, women's roles as human rights defenders and as family members of victims who seek truth and justice.[102]

As discussed at the outset of this chapter, therefore, the foregoing underscores the nature of international law as a discipline capable of asserting

[96] See SR Ratner, 'Book Review and Note: Unspeakable Truths: Confronting State Terror and Atrocity. By Priscilla B. Hayner' (2001) 95 *American Journal of International Law* 994 at 995 (noting that, 'truth commissions have not done especially well at describing abuses against women, in part because the stigma against sexual violence makes women reluctant to tell their stories, in part because some commissions are unwilling to consider sexual crimes as political and thus as part of their mandate'.).

[97] *Prosecutor v Kunarac, Kovać and Vuković*, Judgment, IT-96–23-T, 22 February 2001 at 257, 258; *Prosecutor v Kunarac, Kovać and Vuković*, Judgment, IT-96–23-A, 12 June 2002 at 254, 257.

[98] *Prosecutor v Kvočka*, Judgment, IT-98–30–1/T, 2 November 2001 at 259, 323.

[99] *Prosecutor v Akayesu*, Judgment, ICTR-96–4-T, 2 September 1998 at 170, 179, 314. *Prosecutor v Akayesu*, Judgment, ICTR-96–4-A, 1 June 2001 at 16, 252–3.

[100] Wells, 'Gender, Violence and Prospects for Justice at the Gacaca Courts in Rwanda' (n 66 above) at 186.

[101] K Samuel, 'Gender and Transitional Justice in Sri Lanka,' paper submitted to *Sri Lanka Transitional Justice Working Group* (on file with author).

[102] *Ibid*. See also Wells, 'Gender, Violence and Prospects for Justice at the Gacaca Courts in Rwanda' (n 66 above) at 194–5, discussing priorities of female survivors in Rwanda.

the rights of victims. At the same time, the discussion highlights the need to constantly critique and challenge international law in order to ensure that the rights and experiences of women, for example, are acknowledged and addressed comprehensively rather than narrowly construed.

C Participation and Ownership

Finally, developments in international law increasingly highlight the centrality of participation and ownership in transitional justice processes. As noted above, in 2004, the Secretary-General of the United Nations issued a report which reflected on the 'lessons learned' in the fields of transitional justice and the rule of law. In particular, he acknowledged the formulaic tendencies of the international community to emphasise the importance of establishing a specific type of transitional justice process, 'without first affording victims and national constituencies the opportunity to consider and decide on the proper balance'.[103] In this respect, he outlined the challenge for the international community in learning 'how to respect and support local ownership, local leadership and a local constituency',[104] and reflected that, to date, the transitional justice processes which have involved substantial local consultations have provided, 'a better understanding of the dynamics of past conflict, patterns of discrimination and types of victims'.[105] As a result, the Secretary-General emphasises the policy shift of the United Nations towards the

> active and meaningful participation of national stakeholders, including justice sector officials, civil society, professional associations, traditional leaders and key groups, such as women, minorities, displaced persons and refugees.[106]

Similarly, the UN Set of Principles on Impunity underscores, 'the broad participation of victims and other citizens' in 'designing policies for combating impunity'. In addition, they highlight that

> [b]road consultations also help ensure that policies for combating impunity are themselves rooted in processes that ensure public accountability.[107]

International law also sets out the role of outreach programmes in making the right to a remedy and reparation effective. Principle 33 of the Set of Principles to Combat Impunity directs the 'widest possible publicity' of

[103] Secretary-General's Report to the UN Security Council (n 54 above) at para 25.
[104] Secretary-General's Report to the UN Security Council (n 54 above) at para 17.
[105] Secretary-General's Report to the UN Security Council (n 54 above) at 16.
[106] Secretary-General's Report to the UN Security Council (n 54 above) at para 15. See also Lundy and McGovern's chapter in this collection.
[107] UNHRC, 'Promotion and Protection of Human Rights—Impunity: Report of the Independent Expert to Update the Set of Principles to Combat Impunity' (n 24 above) at para 7.

'reparation procedures', and Principle 12(a) of the Basic Principles and Guidelines on the Right to a Remedy and Reparation for Victims of Gross Violations of International Human Rights Law and Serious Violations of International Humanitarian Law[108] (Basic Principles on Reparations) requires the dissemination of information of 'all available remedies for gross violations of international human rights law and serious violations of international humanitarian law'.[109] The Independent Expert tasked with updating the Set of Principles to Combat Impunity[110] explains the purpose of Principles 33 and 12(a) as

> to make the right to a remedy *effective* by undertaking outreach programmes aimed at informing as many victims as possible of procedures through which they may exercise this fundamental right ... This ... should be understood to include other appropriate measures for identifying potential beneficiaries of reparation programmes that may, under some circumstances, be more effective than dissemination through public media.

Beyond direct victims, international law also sets out the role of outreach to society as a whole. As with the discussion on amnesties, the role of outreach to broader society was developed within the Inter-American system jurisprudence. In the *Bámaca Velásquez* case, the Court held that

> [s]ociety has the right to know the truth regarding such crimes, so as to be capable of preventing them in the future.[111]

As a result, not only was the state under a duty to investigate but also to 'publicly divulge the results of said investigation'[112] both in the *Official Gazette* and also a daily newspaper with 'national circulation'.[113] The Secretary-General of the United Nations has interpreted these cases as demonstrating the 'preventative and reparatory role that disclosure of truth plays for family members and society as a whole'.[114] Moreover, as noted in the report on the updating of the impunity principles, engagement with

[108] Adopted by the General Assembly in Resolution 60/147 on 16 December 2005.

[109] Notably, the Preamble to the Basic Principles on Reparation provides that the principles 'do not entail new international or domestic legal obligations but identify mechanisms, modalities, procedures and methods for the implementation of existing legal obligations'.

[110] UNHRC, *Promotion and Protection of Human Rights—Impunity: Report of the Independent Expert to Update the Set of Principles to Combat Impunity: Addendum* (n 88 above).

[111] *Bámaca Velásquez v Guatemala*, Inter-American Court of Human Rights (22 February 2002) at para 77. In *El Caracazo v Venezuela*, Inter-American Court of Human Rights (29 August 2002) the Court found that the results of investigations 'must be made known to the public, for Venezuela society to know the truth' at para 118.

[112] *Bámaca Velásquez* (n 111 above) at para 78.

[113] *Bámaca Velásquez* (n 111 above) at para 106(3).

[114] Secretary-General's Report to the UN Security Council (n 54 above) at para 18.

affected communities ensures 'that policies for combating impunity are themselves rooted in processes that ensure public accountability'.[115]

In this respect, the International Criminal Court is perhaps the most prominent example of the shifts in international law towards participation. Article 75 of the Rome Statute enables the Court to make reparations to victims,[116] and Article 68(3) provides that

> [w]here the personal interests of victims are affected, the Court shall permit their views and concerns to be presented and considered at stages of the proceedings determined to be appropriate by the Court.

Victims may exercise their right to participate in the proceedings directly or through a legal representative. In fact, Articles 68 and 75 of the Rome Statute are cited in the Preamble to the recently-adopted Basic Principles on Reparations as providing for a 'right to a remedy for victims of violations of international human rights law'. Equally, however, the extent of the participation of victims in ICC proceedings remains a contested and ongoing issue before the Court. The Prosecutor and the Defence have made a number of challenges on the participation of victims including the capacity of the Court to manage a large number of applications to participate, and the extent of the participation concerned, particularly at the pre-trial stage.[117] The issue is compounded by questions surrounding the representational capacity of individual victims to speak to the diverse needs and interests within affected victim communities and the need to ensure that participation and reparation before the ICC complements broader reparation strategies rather than provides states with a means to avoid their own continuing responsibility.

Beyond participation and reparation, the work of the International Criminal Tribunal for the Former Yugoslavia was 'frequently politicised and used for propaganda purposes by its opponents', and seen as 'remote and disconnected from the population',[118] the ICC learned from the experience of the ad hoc tribunals by establishing an outreach programme at the outset. Outreach is defined by the Court as:

[115] UNHRC, 'Promotion and Protection of Human Rights—Impunity: Report of the Independent Expert to Update the Set of Principles to Combat Impunity' (n 24 above) at para 7.

[116] However, the trust fund established to 'channel money to victims' continues to be under-resourced. See 'The Report to the Assembly of States Parties on the Activities and Projects of the Trust Fund for Victims for the Period 16 July 2004 to 15 August 2005', ICC-ASP/4/12 (29 September 2005).

[117] See International Bar Association, 'ICC Monitoring Report' (September 2006) at 8.

[118] See Security Council, 'Report of the International Tribunal for the Prosecution of Persons Responsible for Serious Violations of International Humanitarian Law Committed in the Territory of the Former Yugoslavia Since 1991' (n 17 above) at 148.

> a process of establishing a sustainable, two-way communication between the Court and communities affected by situations that are subject to investigations and proceedings.[119]

At this stage in the ICC's development, however, the outreach function is not optimal and has also received criticism on a number of levels including a lack of prominence accorded to outreach as an integral component of the Court's work; belated and insufficient activities and a lack of tailoring to the context in which they are conducted.[120] At the same time, such feedback to the Court does appear to be contributing to the development of strategic plans which should and are resulting in enhanced outreach activities.

V CONCLUSION

In exploring the relationship between indigenous processes and formal justice mechanisms, the debate should not regress to a stark neo-colonialist versus cultural relativism stand-off. As Ibhawo argues, in Africa at least the debate is now much more nuanced, particularly as societies are not static, 'monolithic or unchanging'[121] and

> has led to calls for a regime of human rights founded on the basic human rights standards but also enriched by the African cultural experience.[122]

She continues that

> [i]t is not enough to identify the cultural barriers and limitations to modern domestic and international human rights standards. It is even more important to understand the social basis of these cultural traditions and how they might be adapted to or integrated with national legislation to promote human rights ... such adaptation and integration must be done in a way that does not compromise the cultural integrity of peoples. In this way, the legal and policy provisions of national human rights can derive their legitimacy not only from state authority but also from the force of cultural traditions.[123]

In considering options for transitional justice, the choice between local and 'international' approaches should not be viewed as exclusive. Rather, as discussed throughout this chapter, it is the challenge for both to meet the requirements of international law in ensuring the rights of victims and

[119] Statement made by President Philippe Kirsch, www.icc-cpi.int/library/asp/060323_Compilation_of_Statements.pdf (March 2006).

[120] See International Bar Association (June 2006) (for an overview of responses to the outreach activities of the ICC).

[121] Ibhawo, 'Between Culture and Constitution' (n 13 above) at 841.

[122] Ibhawo, 'Between Culture and Constitution' (n 13 above) at 839. See also J Donnelly, 'Cultural Relativism and Universal Human Rights' (1984) 6 *Human Rights Quarterly* 400.

[123] Ibhawo, 'Between Culture and Constitution' (n 13 above) at 840.

traditionally marginalised groups. Just as discussed in relation to formal mechanisms, Ibhawo points out that

> it is important to create a dialogue between the weaker and the stronger within the cultural community and society at large. Women and minority groups must be able to dialogue over interpretations of cultural values with politicians, officials, traditional leaders, and family heads in both the rural and urban areas.[124]

This perspective is buttressed by Coomaraswamy, who concludes that

> [b]eing sensitive to cultural relativism cannot imply putting hard-won battles on human rights up for grabs. There is a shared history and collective memory at the international level. What must be seen as negotiable are the strategies of enforcement and implementation.[125]

[124] Ibhawo, 'Between Culture and Constitution' (n 13 above) at 855.

[125] R Coomaraswamy, 'Identity Within: Cultural Relativism, Minority Rights and the Empowerment of Women' (2002–03) 34 *George Washington International Law Review* 483 at 494.

4

Constitution-making, Transition and the Reconstitution of Society

KIRSTEN MCCONNACHIE AND JOHN MORISON*

I INTRODUCTION

THIS CONTRIBUTION TAKES up the 'from below' perspective that infuses this collection and develops it in the context of constitution-making in periods of transition. Traditionally constitutional theory has related to a largely top-down process in which interest is located within ideas of the nation, the parliament and the law. These stand in for 'the people' and provide the impetus for developing machinery to convert the rough world of the political into safer structures for governance. The spectre of sovereignty looms and constitutional action is focused on the foundational activity of transforming a 'constitutional moment' into a structure of government—what Loughlin describes as the 'third order' of the political, where institutional form is given to the political conflicts that difficult societies contain.[1] In recent times conflicted societies are not only given parliaments, power-sharing and rights mechanisms but also more specific mechanisms of conflict resolution in the form of prisoner-release schemes, amnesties, and truth commissions as well as the establishment of a range of commissions to oversee key functions such as policing, judicial appointments systems and the like.

It is argued here, however, that the remit of constitutional law in a context where societies are in transition is far from exhausted by such formal actions. Developing and extending earlier work exploring how ideas of governmentality may alter the remit of constitutional theory,[2] this

* The authors would like to thank the editors of this collection and Michael Hamilton for comments on earlier drafts.

[1] See M Loughlin, 'Constitutional Law: the Third Order of the Political' in N Bamforth and P Leyland (eds), *Public Law in a Multi-Layered Constitution* (Oxford, Hart Publishing, 2003).

[2] See, eg, J Morison, 'Government-Voluntary Sector Compacts: Governance, Governmentality and Civil Society' (2000) 27 *Journal of Law and Society* 98; J Morison, 'Democracy,

chapter explores the role of law in transforming power, creating authority and developing legitimacy. It suggests that the theatre of constitutional action is not exhaustively explored by looking at the details of elite political deals and the structures that they bequeath to conflicted societies. Indeed, it argues that these structures provide only a place where conflicts can be contained and worked upon over time with the instruments of rights, equality and governance that are provided in the frameworks. As understandings of law and of power more generally are developed, along with a better appreciation of what is really involved in a proper constitutional settlement, the importance of the active subject as the entity through which and by means of which power is actually exercised can be understood, and a fuller range of governmental activity can be mapped. In doing this, the chapter will initially highlight the particular difficulties of traditional constitutional law in moving beyond the notion of a 'constitutional moment', and of recognising a constitution-drafting process as something more than a political opportunity to re-engage with traditional ideas of territory, sovereignty and law. It will then turn to accounts of 'transition' and 'transitional constitutionalism' to evaluate whether the frameworks there really move our understanding much further than the high level concerns of more traditional constitutionalism.

The account will then turn to ideas of governmentality, which perceive government by itself as unable to achieve its ends without the willing co-operation of the individual subject participating in his/her own governance. With this challenge to the dominant paradigm thrown down, the account then looks to how versions of constitutionalism that emphasise the participatory nature of governance and democracy can accommodate the re-orientation of subject-matter that we believe is necessary for constitutions to be properly made.

II CONSTITUTION-MAKING: FROM NATION-BUILDING TO TRANSITION

There are at least two sets of approaches to constitution-making. The first holds that, historically, constitutions tended to be drafted with the intention of performing a centuries-long role in governance, in so much as they mark a new beginning and a change from what has gone before. Tully describes this model of the constitution as a discontinuous founding moment in which 'the plurality of existing ancient authorities is eliminated'

Governance and Governmentality: Civic Public Space and Constitutional Renewal in Northern Ireland' (2001) 21 *Oxford Journal of Legal Studies* 287; J Morison, 'Modernising Government and the E-Government Revolution: Technologies of Government and Technologies of Democracy' in Bamforth and Leyland (eds), *Public Law in a Multi-Layered Constitution* (n 1 above).

in the creation of a uniform government.[3] While such an approach may seem to have particular application in a colonial or post-colonial situation, it does also serve for the sort of regime change that is more commonplace in the history of European constitutionalism.[4] Constitution-making here is linked to an assertion of (sometimes) popular sovereignty and it purports to represent a new beginning. Of course such a paradigm, however, does not necessarily convey adequately the role of a constitution where it is more than a declamatory 'end' of one dispensation and the birth of another. It does not cover the idea of a constitution as part of a dynamic and transformative social process. A constitution in this second sense may be a framework for development rather than a fully-fashioned machine for government.[5]

The contrast between these approaches reflects contested visions of the role and impact of a constitutional document more generally. There is an initial attraction to the belief that constitutions and the institutions they create have a symbiotic relationship with societies, in which they both shape and are shaped by the external political environment. As Sadurski suggests, institutions 'matter' in the sense that they are not neutral; they do not merely channel and organise pre-political forms of collective life. Rather, they crucially affect, influence and change the way politics develop.[6] Mediation of a constitutional document through a range of institutions and individuals suggests an element of praxis, which accords with Pitkin's construction of constitutions as not only something that we *have,* but also something that we *are,* and that we *do.*[7] This supports a more expansive understanding of a constitution than some conventional theory, which tends to emphasise an almost exclusively top-down distribution of power through sovereign and state to subjects.

This latter approach is particularly evident in the dualist democracy framework of constitutional analysis, which conceives constitutional politics and normal politics as dichotomised, and punctuated by periodic

[3] J Tully, *Strange Multiplicity: Constitutionalism in an Age of Diversity* (Cambridge, Cambridge University Press, 1995) 67.

[4] See further RC Van Caenegem, *An Historical Introduction to Western Constitutional Law* (Cambridge, Cambridge University Press, 1995).

[5] Indeed, as Jurgen Habermas maintains, 'a constitution can be thought of as a historical project that each generation of citizens continues to pursue': J Habermas, *The Inclusion of the Other: Studies in Political Theory*, C Cronin and P de Greiff (eds) (Cambridge MA, MIT Press, 1997) 203.

[6] W Sadurski, 'On the Relevance of Institutions and the Centrality of Constitutions in Post-communist Transitions' in J Zielonka (ed), *Democratic Consolidation in Eastern Europe Volume 1* (Oxford, Oxford University Press, 2001) 456.

[7] HF Pitkin, 'The Idea of a Constitution' (1987) 37 *Journal of Legal Education* 167–9, ted in Sadurski (n 6 above) at 461.

'constitutional moments'.[8] The harnessing of such a constitutional moment creates a defining role for law (as both encapsulating and transcending external events), yet one which is ultimately passive and reactionary. This analysis is perhaps better suited to an autocratic age, where governors could presume the existence of a homogenous people and the right of political elites to speak on their behalf.[9]

The levelling effect of globalisation has made such presumption at least unfashionable, if not quite obsolete. This levelling is just one product of seismic political shifts, which have also resulted in increasingly multicultural societies, a radical repositioning of the nation-state, and a range of new or altered supra-national and sub-national identities. The multi-faceted implications of these changes are now well known and have been analysed in a variety of fields, including economics, political structures and empire.[10] Constitutional scholars have risen to the challenges of shifting sites of power with sophisticated theories for the management of diversity[11] or mediation of entrenched group identities.[12] However, in constitutionalism as in other fields, these new voices and the theoretical frameworks they propose have tended to speak more to the global trend for supra-national cohesion than for sub-national implosion.[13]

The persistence of this imbalance towards what might be termed an imperium rather than a community approach[14] is unfortunate, as constitution-making increasingly takes place during a period of political volatility or during the creation of a new state. In 1997, Sartori wrote that of approximately 170 written constitutions in existence, more than half

[8] See the B Ackerman trilogy, *We the People*, vols 1–3 (Cambridge MA, Belknap Press, 1991); J Morison and K McEvoy, 'Beyond the Constitutional Moment: Law, Transition and Peacemaking in Northern Ireland' (2003) 26 *Fordham International Law Review* 961.

[9] For example, as in the—possibly apocryphal—pronouncement by Louis XIV, '*L'etat c'est Moi*' (see G Poggi, *The Development of the Modern State: A Sociological Introduction* (London, Hutchinson, 1978) fn 15). 'We, the people', the most—perhaps the only—universally recognised constitutional excerpt, illustrates a similar presumption. Notably, the post-war Constitution of Japan (1947) begins with the phrase: 'We, the Japanese people', although the text was drafted by American lawyers.

[10] A Sen, *Development as Freedom* (Oxford, Oxford University Press, 1999); D Held, AG McGrew, D Goldblatt and J Perraton, *Global Transformations: Politics, Economics and Culture* (Oxford, Polity Press, 1999); M Hardt and A Negri, *Empire* (Cambridge MA, Harvard University Press, 2000).

[11] N Walker, 'The Idea of Constitutional Pluralism' (2002) 65 *Modern Law Review* 317; J Tully, 'The Unfreedom of the Moderns in Comparison to their Ideals of Constitutional Democracy' (2002) 65 *Modern Law Review* 204.

[12] A Lijphart and CH Waisman (eds), *Institutional Design in New Democracies* (Boulder CO, Westview Press, 1996); D Horowitz, 'Democracy in Divided Societies' (1993) 4 *Journal of Democracy* 18.

[13] Eg C Harvey, J Morison and J Shaw, 'Voices, Spaces and Processes in Constitutionalism' (2000) 27 *Journal of Law and Society* 1–3; G de Búrca and N Walker, 'Law and Transnational Civil Society: Upsetting the Agenda?' (2003) 9 *European Law Journal* 387.

[14] See R Cotterrell, *Law's Community: Legal Theory in Sociological Perspective* (Oxford, Clarendon Press, 1995).

had been written since 1974.[15] The intervening decade has seen constitutional texts or processes in Sierra Leone, East Timor, Northern Ireland, Rwanda, the Democratic Republic of Congo and many more.

Against this background questions such as whether the relationship between a constitutional document and the social polity is endogenous or exogenous, or whether democracy can be 'designed', are therefore of deep practical significance. In a volatile post-conflict environment, in addition to traditional tasks of determining and reconstructing functioning institutions of government, constitution-making may play an important role in distancing a new regime from its predecessor through adherence to democratic standards and the rule of law, according status to previously disenfranchised groups and perhaps making provision to address past institutional abuses.[16] Increasingly, and as a reflection of changed conflict patterns and motivations, constitutional processes must seek to manage questions of group rights or contested identity.[17]

The 'dynamic, mediating'[18] nature of such constitution-making adds weight to the contention that there is a place for constitutionalism in not just delineating the normative basis for executive governance, but in shaping the course of conflict resolution. The peace-making role of this approach is gathering increasing attention and ambition.[19] Ghai and Galli describe modern constitutions as

> instruments to enhance national unity and territorial integrity, defining or sharpening a national ideology, and developing a collective agenda for social and political change.[20]

[15] G Sartori, *Comparative Constitutional Engineering: An Inquiry into Structures, Incentives and Outcomes*, 2nd edn (New York, New York University Press, 1997) 197.

[16] M Rosenfeld, 'Constitution-Making, Identity Building and Peaceful Transition to Democracy: Theoretical Reflections Inspired by the Spanish Example' (1998) 19 *Cardozo Law Review* 1891 at 1902.

[17] D Horowitz, 'Democracy in Divided Societies' (1993) 4 *Journal of Democracy* 18; D Horowitz, *Ethnic Groups in Conflict* (Berkeley, University of California Press, 1985); B Reilly, *Democracy in Divided Societies* (Cambridge, Cambridge University Press 2001); A Lijphart, *Democracy in Plural Societies* (New Haven CT, Yale University Press 1977); A Lijphart and CH Waisman (eds), *Institutional Design in New Democracies* (Boulder CO, Westview Press, 1996).

[18] R Teitel, *Transitional Justice* (Oxford, Oxford University Press, 2000) 8.

[19] *Ibid* at ch 6 'Constitutional Justice'; V Hart, 'Constitution-Making and the Transformation of Conflict' (2001) 26 *Peace and Change* 153; J Benomar, 'Constitution Making after Conflict: Lessons for Iraq' (2004) 15 *Journal of Democracy* 81; K Samuels, 'Post-Conflict Peace-Building and Constitution-Making' (2006) 6 *Chicago Journal of International Law* 663.

[20] Y Ghai and G Galli, *Constitution Building Processes and Democratization* (International Institute for Democracy and Electoral Assistance, 2006) 13. Available online at http://www.idea.int/conflict/cbp/ (visited 20 July 2006); also International IDEA, *Democracy, Conflict and Human Security: Further Readings* (International IDEA, 2006).

Klare recognises the potentially transformative peace-making role of a constitution as inviting

> a new imagination and self-reflection about legal methods, analysis and reasoning consistent with its transformative goals ... where judicial mindset and methodology are ... examined and revised so as to promote equality, a culture of democracy and transparent governance.[21]

Such claims and objectives are closely rhetorically linked to transitional justice. Certainly, both discourses have an express interest in state-building, are preoccupied with questions of rights, justice and democracy and prioritise the role of law in societal reconstruction. A constitutional text can perform functions of securing and sustaining short-term and long-term governance, which place it within a quintessentially transitional justice rubric, for example, in the acknowledgement of past atrocities and other contributions to victim recognition and redress.[22] A constitutional text is also well placed to tackle structural causes or provocations of conflict, such as land reform[23] or freedom of assembly (for example, regarding Orange Order parades in Northern Ireland). Through a combination of historical acknowledgement, institutional creation and protection for social and economic rights, a constitution can make a potent contribution to transitional justice.[24]

Despite this evident overlap, transitional justice has to date not been overly concerned with political structures, focusing instead on mechanisms of adversarial justice, truth-seeking, reparation and memorialisation.[25] Even the phrase 'transitional constitutionalism' has been a relatively late and undeveloped addition to the lexicon of transitional justice, referring only to the practice of constitution-making after regime change and not to

[21] K Klare, 'Legal Culture and Transformative Constitutionalism' (1998) 14 *South African Journal on Human Rights* 146 at 156.

[22] Teitel, *Transitional Justice* (n 18 above); Hart, 'Constitution-Making and the Transformation of Conflict' (n 19 above); A Czarnota, M Krygier and W Sadurski (eds), *Rethinking the Rule of Law after Communism* (Budapest/New York, CEU Press, 2005).

[23] Eg Art XIII of the 1987 Constitution of the Philippines addresses urban land reform, obligating the state to make available low-cost housing and protecting dwellings of the urban and rural poor from unlawful destruction.

[24] Aeyal Gross identifies five areas in which a constitution might make a contribution to transitional justice: (1) as part of a reconciliation process; (2) in defining the nature of the state; (3) addressing the past, history and 'collective memory'; (4) addressing the distribution of property and land rights; and (5) addressing the distribution of social economic rights. See AM Gross, 'The Constitution, Reconciliation and Transitional Justice: Lessons from South Africa and Israel' (2004) 40 *Stanford Journal International Law* 47 at 57.

[25] For a representative selection of the vast literature on transitional justice see, eg E Barkan, *The Guilt of Nations: Restitution and Historical Injustices* (New York, Norton, 2000); B Hamber (ed), *Past Imperfect: Dealing with the Past in Northern Ireland* (INCORE, 1998); AH Henkin, *The Legacy of Abuse: Confronting the Past, Facing the Future*, (New York, Aspen Institute, 2002); NJ Kritz (ed), *Transitional Justice: How Emerging Democracies Reckon with Former Regimes* (Washington DC, US Institute of Peace, 1995); M Cherif Bassiouni (ed), *Post-Conflict Justice* (Ardsley NY, Transnational Publishers, 2002).

the principles which might underlie such practice.[26] Where institutional reform is identified as a tool of transitional justice, it is typically not extended to the constitutional sphere—at least in the fundamental sense of how constitutions can become frameworks to allow peoples to work out how to live together. Instead the emphasis remains on the reform of specific state institutions such as the judiciary, security services or civil service.[27]

Although transitional justice has not wholly embraced constitutionalism as such it is interesting that the actual practice of constitution-making, in contrast, is increasingly preoccupied with the creation of mechanisms to manage transition. This is particularly apparent in the strong trend for constitutions with a life-span of only a few years. Explicitly styled as 'transitional' or 'interim' constitutions—as adopted in countries including South Africa,[28] Sudan,[29] the Democratic Republic of the Congo[30] and Iraq[31]—these texts are considered a means by which a new regime may disentrench itself from its predecessor, gain negotiation time to assess the priorities and values of a desirable post-transition society and perhaps bridge over a particularly volatile political moment.[32] The temporary and negotiated nature of these texts situates them in a hazy area between constitution and peace agreement. Indeed, a leading text on peace agreements suggests 'peace agreements are best understood as a form of transitional constitution'.[33] This recommendation is supported with reference to the role of peace agreements in establishing political institutions and in adopting a simultaneously backward- and forward- looking approach to social structures (although with the caveat that, unlike a

[26] See, eg W Sadurski, 'Transitional Constitutionalism: Simplistic and Fancy Theories' in Czarnota, Krygier and Sadurski, *Rethinking the Rule of Law after Communism* (n 22 above); R Teitel, 'Post-Communist Constitutionalism: A Transitional Perspective' (1994) 26 *Columbia Human Rights Law Review* 167 at 168; Samuels, 'Post-Conflict Peace-Building and Constitution-Making' (n 19 above) at 667.

[27] Eg R Mattarollo, 'The Transition to Democracy and Institution Building: The Case of Haiti' in M Cherif Bassiouni (ed), *Post-Conflict Justice* (n 25 above). This appears to be the type of institutional reform recognised by the International Centre for Transitional Justice as a 'pillar' of transitional justice (in the company of prosecutions, truth-seeking, reparation and reconciliation): see www.ictj.org.

[28] Interim Constitution, adopted 27 April 1994.

[29] Transitional Constitution, adopted 6 July 2005.

[30] Transitional Constitution, adopted 2 April 2003.

[31] Interim Constitution (Law of Administration for the State of Iraq for the Transitional Period), adopted 8 March 2004.

[32] The first recognition of this phenomenon appears to have been by Arthur Jacobson in 1993 ('Transitional Constitutions' (1993) 14 *Cardozo Law Review* 947), offering the somewhat opaque definition: 'a transitional constitution postpones the accommodation of political paradoxes using unstable principles instead for carrying on in the absence of agreement on one or more elements of the basic framework'.

[33] C Bell, *Peace Agreements and Human Rights* (Oxford, Oxford University Press, 2000) 9.

traditional constitution, peace agreements may also be intentionally partial, short-lived and overtly political in both intent and implementation).[34] Frequently transitional constitutions codify prior peace agreements, as with Sudan's Transitional Constitution of 2005, and final constitutions incorporate transitional constitutions.[35]

This is significant, not least because one of the defining characteristics traditionally assumed of a constitution is permanence. It is viewed as a durable bedrock upon which legal and political structures can be constructed, and reinforced by complex processes for amendment. The notion that a constitution is a permanent template is an important symbolic attribute. Commentaries of Central and Eastern European constitutional processes acknowledge that—at least for the first countries to exit communism—underlying the 'constitutional compulsion' which prevailed was a belief in the capacity of a constitution to cement an independent, indivisible state.[36]

In current transitional contexts, a very different understanding of constitutional texts is emerging. In addition to explicitly transitional constitutions as described above, recent peace processes also evidence a trend for documents of ambiguous status and function. For example, Noah Feldman has suggested that the Transitional Administrative Law adopted by the Coalition Provisional Authority in Iraq should be considered a constitutional document.[37] Both the Dayton Accord for the Former Yugoslavia and the 1998 Belfast Agreement in Northern Ireland are documents of considerable constitutional significance not immediately recognisable as constitutional texts. The Belfast Agreement is not just a constitutional settlement which addressed issues of government and parliamentary composition—the future 'shape' of Northern Ireland's political society—but also a peace agreement which looked backwards to untangle problems of disarmament, prisoner release and the recognition of victims of the conflict.[38]

[34] *Ibid* at 310.

[35] Embassy of the Sudan, 'Adoption of the Transitional Constitution and Performance of Oath Ceremonies of the Presidency Institution', 8 July 2005: see www.sudanembassy.org (visited 30 May 2006).

[36] R Elgie and J Zielonka, 'Constitutions and Constitution Building: A Comparative Perspective' in J Zielonka (ed), *Democratic Consolidation in Eastern Europe: Volume 1* (Oxford, Oxford University Press, 2001) 30; R Ludwikowski, 'Constitutional Culture of the New East-Central European Democracies' (2000) 29 *Georgia Journal of International and Comparative Law* (2000) 14.

[37] N Feldman, 'Imposed Constitutionalism' (2005) 37 *Connecticut Law Review* 857.

[38] J Morison and M Lynch, 'Litigating the Agreement: Towards a New Judicial Constitutionalism for the UK from Northern Ireland?' in J Morison, K McEvoy and G Anthony (eds), *Judges, Transition and Human Rights* (Oxford, Oxford University Press, 2007) 214; C Campbell, F Ní Aoláin and C Harvey, 'The Frontiers of Legal Analysis: Reframing the Transition in Northern Ireland' (2003) 68 *Modern Law Review* 317.

It is clear that, contrary to the historic paradigm of a constitutional document as a definitive text, enduring and transcendent of context, modern constitutional theory must display considerable flexibility in defining and recognising a wide array of documents as 'constitutional'.

Similar issues tend to be addressed in a peace agreement, transitional constitution and final constitution, such as the form of political institutions and mechanisms of conflict resolution or transitional justice such as amnesty, tribunals and truth commissions.[39] The notion that the past must be addressed in a constitutional document has become increasingly mainstreamed since the South African transition. Peace negotiations and the transitional constitution created a truth commission in the Democratic Republic of Congo, while the Truth and Reconciliation Commission and national Human Rights Commission for Sierra Leone were provided for in the Lomé Peace Accord of 1999,[40] and Malawi's transitional constitution established a national compensation tribunal. That a process of fine-tuning and re-thinking constitutional arrangements has apparently become an accepted part of the constitution-making process suggests an expansion in the roles which a constitution is expected to perform; not only setting rules and standards for political engagement but also addressing past harms, mediating political or ethnic tensions and redressing social inequalities.

However, this is less innovative than it may first seem. Constitutionalism—and, indeed, transitional justice—is increasingly mediated through the language and goals of state-building and democracy in an almost identikit format.[41] Even the South African constitutional process—described by Sunstein as 'the most admirable constitution in the history of the world' and by Teitel as 'exemplifying' the uses of transitional constitutions[42]—is surprisingly conventional in process and content, encompassing a pathway of peace agreement, interim constitution and final constitution which addressed prisoner release, amnesty, the creation of a Constitutional Court, the adoption of a Bill of Rights and provision for reparations.

Post-Cold War, free market liberal democracy has been globally consolidated to the extent that it is truly, as Linz and Stepan predicted, the 'only

[39] C Bell, *Peace Agreements and Human Rights* (n 33 above) at 295–300, 304–12.

[40] Art VI(2), Peace Agreement between the Government of Sierra Leone and the Revolutionary United Front of Sierra Leone (Lome Peace Accord) 7 July 1999.

[41] D Horowitz acknowledges the prevailing conservatism in constitution-making in 'Constitutional Design: Proposals Versus Processes' in A Reynolds (ed), *The Architecture of Democracy* (Oxford, Oxford University Press, 2002) 16–18. The US Department of State Office of the Coordinator for Reconstruction and Stabilization in April 2005 issued a matrix of *Post-Conflict Reconstruction Essential Tasks*. Constitutional Processes are addressed in ch II ('provide technical and legal advisors with expertise'; 'ensure adoption of constitution'). Available online at http://www.state.gov/s/crs/.

[42] CR Sunstein, *Designing Democracy: What Constitutions Do* (New York, Oxford University Press, 2001) 261; Teitel, *Transitional Justice* (n 18 above) at 198.

game in town'.[43] Stoker writes equivocally of the 'triumph of democracy' while at the same time reporting on a global dissatisfaction with political endeavor.[44] Democracy in practice often seems to be of thin, top-down and incumbent variety, where the emphasis is on the formal state, and the conflation of government institutions with the sole or even main expression of democracy appears to exhaust the project of democracy.[45] Indeed, this idea of democracy seems to involve an almost exclusively vertical relationship between the state and its subjects, where the emphasis is more on building state capacity to function within the 'club' of democratic states than it is on winning a genuinely more integrative, thicker and bottom-up version of democracy that delivers the promise of democracy to all its citizens alike.[46] Despite advanced theoretical understanding of the complex, networked nature of power flows beyond the state structure (see further below), constitutional change (and the pursuit of democracy) remains focused on the creation or reformation of big-bang, top-down national institutions and reliant upon classical notions of state, sovereign and government. Even in the inescapable dynamism of a transitional context, populations continue to be conceived as passive subjects of political institutions rather than as engaged and active power-holders. This suggests that an alternative understanding of power is necessary.

III GOVERNMENTALITY AND THE NATURE OF CONSTITUTIONAL POWER

It is apparent that the primary task of a constitution, and of a political transition more generally, is a realignment of power relationships. The persistence of Westphalianism is therefore particularly disappointing in light of the sophisticated theoretical constructs which exist as interpretive aids to power in modern society. Most constitutional theorists now accept in general terms that there has been a movement from government to governance, and that the role of the state has moved from being a guarantor and provider of security, wealth and law towards being more of a partner or facilitator for a variety of other bodies and agencies as they concern themselves with such issues. Nevertheless, constitutionalists

[43] J Linz and A Stepan, *Problems of Democratic Transition and Consolidation: Southern Europe, South America, and Post-Communist Europe* (Baltimore MD, Johns Hopkins University Press, 1996)

[44] G Stoker, *Why Politics Matters: Making Democracy Work* (Basingstoke, Palgrave Macmillan, 2006)

[45] See J Morison, 'Models of Participation: From Representation to Participation' in J Jowell and D Oliver (eds), *The Changing Constitution*, 6th edn (Oxford, Oxford University Press, 2007).

[46] See further R Dworkin, *Is Democracy Possible Here?* (Princeton NJ, Princeton University Press, 2006).

remain focused too exclusively on models of power that fail to capture how government now works.[47] Critical scholars have offered subtle readings of power and society which go far beyond a blunt, vertical construct of the exercise of government solely or primarily by a national executive to describe the postmodern phenomena of de-centering of governance, or 'governance without government'.[48]

An important strand within this work was pioneered three decades ago by Michel Foucault's schema and conceptual vocabulary of governmentality.[49] Mitchell Dean describes the scope and impact of such work as follows:

> [Governmentality] asks questions concerned with how we govern and how we are governed, and with the relation between the government of ourselves, the government of others and the government of the state. It thus resumes older and broader meanings of government and governing that are not necessarily tied to the nation-state and, in some ways, have become obscured by the rise of the liberal constitutional national state and its identification of government with *the* government, i.e. with the body that claims supreme authority within a given territory and its various apparatuses.[50]

As Foucault himself reminds us,

> the analysis of power relations within a society cannot be reduced to the study of a series of institutions, not even to the study of all those institutions which would merit the name 'political'.[51]

Thus, in addition to the formal state there are other bodies that have a role in the operation of government. Power relations are rooted in the system of social networks. Civil society, local government, the private sector, the individual consumer, citizen, voter, expert are all 'active subjects' who not only collaborate in the exercise of government but also shape and inform

47 See J Morison, 'The Case Against Constitutional Reform' (1998) 25 *Journal of Law and Society* 510.

48 JN Rosenau (ed), *Governance without Government* (Cambridge, Cambridge Studies in International Relations, 1992).

49 See particularly, M Foucault, 'Governmentality' in JD Faubion (ed), *Power: The Essential Works of Michel Foucault Volume 3* (London, Allen Lane Penguin Press, 2000); L Martin, H Gutman and P Hutton (eds), *Technologies of the Self: A Seminar with Michel Foucault* (London, Tavistock, 1998); P Rabinow (ed), *Ethics: Subjectivity and Truth: The Essential Works of Michel Foucault Volume 1* (London, Penguin Books, 1997). Perhaps most important among those who have developed Foucault's work in general terms are N Rose, *Powers of Freedom: Reframing Political Thought* (Cambridge, Cambridge University Press, 1999); *The Politics of Life Itself* (Princeton, Princeton University Press, 2007) and M Dean, *Governmentality: Power and Rules in Modern Society* (London, Sage, 1999).

50 Dean, *Governmentality* (n 49 above) at 2–3.

51 M Foucault, 'Afterword, The Subject and Power' in H Dreyfuss and P Rabinow (eds), *Beyond Structuralism and Hermeneutics* (Chicago, University of Chicago Press, 1982) 224.

it.[52] The emphasis within this approach is less on the conventional subjects of constitutionalism such as government of a territory, and ideas of judicial sovereignty and law, and more on the management of things—people, resources, ideas—as part of the multi-form tactics of government. The direct action of the state in terms of law-making or institution-creating is to be augmented by the important quality of the freedom of the subject. It is not direct governmental action alone that achieves what governments want. This can be done successfully only with the willing co-operation of the individual subject participating in his/her own governance. In other words, the site and the agents of government are more than the state and passive subjects; they include also a whole range of persons and agencies co-opted into a wider exercise of power.[53]

Rather than simply concentrating on how the state controls and disciplines the body, governance is now involved in two aspects: there are the forms of rule by which authorities govern populations, and there are the 'technologies of the self' through which people shape their own subjectivity and 'make themselves up' as active subjects of power who can make choices. As one of us has argued before,[54] a proper understanding of power must acknowledge an idea of freedom, of individuals 'making themselves up' as active subjects or as citizens capable of bearing a regulated freedom within complex chains of constraints, calculations of interests, patterns and habits, and obligations and fears. Government is thus a domain of strategies, techniques and procedures (or 'technologies') through which different forces and groups (including the formal state but reaching far beyond it too) attempt to render their own various programs operable. The governmentality approach also locates the activity of government generally within the micro level and, in particular, within specific ways of thinking (or 'rationalities') which structure how we see and understand problems, their solutions, and the framework within which they exist. As Foucault sees it, power should not be analysed from 'the inside' but rather where 'it is completely invested in real and effective practices' and the goal should be

> to study power by looking at, as it were, at its external face, at the point where it relates directly and immediately at what we might ... call its object, its target,

[52] See J Morison, 'The Government—Voluntary Sector Compacts: Governance, Governmentality and Civil Society' , n2 above.

[53] As Foucault expresses it, power must be analysed 'as something that circulates, or rather as something that functions only when it is part of a chain ... Power functions. Power is exercised through networks and individuals do not simply circulate in those networks; they are in a position to both submit to and exercise power; they are always in its relays. In other words, power passes through individuals. It is not applied to them'. M Foucault, *Society Must be Defended: Lectures at the Collège De France 1975–1976* (trans D Macey) (Harmondsworth, Penguin Books, 2004) 28.

[54] J Morison, 'Government-Voluntary Sector Compacts: Governance, Governmentality and Civil Society' (2000), n 2 above.

> its field of application or, in other words, the places where it implants itself and produces its real effects.[55]

Without this understanding government is simply the imposition of the sovereign will on variously compliant or recalcitrant subjects. Without this wider concept of power, we may see constitutions in a one-dimensional way with the focus only on structures and norms. As Foucault puts it in an often quoted remark,

> [p]olitical theory has never ceased to be obsessed with the person of the sovereign. Such theories still continue today to busy themselves with the problem of sovereignty. What we need, however, is a political philosophy that isn't erected around the problem of sovereignty, nor therefore around the problems of law and prohibition. We need to cut off the King's head: in political theory that still has to be done.[56]

In a sense this needs to be done too in constitutional legal theory. Foucault complains that the 18th century

> invented a juridico-political theory of power centered on the notion of the will and its alienation, transfer, and representation in a governmental apparatus.[57]

This understanding has persisted and constitutionalists persist in seeing power mainly or exclusively in these terms.[58]

The fundamental insights that stem from such a relocation of focus as the governmentality approach requires include recognition of the existence of multiple sites of government, multiple sites of governance, and a more complex relationship between governor and governed. The exercise of governance is best understood as multi-textual and multi-form, wherein power is distributed in complex networks and subtle flows at all levels of society, and the state executive is constructed as a facilitator or partner in the exercise of rhizomatic governance. The 'objects' of governance are also reconstructed, not as a uniform herd, but as co-participants in a complex, networked relationship. People *choose* to behave in accordance with or to reject rules and demands from above. Governing cannot then be an exercise of brute power in commanding and demanding obedience, but

[55] M Foucault, *Society Must be Defended* (n 53 above) at 28.

[56] C Gordon (ed), *Power/Knowledge: Selected Interviews and Other Writings 1972–1977* (New York, Pantheon, 1980) 121.

[57] M Foucault, *Abnormal: Lectures at the Collège de France 1974–1975* (New York, Picador, 2003), 49.

[58] As Foucault again puts it, 'all jurists try to do the same thing, as their problem is to discover how a multiplicity of individuals and wills can be shaped into a single will or even a single body that is supposedly animated by a soul known as sovereignty'. Rather than searching for the heart or head of the state for something that is constitutive in the sense of being sovereign, we should 'study the multiple, peripheral bodies, the bodies that are constituted as subject by power-effects'. M Foucault, *Society must be Defended* (n 53 above) at 29.

must seek to achieve willing compliance and engagement with various projects of governance. Thus, 'multi-form' tactics of governance seek to mobilise, manage and inspire, and citizens must be understood as both exercisers and subjects of power. A governmentality-infused approach to constitutionalism would look beyond the state and centralised institutions to seek to understand how power is deployed through a whole series of networks and alliances.[59] This would include the role of the voluntary sector, national and international NGOs and local interest groups as well as state and non-state armed groups. By building an understanding of the complexity and fugitive nature of power, steps could be taken which would build space for facilitation of a genuine process of negotiation and the pursuit of democratic control in all sites of power. Through this process of acknowledgement and action, constitutive change may be effected at a profound level.

It is clear that what is required is not a rejection of a continued role and influence for the state, but a reconstruction of the state-community relationship, and

> relocat[ion] of this familiar vocabulary [of state and state institutions] as one important and enduring family in larger and more complex languages of networks of rule and democratic freedom.[60]

In particular, rather than seeing a constitution as an assertion of new sets of rules, we must develop those various approaches. For example, the constitution may be conceived as an operational framework, creating institutional conditions that can exert pressure on society to constantly re-order itself in ways that emphasise participation, dialogue, deliberation and mutual recognition as a means of renewing democracy.[61] This is the nature of constitutional transformation.

IV CONSTITUTIONAL PROCESS: PARTICIPATION, DEMOCRATIC DECISION-MAKING AND RIGHTS DISCOURSES

The final sections of this chapter explore what a constitution-making process conditioned by an understanding of governmentality might address. It is apparent that in modern contexts of constitution-making, the traditional roles of a constitution—reconstruction of power relationships and a realignment of the state in the eyes of its citizens—are augmented

[59] See further J Morison, 'Democracy, Governance and Governmentality: Civic Space and Constitutional Renewal in Northern Ireland' (2001) 21 *Oxford Journal of Legal Studies* 287.

[60] Tully, 'The Unfreedom of the Moderns in Comparison to their Ideals of Constitutional Democracy' (n 11 above) at 220.

[61] See further U Preuss, *Constitutional Revolution: The Link Between Constitutionalism and Progress* (trans D Schneider) (Amherst NY, Prometheus Books, 1995)

with a conflict resolution, peace-making facet. This is compounded by the recognition that nearly all contemporary transitional states adopt constitutions, and that the quasi-peace agreement model of a 'transitional constitution' creates a space for innovative political mediation which is responsive to broader societal needs and aspirations. Governmentality theory provides a lens through which we can challenge the potential of constitutional texts and processes to leave behind the formulaic and formalised institutional focus of a state-building agenda and instead progress profound structural, cultural or attitudinal change. A governmentality-infused constitution-making process would be oriented less towards elite negotiated, quantifiable outcomes such as elections, the creation of new institutions or the drafting of legal texts, and more focused on the recognition and reconstruction of relationships both horizontally and vertically. As a result, a governmentality approach would support a constitution-making process that seeks the participation and engagement of entire societies and is aware of how those who are traditionally seen as merely governed are themselves involved in a wider process of governance. In seeking to plot the constitutional relationships that exist at this level, and to understand more fully how society in this sense is actually *constituted*, attention must be given to developing further ideas of participation, a deeper and more fully articulated rights framework and a re-working of certain elemental relationships.

A Participation

The fact of power and social relationships existing as networked and multi-form is not entirely absent within traditional constitution-building. Indeed, the attention to the *process* of constitution-making is evidence of its partial recognition. However the interpretation often accorded to ideas of process, with an increasingly prominent role being accorded to international experts in constitution-making, has prompted some commentators to question whether entrenchment of democratic standards and fundamental rights may not be better achieved by empowering local societies rather than imposing rules from the outside.[62]

'Participatory constitutionalism', which prioritises public consultation and outreach, has been undertaken to varying degrees in countries including Brazil, Nicaragua, East Timor, Fiji and South Africa. There is even

[62] For a trenchant critique of international co-option of a post-conflict constitutional process see D Chandler, *Bosnia: Faking Democracy After Dayton*, 2nd edn (London, Pluto Press, 2000).

some claim of a *right* to public participation in constitution-making.[63] Although precise goals and impact will obviously vary according to context, participation in a constitution-making process is generally intended to encourage an emerging public voice, to give voice to previously excluded groups, and to ensure the constitution is representative of a wider range of social concerns. It is this aspect of constitution-making which has received most attention to date in terms of its potential contribution to peace-making.[64]

Neil Kritz has identified constitution-making processes in Eritrea, Rwanda and South Africa as three of the more successful processes of participatory constitution-making, and notable achievements were indeed attained in each jurisdiction.[65] Almost three quarters of the South African population was reached by the constitutional process outreach campaign and the Constitutional Assembly received two million public submissions.[66] In Rwanda, the constitution-building process was explicitly designed to counter the circumstances of a feudal society with no heritage of popular participation in decision-making, through an outreach process that placed thousands of individuals in outlying provinces for periods of up to six months to educate and engage communities in constitutional debates.[67] In Eritrea, a comprehensive outreach process was conducted over three years, utilizing a variety of creative media for education and communication such as poetry, storytelling and drama.

Encouraging public participation can enhance the peace-making role of a constitution by moving beyond the constitution as a mere statement of intent towards establishing a model of democracy in action. In both Northern Ireland and South Africa, women's coalitions contrived to ensure a prominent role for gender issues on the constitutional agenda, despite

[63] The UN Human Rights Committee recognised a right to public participation in constitution making in 1991 and again in 1996: V Hart, *Democratic Constitution Making*, United States Institute of Peace Special Report 107 (Washington DC, USIP, 2003) 7. Available online at http://www.usip.org/pubs/specialreports/sr107.pdf.

[64] Illustrated by ongoing comparative studies of constitution-making under the auspices of the United States Institute of Peace and the International Institute for Democracy and Electoral Assistance:' Hart *Democratic Constitution Making* (n 63 above) at 7. International IDEA, *The Role of Constitution Building Processes in Democratization*,project overview and additional resources available online at http://www.idea.int/conflict/cbp/ .

[65] N Kritz, *Constitution-Making Process: Lessons for Iraq*. Testimony before a Joint Hearing of the Senate Committee on the Judiciary, Subcommittee on the Constitution, Civil Rights and Property Rights and the Senate Committee on Foreign Relations, Subcommittee on Near Eastern and South Asian Affairs (25 June 2003). Available online at http://www.usip.org/congress/testimony/2003/0625_kritz.html.

[66] Hart, *Democratic Constitution Making* (n 63 above) at 7.

[67] Hart, *Democratic Constitution Making* (n 63 above). See also the Republic of Rwanda Legal and Constitutional Commission, *Towards a Constitution for Rwanda: Action Plan 2002–2003* (Kigali, 2002), available online at http://www.cjcr.gov.rw/eng/actionplancjc.PDF.

initial exclusion from the negotiations process.[68] These situations offer instructive examples of the capacity of civil society to effect genuine social change as with, for example, the impressive political sophistication displayed by the Northern Ireland Women's Coalition in their negotiation skills and ability to rise above tired posturing from other (male) delegates and strategically mobilise social capital.[69]

However, there is a more complex story. In Eritrea, the constitution as drafted was never implemented. The Rwandan process, although innovative in many respects, was entirely elite-driven, under the auspices of a government frequently criticised for its authoritarian tendencies.[70] Other participatory processes have resulted in excellent constitutional texts which were not adhered to in practice (Thailand) or which were manipulated by elites (Uganda).[71] These discrepancies are borne out by a comparative analysis of 12 recent constitution-building processes, which suggests that while participatory processes do tend to have an empowering effect on a local populace and result in more inclusive and representative constitutional documents, this outcome may be perceived by local elites as threatening to their interests, thus potentially raising the likelihood of 'spoiling' activities.[72] Of course, the multiple variables within a constitution-making process and the politics of a transitional process militate against any but the broadest of generalisations. However, these findings offer a useful reminder that constitution-making processes operate in a complex dialectic with a similarly complex multi-dimensional political context—and, perhaps, reinforce Bastian and Luckham's 'iron law of the perverse consequences of institutional design'.[73]

[68] D Pottie and S Hassim, 'The Politics of Institutional Design in the South African Transition' in S Bastian and R Luckham (eds), *Can Democracy be Designed?* (New York, Zed Books, 2003); K Fearon, *Women's Work: the Story of the Northern Ireland Women's Coalition* (Belfast, The Blackstaff Press, 1999).

[69] K Fearon, 'Northern Ireland Women's Coalition: Institutionalizing a political voice and ensuring representation', *Accord: An International Review of Peace Initiatives* (2000).

[70] See, eg J Kimonyo, N Twagiramungu and C Kayumba, *Supporting the Post-Genocide Transition in Rwanda*, Working Paper 32 (Netherlands Institute of International Relations, 2004). Available online at http://www.clingendael.nl/publications/2004/20041200_cru_working_paper_32.pdf.

[71] Y Ghai and G Galli, *Constitution Building Processes and Democratization* (n 20 above).

[72] K Samuels, 'Constitution Building Processes and Democratization: A Discussion of Twelve Case Studies' (International IDEA). Available online at http://www.idea.int/conflict/cbp/upload/IDEA%20CBP%20Comparative%20paper%20by%20Kirsti%20Samuels-2.pdf. See also Samuels, 'Post-Conflict Peace-Building and Constitution-Making' (n 18 above) at 669–71.

[73] S Bastian and R Luckham, 'Conclusion—The Politics of Institutional Choice' in S Bastian and R Luckham (eds), *Can Democracy be Designed?* (London/New York, Zed Books, 2003) 314.

B Rights

A constitution is at best a starting point for societal reconstruction and not a conclusive solution. It has been argued by one of the authors elsewhere that one of the most valuable contributions of the Good Friday Agreement in Northern Ireland was the space it created to facilitate legitimate political dissent.[74] However, creating the space for both dissent and resolution of disputes may be aided by the articulation of a more nuanced framework of rights and responsibilities which makes rights universally relevant and resonant. Rights can provide the vocabulary within which discussion can take place and the language within which any solution must be couched, overseen by a grammar of international rules and enforcement mechanisms.

The contemporary constitutional template of a Bill of Rights, with observance monitored by a Constitutional Court or similar mechanism of judicial review epitomises the role of a constitution here as a 'commitment device'. Ferejohn and Sager recognise the importance of this role where they comment that

> by enshrining various aspects of procedure or substance in a written document that announces itself as the supreme source of law, and by making that document difficult to change, a people can achieve a future better than any they could otherwise attain.[75]

Rights are now seemingly ineradicably linked to progress towards successful development, properly functioning politics and the pursuit of a good life.[76] This desire to entrench an international rights framework reflects the opportunity that a constitution presents to harness a point of political momentum and assert the normative principles by which government and citizenry will operate in the future as they struggle to find ways of living together. Human rights offer a framing device which can further inclusive social policy, create an avenue for enforcement of entitlements by citizens against the state and permit the mediation of disputes in a universally-recognised language. Rights also offer a language in which to move towards recognition, strive towards agreement and couch disagreement. This is in contrast to more traditional constitutions of the 19th century, where themes of national identity provided the impetus for constitutional

[74] See J Morison, 'Democracy, Governance and Governmentality: Civic Public Space and Constitutional Renewal in Northern Ireland' (n 2 above).

[75] J Ferejohn and L Sager, 'Commitment and Constitutionalism' (2003) 81 *Texas Law Review* 1929 at 1929.

[76] Indeed, there is even a view that a right to democratic governance and a democratic standard of governmental legitimacy today belong in international law: see S Marks, *The Riddle of all Constitutions: International Law, Democracy and the Critique of Ideology* (Oxford, Oxford University Press, 2000) esp ch 2.

development, and thus introduced what Balibar has described as the 'obsessive, spectral return of popular sovereignty in regimes of democratic citizenship'.[77] Rights in this context simply offer a better foundation for beginning rather than ending the constitutional process of negotiating a shared future.

Of course it must be remembered that human rights standards are more vivid and nuanced—and thus more valuable in this process—than legal systems often credit, and the exclusive recourse to standards, systems and courts for advancing complex normative principles has arguably unduly restricted their conceptual core.[78] As Anthony Woodiwiss concludes,

> just as there is far more in rights than law alone, so for rights to work far more than law itself is required.[79]

We cannot here develop fully what is additionally required but will restrict ourselves to highlighting one element beyond law essential to make rights 'work'. This pertains to genuine dialogue, designed to foster the environment that Habermas calls 'democratizing rights discourse'; founding a nation-building process on principles of democracy and human rights, but seeking to entrench those principles by encouraging the percolation of rights discourse through debate regarding the terms and standards for participation in society.[80] Indeed, this is the thrust of many approaches to deliberative or discursive democracy which seek to make rights meaningful through a process of open and authentic public debate.[81] Moving beyond

[77] E Balibar, *We the People of Europe? Reflections on Transnational Citizenship* (trans J Swenson) (Princeton NJ, Princeton University Press, 2004).

[78] For a range of critiques of human rights discourse and the risks of excessive formalism see, for example, D Kennedy, 'The International Human Rights Movement: Part of the Problem?' (2002) 15 *Harvard Human Rights Journal* 99; D Kennedy, 'The Critique of Rights in Critical Legal Studies' in W Brown and J Halley (eds), *Left Legalism/Left Critique* (Durham/ London, Duke University Press 2002),178–226; S Meckled-García and B Çali (eds), *The Legalization of Human Rights* (London/New York, Routledge, 2006); V Nesiah and A Keenan, 'Human Rights and Sacred Cows: Framing Violence, Disappearing Struggles' in N Gordon (ed), *From the Margins of Globalization: Critical Perspectives on Human Rights* (Lanham, Lexington Books, 2004); B Rajagopal, *International Law from Below: Development, Social Movements and Third World Resistance* (Cambridge, Cambridge University Press, 2003); R Hirschl, *Towards Juristocracy: The Origins and Consequences of the New Constitutionalism* (Cambridge MA, Harvard University Press, 2004).

[79] A Woodiwiss, 'The law cannot be enough: Human Rights and the limits of legalism' in S Meckled-García and B Çali (eds), *The Legalization of Human Rights* (London/New York, Routledge 2006) 49.

[80] J Habermas, *Between Facts and Norms* (trans W Rehg) (Cambridge MA, MIT Press, 1996).

[81] Eg JS Dryzek, *Discursive Democracy* (Cambridge, Cambridge University Press, 1990); JS Dryzek, *Deliberative Democracy and Beyond* (Oxford, Oxford University Press, 2000) 11–12; A Gutmann and D Thompson, *Democracy and Disagreement* (Cambridge MA, Belknap Press 1996); J Habermas, *Theory of Communicative Action* (trans T McCarthy) (Boston, Beacon Press, 1987); C Pateman, *Participation and Democratic Theory* (Cambridge, Cambridge University Press, 1970). For an overview see J Fiskin and P Laslett (eds), *Debating Deliberative Democracy* (Oxford, Blackwell, 2003).

legalism to embrace multi-textural interpretations of human rights would add another bi-directional perspective to the backwards/forwards nature of transitional constitutionalism, ensuring that constitutional processes continue to look upwards to universal rights frameworks and democratic standards, yet diffuse the essential meaning of these frameworks throughout the diverse cultures and social groups which constitute a nation.

C Relationships

Although discursive shifts promoting the language of rights, democracy and individual freedoms are valuable, they will always be an insufficient means to engender deep social change. In addition to creative use of a rights framework to establish a dialogic and participative grammar of political discourse, questions of institutional architecture and the sorts of relationships that they create and foster must also be considered.[82]

Many theorists and practitioners have addressed the question of constitutional engineering, for example, exploring different modes of power-sharing and the potential to manage divisions through electoral policy and so forth.[83] Such explorations of the relationship between constitutional processes and national political dynamics represent an important contribution to the theory and practice of constitution-making in transitions. However, the focus continues to be on institutions and elite pacts, imagined through an explicitly top-down lens. There is a need for a parallel focus on the broader constellation of institutional bonds and the universe of constitutional architectures that might exist, particularly in terms of how these may recognise and re-work relationships within societies.

Moving beyond the national political landscape takes us into the territory of this collection: the grassroots, subaltern or 'from below'. James Tully rightly comments that to define 'from below' as the lowest stratum of the social hierarchy is to miss the critical meaning of the networked governmentality metaphor, which is that debate and praxis occurs in a multi-layered fashion throughout all society.[84] This is a very important

[82] S Chesterman, 'Imposed Constitutions, Imposed Constitutionalism and Ownership' (2005) 37 *Connecticut Law Review* 947.

[83] G Sartori, *Comparative Constitutional Engineering: An Inquiry into Structures, Incentives and Outcomes*, 2nd edn (New York, New York University Press, 1997); B Reilly, *Democracy in Divided Societies* (Cambridge, Cambridge University Press, 2001); A Lijphart and CH Waisman (eds), *Institutional Design in New Democracies* (Boulder CO, Westview Press, 1996); A Reynolds (ed), *The Architecture of Democracy: Constitutional Design, Conflict Management and Democracy* (Oxford, Oxford University Press, 2001). See also the literature on democratic experimentalism, eg M Dorf and C Sable, 'A Constitution of Democratic Experimentalism' (1998) 98 *Colombia Law Review* 267.

[84] Tully, 'The Unfreedom of the Moderns in Comparison to their Ideals of Constitutional Democracy" (n 11 above) at 220.

insight and one that we endorse wholly. Civil society as well as other private, public and semi-public entities, and the whole range of groups and individuals, are all involved immediately within our understanding of power. The local, national, regional and international or transnational dimensions too are all implicated. Language, resources, people and ways of seeing the world are as involved in governance as law, money or state structures. Even the very terms that we use to understand the issues are part of the exercise of power.[85] For a discourse to be legitimately 'from below' it must concern itself with all of these aspects and more.

Having acknowledged this, we would argue however that there is a particularly important dimension within transitional constitution-making which relates to the issue of inclusion of the disempowered or disenfranchised within the mainstream institutions. Inclusion at this level does not of course exhaust the obligation to include the disempowered and neither is it the only way that they are to be factored in. However, there is perhaps a special need to adjust the general process whereby social demands are translated into a national political agenda so that it includes those who are otherwise excluded.[86] While we would argue generally that governance, with all its multi-form tactics, is the proper site to factor into the exercise of power all those aspects that we would want to see, there is perhaps good reason for engineering the traditional structures of the constitution to ensure that at that level too there is an appropriate level of involvement.

For example, there is no reason why a traditional Constitutional Court is incapable of playing a role in this task, provided there is sufficient political will and independence. This appears to have been the case in Colombia, where the Constitutional Court established in 1991 has taken a leading role in acknowledging inequality and catalysing social change.[87] As a result of a combination of institutional personality and structural legal

[85] Eg P Millar and N Rose refer to 'the fundamental role that knowledges play in rendering aspects of existence thinkable and calculable, and amenable to deliberated and planful initiatives': see 'Governing Economic Life' (1990) 19 *Economy and Society* 1 at 3.

[86] This is also the direction of the emergent discourse of 'globalisation from below', as represented by, among others, J Brecher, T Costello and B Smith, *Globalization from Below* (London, South End Press, 2000); R Falk, *Predatory Globalization* (London, Polity Press, 1999); B de Sousa-Santos and C A Rodríguez-Garavito, *Law and Globalisation from Below* (Cambridge, Cambridge University Press, 2005); N Klein, *Fences and Windows: Dispatches from the Front Lines of the Globalization Debate* (London, Picador 2002).

[87] Materials available in English about this interesting phenomenon are unfortunately scant. See, eg M Garcia-Villegas, 'Law as Hope: Constitutions, Courts, and Social Change in Latin America' (2004) 16 *Florida Journal of International Law* 133; M Cepeda-Espinosa, 'Judicial Activism in a Violent Context: The Origin, Role and Impact of the Colombian Constitutional Court' (2004) 3 *Washington University Global Studies Law Review* 529 at 531; MI Morgan, 'Taking Machismo to Court: The Gender Jurisprudence of the Colombian Constitutional Court' (1998) 30 *University of Miami Inter-American Law Review* 253.

innovation (including the introduction of a writ for protection of fundamental rights, *acción de tutela*, which makes possible a form of constitutional judicial review providing swift concrete resolution of individual cases), there appear to have been important developments in this regard. Cepeda-Espinosa, for example, suggests that the Constitutional Court has

> infused the Colombian legal system with an entirely new outlook and perspective [and] substantially altered imbalances of power in the Colombian social, political, and economic spheres.[88]

More often however, profiling subaltern demands will require tackling conflicted or negative relationships between citizenry and state. Martin Loughlin has identified a tension between legitimacy and effectiveness, in which governments become separated from citizenry by their preoccupation with supra-national politics, while citizenry in turn reject national structures of governance and revert to local or informal dispute resolution.[89] In other contexts, citizen withdrawal from the state may be a reaction to weakened or predatory state institutions.[90] This withdrawal can render large swathes of population invisible to central government, and vice versa. Further, where judicial institutions have been complicit in state abuses of human rights, a judicial model for protection of constitutional rights will obviously be less convincing as a mechanism for the pursuit of radical change.

A focus on political culture and executive government views these antagonisms only peripherally. Ironically, by centering and centralising the state within constitution-making, executive responsibility for social and structural change (both positive and negative) is de-emphasised. This has been critiqued by Luckham, Goetz and Kaldor, who claim that it is a result of disproportionate attention paid to 'high politics of state rather than the deep politics of society', that 'institutional development tends to be seen as a good in itself' and

> elite pacts defining 'rules of the game' are given more attention than the political struggles of marginalised groups, including women, minorities and the poor.[91]

[88] Cepeda-Espinosa, 'Judicial Activism in a Violent Context' (n 87 above) at 536.

[89] M Loughlin, 'Constitutional Theory: A 25th Anniversary Essay' (2005) 25 *Oxford Journal of Legal Studies* 183.

[90] For example, International Crisis Group reports the findings of a recent study in which citizens of the Democratic Republic of Congo were asked how they would treat the state if it were a person. 'Kill him' was a frequent answer. International Crisis Group, Escaping the Conflict Trap: Promoting Good Governance in the Congo (Africa Report No 114). Available online at http://www.crisisgroup.org/home/index.cfm?id=4276&l=1 (visited 30 July 2006).

[91] R Luckham, A Goetz and M Kaldor, 'Democratic Institutions, Democratic Politics and Political Violence' in S Bastian and R Luckham (eds), *Can Democracy be Designed?* (New York, Zed Books, 2003) 21.

V CONCLUSION

If constitution-making is to maximise its transformative potential in the reconstitution of societies, it must seek a more dynamic task than merely a re-shuffling of elites as the traditional institutions of formal government are re-populated. As the foregoing has outlined, there are multiple points in a constitution-building process where a participative, discursive and rights-orientated approach could be integrated in pursuit of a fundamental shift in understanding of a state's position vis-à-vis its citizens in the pursuit of genuinely constitutive change. There must be more too than a tokenistic involvement of some of those who were previously excluded—a 'post hoc inclusion of the excluded', as de Sousa Santos and Rodríguez-Garavito describe it.[92] We need instead to develop a better understanding of how power operates and then apply ourselves more directly to ensuring that interventions are effective, appropriate and based on facilitating a discursive, participative and rights-based approach. This will produce the constitutional raw materials that will allow the basic constitutional issue of how to live together to be worked upon in an inclusive and democratic process welling up from below.

This involves first and foremost moving away from the sort of classic age, juridico-political theory of power that is centred almost exclusively on the notion of the will and its alienation, transfer and representation in a governmental apparatus. We must understand that the sites and indeed formats of power are much more diverse and diffuse, and that it is there that the activity of government occurs just as much as it does at the high level of constitutional courts and legislative chambers. Transformation must occur at an ethical level where the level of 'conduct of conduct' is being considered. A constitution which recognises this would engage people in determining the details of how they want to live themselves and in establishing the basis of participation and democracy. It would be properly constitutive in an evolving and continuing sense.[93]

With this objective in mind we can see constitution-making as only a first stage in creating some of the conditions in which this negotiation and re-negotiation of how we wish to govern ourselves is carried out. The governmentality approach, which downgrades the importance of the state and looks instead at how power is actually constituted through society, offers a better way to approach the issue than does a formal constitutionalism emphasising state and structure. It recognises that real constitutional agreement cannot be imposed or conferred from outside no matter how

[92] B de Sousa-Santos and CA Rodríguez-Garavito, 'Law, politics and the subaltern in counter-hegemonic globalization' in *Law and Globalization from Below* (Cambridge, Cambridge University Press 2005) 9.

[93] M Foucault, 'The Ethic of the Concern for Self as a Practice of Freedom' in P Rabinow (ed), *Ethics: Subjectivity and Truth* (Harmondsworth, Penguin Books, 2000) 300.

beneficent the drafters of the constitution think themselves to be. In short, we take up this insight from the governmentality approach and are arguing for a conception of constitution-making in which the text document is merely the backdrop to a vibrant culture of dialogue and debate regarding the meaning and extent of constitutional rights and relationships.

5

*The Role of Community In Participatory Transitional Justice**

PATRICIA LUNDY AND MARK MCGOVERN

I INTRODUCTION

WHAT HAS BEEN coined the 'post-conflict agenda' has its roots in the peace framework developed in the United Nations' Secretary-General Boutros Boutros-Ghali's 'Agenda for Peace' 1992.[1] In this paper we advance the view that a grassroots approach to transitional justice should be regarded as an intrinsic part of this agenda. The international community has recently prioritised justice issues and is financing and supporting the implementation of a plethora of legal initiatives. As one commentator noted, development co-operation has been reformulated in legal terms and more and more international effort has gone into building courts, writing laws, punishing the perpetrators of human rights abuses, supporting human rights NGOs and generally promoting the rule of law abroad.[2] (Re-) establishing the rule of law is now regarded as a prerequisite for the emergence of stable and peaceful societies, and justice packages are frequently part of negotiated peace agreements.[3] However, there is a growing debate about the appropriate model and level (for example the global, national, local or community) at which transitional justice measures should be adopted, and whether these are complementary or viable alternative processes.[4] Critics have argued

* A version of this paper is also published in (2008) 35 *Journal of Law and Society* 2. We are grateful for the permission of the editor to republish it here.

[1] UN Secretary-General's Report, 'An Agenda for Peace: Prevention Diplomacy, Peace-making and Peacekeeping' (17 June 1992) UN Doc A/47/277-S/24111.

[2] C Mokhiber, 'Local Perspectives: Foreign Aid to the Justice Sector', Summary of Findings (Geneva, International Council on Human Rights Policy, 2000).

[3] For a discussion on the notion of a 'dominant script' in transitional justice discourse, see also J Cavallaro and S Albuja (ch 6) and K McConnachie and J Morison (ch 4) in this collection.

[4] A Betts, 'Should Approaches to Post-conflict Justice and Reconciliation be Determined Globally, Nationally or Locally?' (2005) 17(4) *European Journal of Development Research*

that law is increasingly seen by the international community as one of the safest ways in which to engage with, or intervene, in other countries. Such attempts to 'influence the rules of the game' evidence the fact that international justice and rule of law initiatives are not politically neutral.[5] In particular, the tendency to exclude local communities as active participants in transitional justice measures is a primary flaw raising fundamental questions of legitimacy, local ownership and participation. Simply involving local people at the implementation stage of these initiatives is not enough. For a fully participatory process (we will argue) they should also take part at every stage in the process, including conception, design, decision-making and management.

The aim of this paper is to critically examine some of these issues, and while mindful of the dangers of over-eulogising a participatory approach, to explore the value of participation and local agency for transitional justice theory, policy and practice. It is structured in five parts. First, it briefly examines the origins of transitional justice and its application in post-conflict societies. This is followed by a brief assessment of some of the key principles invoked in dominant versions of transitional discourse: transition, democracy and justice. Second, drawing predominantly on insights from the field of international development studies, the ideological assumptions of transitional interventions are analysed in the context of a wider 'post-conflict agenda'. Third, the paper explores evidence suggesting that a move toward a greater emphasis on participation is emerging in transitional debates. Fourth, the roots of participatory principles in radical development theory and the strengths and weaknesses in such an approach are examined. A cautious note is raised, however, about over eulogising the merits of a participatory approach. Finally, using a case study of the Ardoyne Commemoration Project, a bottom-up 'truth-telling' project in Northern Ireland in which the authors were involved, the paper will discuss and explore the contribution of grassroots 'truth-telling' processes to transitional justice,[6] and make some general suggestions as to how these

735; L Bickford, 'Unofficial Truth Projects' (June 2006), unpublished paper on file with authors; P Gready, 'Reconceptualizing Transitional Justice: Embedded and Distanced Justice' (2005) 5 *Conflict, Security and Development* 3; P Lundy and M McGovern, 'The Dialogues Within: Memory, Community and Post-Conflict Transition in a Nationalist Community in the North of Ireland', Paper presented to *Cultures of Political Transition: Memory, Identity and Voice*, Institute of Commonwealth Studies, 13–17 September 2000, University of North London; P Lundy and M McGovern, 'Participation, Truth and Partiality: Participatory Action Research, Community-based Truth-telling and Post-conflict Transition in Northern Ireland' (2006) 40 *Sociology* 71.

[5] J Hearn, 'Aiding Democracy? Donors & Civil Society in South Africa' (1990) 21 *Third World Quarterly* 815; B Oomen, 'Donor Driven Justice and it Discontents: The Case of Rwanda' (2005) 36 *Development and Change* 887.

[6] Ardoyne Commemoration Project, *Ardoyne: The Untold Truth* (Belfast, Beyond the Pale, 2002); P Lundy and M McGovern, *Community, 'Truth-telling' and Conflict Resolution* (Belfast, Northern Ireland Community Relations Council, 2005).

might be translated into values underpinning transitional justice practice. The aim is therefore to make a positive contribution to the debate on the future direction of transitional justice and, at a practical level, of discussions and policy initiatives on 'bottom-up' approaches to transitional justice.

II TRANSITION AND JUSTICE

For many, recent years have seen the increased appropriation of the language of 'human rights' and 'transition' as part of an essentially unilateralist global project of 'democracy promotion'.[7] The dominant paradigm for understanding democratisation within the international community embraced the assumption that the move away from dictatorial rule (evident in many parts of the world in the past 25 years), understood as the essence of transitional societies, invariably involves democratisation. 'Transition', as normally conceived within transitional justice theory, tends to involve a particular and limited conception of democratisation based on liberal and essentially Western formulations of democracy. Moreover the assumption that 'transition' implies a move away from dictatorship and toward democracy ignores the problem that human rights abuses may continue to take place in circumstances where, in theory at least, the norms of liberal democratic accountability prevail.[8] Challenging this permits a radical critique of implicit liberal versions of transition that may otherwise struggle to deal with the subversion of the rule of law, under the guise of law itself, in ostensibly liberal democratic states.

The definition of justice, too, tends to be narrowly conceived and limited to the legal sphere. As Heyzer has noted,

> justice is addressed in a skewed, partial and piecemeal manner, as much by practitioners as by scholars, and the attempt to marry peace and justice after conflict remains largely incomplete.[9]

Rama Mani argues that there are severe philosophical and conceptual shortcomings to the way justice tends to be understood by transitional policy-makers and practitioners, with significant practical consequences. National and international 'peace-builders', it is suggested, fail to recognise and respond to the complexities of restoring the multi-faceted dimensions

[7] See McEvoy's critique of the legalistic understanding of this process in this collection.

[8] C Bell, C Campbell and F Ní Aoláin, 'Justice Discourse in Transition' (2004) 13 *Social and Legal Studies*; F Ní Aoláin and C Campbell, 'The Paradox of Transition in Conflicted Democracies' (2005) 27 *Human Rights Quarterly* 175.

[9] N Heyzer (UNIFEM Exec Director), 'Women, War and Peace: Mobilizing for Security and Justice in the 21st Century', *The Dag Hammarskjold Lecture 2004*, Sweden, 22 September 2004, 1 at 4.

of justice in low income, war-torn societies. The over-riding focus on redressing direct injustices against individuals (in the form of human rights abuses, war crimes and crimes against humanity) tends to leave the injustices that caused the conflict untouched.

Rather, Mani proposes an alternative, holistic and integrated approach to conceptualising justice in transition, with three distinct, but inter-related dimensions: legal, rectificatory and distributive.[10] While the first of these is concerned with the restoration of the rule of law, and the second with direct human rights abuses suffered by individuals, the third is designed to address structural and systematic injustices resulting from political and economic discrimination and inequalities of resource distribution. For Mani, the focus on the rectificatory, in particular, can lead to a neglect of the other dimensions of justice.

The point here is not to suggest that human rights or democracy do not matter; rather, that the agenda being set for transitional justice, as it is currently constituted, tends to marginalise issues, questions and approaches that might either challenge the forms and norms of Western governance, or implicate dominant global economic relations in the causes of conflict, rather than its solution. Marginalising economic justice, as with the desire to determine the forms and limits of democratisation, might then be understood as part and parcel of a wider 'ideological battle'.[11] This also, of course, raises the even thornier 'universalism vs relativism' debate in the conceptualisation of human rights and justice, to say nothing of the debate over sovereignty and the just basis for international intervention. These issues cannot be dealt with substantially here. However, what can be said is that the attempt to apply values uniformly across cultures and societies, where the possibilities for peoples in those societies to participate, influence and impact upon that process are confined and delimited, is in essence a negation of those values by the very means of their supposed implementation. Put another way, the values and ideas informing justice may need to be articulated within and by each community, based on its specific realities and needs, for both conceptual and, indeed, practical reasons. In terms of the latter, for example, as Mani points out,

> if ideas and institutions about as fundamental and personal a value as justice are imposed from outside without an internal resonance, they may flounder, notwithstanding their assertion of universality.[12]

That non-Western scholars, living and working in resource-poor and war-torn societies, have little voice in Western-dominated and -generated

[10] R Mani, *Beyond Retribution: Seeking Justice in the Shadows of War* (Oxford, Polity Press, 2002).

[11] Hearn, 'Aiding Democracy? Donors & Civil Society in South Africa' (n 5 above) at 820.

[12] Mani, *Beyond Retribution: Seeking Justice in the Shadows of War* (n 10 above) at 49.

academic theories and debates, may itself be seen as an injustice impacting upon the study and practice of transitional justice-making. The narrow focus on questions of law, evident in much transitional justice theory, creates problems for understanding the issues at stake and the consequences of transitional processes by removing them from a wider structural social, political and economic context.

III CRITIQUING THE 'POST-CONFLICT AGENDA'?

The problem of a potential 'democratic deficit' lies at the heart of a critique of hegemonic international approaches to 'democracy promotion' in post-conflict situations. What is essentially at issue is the question of agency, of who engenders and controls change, within what has been termed the 'post-conflict agenda'.[13] This raises fundamental questions about power relations and the legitimation of dominant interests. As already noted, justice has become a key feature of international foreign policy and cooperation and is one of the main ways in which the international community has come to engage with countries in the late 1990s. The 'judicialisation of international relations' is apparent in a wide range of internationally driven peace-building, reconciliation, development, democratisation, good governance, nation-building and rule-of-law initiatives.[14] Through such interventions international actors are getting deeply involved in political and social matters that they avoided until recently.

The problem, again, as numerous commentators have argued, is that such initiatives tend to be donor-driven, rather than responsive to the needs or wants of people themselves. From the 1990s onward a new approach to post-conflict development has emerged with aid—primarily from the North to the South—being viewed as a tool of political engineering.[15] The shift toward 'human rights' and 'legal and judicial development' projects

[13] The term 'post-conflict agenda' refers in this paper to the many and varied peace building, conflict management, 'good governance', democratisation and rule of law and justice interventions sponsored by the international community.

[14] Hearn, 'Aiding Democracy? Donors & Civil Society in South Africa' (n 5 above); Oomen, 'Donor Driven Justice and it Discontents: The Case of Rwanda' (n 5 above); P Uvin, 'Difficult Choices in the New Post-Conflict Agenda: the International Community in Rwanda after the Genocide' (2001) 22 *Third World Quarterly* 177.

[15] Hearn, 'Aiding Democracy? Donors & Civil Society in South Africa' (n 5 above); G Knaus and F Martin, '"Travails of the European Raj" Lessons from Bosnia Herzegovina' (2003) 14 *Journal of Democracy* 60; Oomen, 'Donor Driven Justice and it Discontents: The Case of Rwanda' (n 5 above); W Robinson, *Promoting Polyarchy: Globalisation, US Intervention, and Hegemony* (Cambridge, Cambridge University Press, 1996); Mani, *Beyond Retribution: Seeking Justice in the Shadows of War* (n 10 above); R Paris, 'International Peacebuilding and the "Mission Civilisatrice"' (2002) 28 *Review of International Studies* 637; M Pugh (ed), *Regeneration of War-Torn Societies* (London, Macmillan Press, 2000); Uvin, 'Difficult Choices in the New Post-Conflict Agenda' (n 14 above).

has been central to this process. Certainly there has been a proliferation of such programmes. For example, aid from the Organization for Economic Co-operation and Development (OECD) to 'transitional' countries for legal, judicial and human rights initiatives grew from less than US$500,000 in 1988 to a staggering US$581 million in 2002.[16] The number of such projects increased from one in 1988 to 1,836 in 2002. However, of equal significance is the nature of such work. For many critics these projects are primarily donor-driven. For example, in Rwanda the number of OECD-funded legal and 'judicial development' and 'human rights' projects rose from zero to 35 during the 1990s, at an estimated cost of US$30 million. Yet, as has already been touched upon, the extent to which such work impacts on the lives of ordinary Rwandans is extremely limited. In another instance, in Sierra Leone, the annual budget of the Special Tribunal has been calculated at over US$58 million, while the national judicial infrastructure, with only two judges and 12 lawyers, stands in ruins.[17]

As already noted, the vast majority of countries emerging from conflicts are poor and therefore highly dependent on international financial institutions ('IFI's), such as the World Bank and the International Monetary Fund (IMF), for reconstruction aid. IFIs act as catalysts and guarantors for bilateral donors. As a result, poorer countries are dependent on (and often have no option but to agree to) such imposed conditionality. While, in theory, there may be positive political outcomes of such arrangements, in practice the external leverage resulting from conditionality has provoked considerable criticism. Indeed, several commentators have argued that the 'urge to engineer' that is evident in such policies is concerned, at a strategic level, to make way for the integration of war-torn societies into the world economy. Even in countries without debilitating conflict, the role of aid and its efficiency is disputed. Uvin argues that the ethical and strategic challenges encountered in post-conflict situations are an extreme example of those posed in relation to *all* development aid, and the ideological and operational foundations upon which it rests.[18] The core critique is that such strategies promote a pattern of development determined by the dominant ideology of neo-liberal economic modernisation that imbues the IFIs. In other words, wider geo-political and economic interests too often

[16] Oomen, 'Donor Driven Justice and it Discontents: The Case of Rwanda' (n 5 above) at 891.

[17] Oomen, 'Donor Driven Justice and it Discontents: The Case of Rwanda' (n 5 above) at 891.

[18] See, eg J Ferguson, *The Anti-politics Machine: 'Development', Depoliticisation, and Bureaucratic Power in Lesotho* (Minneapolis, University of Minnesota Press, 1994); D Dollar and I Pritchett, *Assessing Aid: What Works, What Doesn't and Why', A World Bank Policy Research Report* (Oxford, Oxford University Press, 1998); M Anderson, *Do No Harm: How Aid Can Support Peace or War* (London, Lynne Rienner, 1999); N Middleton, P O'Keefe and S Moyo, *Disaster and Development: the Politics of Humanitarian Aid* (London, Pluto Press, 1998).

shape what tend to be represented as politically and economically neutral post-conflict and transitional justice initiatives. Far from being neutral, technocratic and apolitical, as proponents would claim, it is argued rather that they are directed at reconstituting post-conflict societies in the image of Western liberal democracies, establishing such models as the ideal-type and setting externally defined limits to the field of permissible action.[19] Indeed this has been likened to a new form of neo-colonialism, resting ultimately on a theory and system of subjugation underwritten by a romanticised vision of the West on the one hand and 'the other' constituted as racially and culturally inferior.[20] There is a danger that transitional justice strategies can, as a consequence, be implicated in this process.

This is clearly closely tied to fundamental changes in international relations revolving around a re-conceptualisation of notions of national sovereignty.[21] The international mission in Bosnia-Herzegovina, regarded as 'government by international experts' that not only shapes but sets and imposes a political agenda, is an obvious case in point.[22] UN transitional administrations in places such as East-Timor and Kosovo, often referred to by terms such as 'trusteeship' or 'protectorate', involve locally unaccountable agencies in drawing up and implementing laws.[23] In Afghanistan, Iraq and Liberia prefabricated 'justice packages' are similarly being readied for introduction.[24] These include a wide range of legal activities formerly considered to be within the remit of national states.

Yet this rise in interventionism, based on Western conceptions of justice, has also been paralleled by reluctance on the part of many rule-of-law experts to acknowledge the political dimensions of such activities. Expressing transitional justice questions as a series of technical issues offsets this potentially troubling recognition.[25] Indeed, critics have argued that the

[19] Knaus and Martin, 'Travails of the European Raj' (n 15 above); Uvin, 'Difficult Choices in the New Post-Conflict Agenda (n 14 above).

[20] Hearn, 'Aiding Democracy? Donors & Civil Society in South Africa' (n 5 above); Knaus and Martin, 'Travails of the European Raj' (n 15 above); Oomen, 'Donor Driven Justice and it Discontents: The Case of Rwanda' (n 5 above); R. Paris, 'International Peacebuilding and the "Mission Civilisatrice"' (n 15 above); Uvin, 'Difficult Choices in the New Post-Conflict Agenda (n 14 above).

[21] Oomen, 'Donor Driven Justice and it Discontents: The Case of Rwanda' (n 5 above) at 892.

[22] Knaus and Martin, 'Travails of the European Raj' (n 15 above).

[23] M Berdal and R Caplan, 'The Politics of International Administration: Introduction (2004) 10 *Special Issue of Global Governance* 1.

[24] Oomen, 'Donor Driven Justice and it Discontents: The Case of Rwanda' (n 5 above) at 891.

[25] A Hurwitz and K Studdard, 'Rule of Law Programs in Peace Operations', International Peace Academy, Policy Paper Report, The Security-Development Nexus Program (2005) at 4.

new 'post-conflict agenda' poses deep, and unresolved, ethical questions for donors and others that are simply not acknowledged or addressed in the literature.[26]

IV PUSHING AN OPEN DOOR? MOVING TOWARD PARTICIPATION[27]

Notwithstanding the criticisms discussed above, there does appear to be a growing recognition, on paper at least, within the international community that, conceptually and operationally, the 'justice enterprise' needs rethinking. Thus, for example, a 2003 UN report on gender, equity and peace agreements endorses a participatory approach.[28] Failure to embrace locals' lived experiences and opinions, it is argued, can lead to a poor understanding of peace transformation. The answer, therefore, is to view local people (in this instance, women) as stakeholders in, and active agents of change. That local ownership of conflict transformation is a 'sensitive' and 'overlooked' issue has also recently been recognised in the UN Secretary-General's Report on the *Rule of Law and Transitional Justice*. Decrying 'one-size-fits-all formulas and the importation of foreign models' of transitional justice, the report advocates instead an approach based on 'national assessments, national participation and national needs and aspirations'. UN norms and standards, it suggests, need to be married to 'respect and support [for] local ownership, local leadership and a local constituency for reform'.[29]

Such official UN responses have followed on from a growing chorus of critical voices raising concerns over the lack of local ownership in transitional processes. Pugh is critical of external actor misconceptions, highlighting their tendency to view entire post-war populations either as traumatised victims, lacking the ability to make decisions about the future, or as people driven by a destructive psychosis that renders them incapable or morally unworthy of positive contributions to peace-building.[30] The

[26] Oomen, 'Donor Driven Justice and it Discontents: The Case of Rwanda' (n 5 above) at 890–92; Uvin, 'Difficult Choices in the New Post-Conflict Agenda' (n 14 above) at 117.

[27] On participation in transitional justice processes, see also the chapter by L McGregor in this collection.

[28] C Chinkin, 'Peace Agreements as a Means for Promoting Gender Equality and Ensuring Participation of Women', UN Division for the Advancement of Women, Expert Group Meeting, 10–13 November 2003, Ottawa, Canada, EGM/PEACE/2003/BP.1.

[29] UN Secretary-General's Report, 'An Agenda for Peace: Prevention Diplomacy, Peacemaking and Peacekeeping' (n 1 above) at 17;see also UN Security Council 5052nd Meeting S/PV.5052; International Peace Academy, 'Rule of Law Programs in Peace Operations: Toward a Conflict-Sensitive Perspective', Concept Paper, 29 October 2004, Millenium Hotel UN Plaza, New York.

[30] M Pugh (ed), *Regeneration of War-Torn Societies* (London, Macmillan Press, 2000) 123.

'other' of peoples in violently divided societies are thus denied their potential contribution to conflict transformation in donor thinking.[31] In similar vein, Hurwitz and Studdard argue that precluding national ownership of legal reform, and focusing instead on changes to rigid legal structures, is unlikely to assist states and populations, creating a 'potentially explosive' problem.[32] As a number of critics have also suggested, initiatives such as the International Criminal Tribunal for Rwanda (ICTR) have largely failed to engender local engagement. As a result, they tend to remain institutions of, and seemingly for the international community, with the development of international criminal law perceived as their chief aim. Echoing the UN report, Hurwitz and Studdard caution against a romantic, unconditional endorsement of indigenous systems and solutions that might perpetuate discriminatory practices against vulnerable groups, but at the same time call for informal mechanisms with a relevance to local populations.

There is, then, a growing awareness that the UN and international actors need to seize the opportunity to develop a 'second generation of rule of law policies'.[33] If this is so it is primarily because the creation of an enduring peace still seems, in far too many instances, an elusive end. Over 40 per cent of post-conflict societies return to conflict within a span of five years.[34] Despite substantial investment in 'top-down' blueprints, projects and mechanisms, the most common outcome of a civil war is another war. Institutionalising and sustaining peace, it is increasingly being suggested, may require placing issues of ownership and participation at the centre of long-term post-conflict justice.

However, if there is now a growing rhetorical recognition of such issues, has this been translated into the reality of policy and practice? Here the evidence is less easy to find. Despite being identified as key issues in international reports and development circles for many years, the virtues of local ownership, empowerment and participatory approaches have tended only to be implemented in a vague, weak and ad hoc manner.[35] It seems that many of these arguments have not been translated in a comprehensive manner into transitional justice theory and practice.

[31] R Gordon and JH Sylvester, 'Deconstructing Development', Villanova University School of Law, School of Law Working Paper Series (2004), Paper 4, 1.

[32] Hurwitz and Studdard, 'Rule of Law Programs in Peace Operations' (n 25 above) at 4.

[33] International Peace Academy, Concept Paper (n 29 above) at 1.

[34] E Mobekk, 'After Intervention: Public Security Management in Post-Conflict Societies—From Intervention to Sustainable Local Ownership', Conference Report, DCAF, Hosted by the Latvian Ministry of Defence in Riga, Latvia (April 2005) at 382.

[35] *Ibid* at 382.

V LEARNING ABOUT A BOTTOM-UP, PARTICIPATORY APPROACH

If a key task today is to consider what principles might underpin a 'bottom-up', participatory approach to transitional justice, there are many lessons to be learnt from how such strategies towards development emerged, what key concepts have underwritten this process and some of the problems and issues that have arisen with their implementation.[36] The roots of radical, bottom-up participatory approaches can be traced to the social struggles, popular unrest and growth of grassroots movements in the South during the late 1960s and 1970s. From their origin, therefore, participatory approaches have formed part of the critique, emerging from the underdeveloped world, to the perceived failure of North-inspired and directed centralised, top-down or 'blueprint' approaches to development.[37] Often closely tied to 'third-world' national liberation campaigns and left-emancipatory struggles, these strategies—designed specifically to challenge dominant paradigms of knowledge control and production—were developed by academic-activists operating in South America, Sub-Saharan Africa and the Asian sub-continent.[38] For Paolo Friere, for example, popular education programmes were designed to create 'conscientisation', a critical state of consciousness rooted in popular experience and people's knowledge of their own structural conditions of oppression. This rests upon a fundamental philosophical proposition; that in order to overcome the reproduction of conditions of alienation and oppression it is necessary for people to identify these themselves and to then conceive of collective actions, based on that knowledge, to overcome them. Agency is therefore placed at the centre of the platform of change.

In many ways this parallels the conception of knowledge and activism evident within radical democratic theory. For example, echoing a Gramscian perspective on the 'praxis' of the 'organic intellectual', Anisur Rahman contends that participatory approaches constitute a political practice challenging not only the idea of oppression through the control of material production, but also forms of domination resulting from control over the 'means of knowledge production [including] the social power to determine what is valid or useful knowledge'.[39] It is in this vein that Orlanda Fals Borda has described the aim of Participatory Action Research

[36] See also McEvoy and McGregor's introductory chapter in this collection for further suggestions concerning potential features of a 'bottom-up' approach to transitional justice.

[37] N Uphoff, 'Grassroots Organisations and NGOs in Rural Development: Opportunities with Diminishing States and Expanding Markets' (1993) 21 *World Development* 607.

[38] O Fals-Borda and MA Rahman (eds), *Action and Knowledge: Breaking the Monopoly with Participatory Action Research* (London, Intermediate Technology Publications, 1991); P Freire, *The Pedagogy of the Oppressed* (New York, Continuum, 1970).

[39] MA Rahman, *People's Self-Development: Perspectives on Participatory Action Research: A Journey Through Experience* (London, Zed Books, 1993) 83.

(PAR) as the legitimation of popular knowledge, and Budd Hall has suggested (*a la* Foucault) that PAR is designed to 'gain a place at the knowledge-creating table' for those generally excluded from such processes.[40] Participatory action can be summed up as a process that facilitates the permanent ability to identify and analyse problems, formulate and plan solutions, mobilise resources and implement them, to gain control over the processes that affect peoples' lives.

These key concepts of participation, empowerment and community-based processes became buzzwords in the 1970s and 1980s within international development circles. Essentially, participation is the means to empowerment. It concerns the ability of local people to define local obstacles or problems, conceptualise, initiate, design and implement programmes to address these problems. The aim is for local actors to be empowered in order for them to generate and 'do' their own 'development' that will therefore also be sustainable after foreign donors leave. The key element is ownership and control: who is consulted, who makes decisions, in whose interests and why. The fundamental change such an approach advocates is therefore a 'transfer of power' from the dominant, decision-making people and institutions to those who are subordinated during the process.[41] The manner in which a given process is initiated, designed, conducted and disseminated is itself intended to form part of a wider emancipatory project by challenging the way in which knowledge is constituted and validated. 'Democratising' the process is umbilically tied to the 'legitimation' of the knowledge produced (or publicly aired) by it. Real participation has therefore to involve what has been termed 'co-generative dialogue'; where local people not only 'advise' on the shape and direction of the process but must also have the opportunity to be collaboratively involved in decision-making'.[42] Community members should not only 'advise' on the shape and direction of the research but must have the opportunity to 'at least collaboratively control'. It relies on a conception of human rights promotion that understands control over decision-making as itself key to the achievement of those rights. Or, as Kenny has recently argued,

> the right to participate in decisions which affect one's life is both an element of human dignity and the key to empowerment—the basis on which change can be

[40] B Hall, 'I Wish This Were a Poem of Practices of Participatory Research' in P Reason and H Bradury (eds), *Handbook of Action Research: Participative Inquiry and Practice* (London, Sage Publications, 2001) 176.

[41] R Chambers, 'Paradigm Shifts and the Practice of Participatory Research and Development', Working Paper No 2 (Institute of Development Studies, Sussex, 1994) at 1.

[42] K Fear and P Edwards, 'Building a Democratic Learning Community Within PDS' (1995) 7(2) *Teaching Education* 7.

> achieved. As such, it is both a means to the enjoyment of human rights, and a human rights goal in itself.[43]

Such perspectives have undoubtedly influenced researchers and activists working on relatively small-scale and community-orientated transitional justice projects in many violently divided societies. This has perhaps been most obvious in parts of Latin America. That participatory theory has been so concerned with processes of 'collective research', the 'critical recovery of history' and the 'diffusion of [such] knowledge' undoubtedly proved to be an influence on the *Nunca Mas* (Never Again) and *testimonio* initiatives that were such a key feature of human rights transitional activism throughout the continent in the 1980s and 1990s.[44] As discussed below, participatory theory undoubtedly influenced the work of the Ardoyne Commemoration Project (ACP), as did the Guatemalan *Nunca Mas* initiative.[45] While local knowledge and experience were the foundation upon which the project proceeded, insights from the sort of theoretical perspectives outlined above, and inspiration from activists in places as distant as Guatemala helped shape and sustain the work.

If transitional justice can learn from the participatory discourse and theory then it also may need to do so from aspects of experience in the development field; in particular, the potential problem of co-option. For example, whatever its radical underpinnings, bottom-up or participatory discourse began to be embraced by mainstream development agencies, and adopted by institutions including the World Bank.[46] It is now a commonplace in the field of mainstream development theory and practice, and is regarded as an essential in good practice. This 'shift' came about due to the disappointment with and realisation of the 'failed' top-down development orthodoxy.[47]

[43] K Kenny, *The Right to Participate in International Human Rights Fieldwork* (Co Meath, Ireland, International Human Rights Network, 2000) at 18

[44] Fals Borda and Rahman, *Action and Knowledge* (n 38 above); see also G Gugelberger, *The Real Thing: Testimonial Discourse in Latin America* (London, Duke University Press, 1996); Recovery of Historical Memory (REHMI), *Guatemala: Never Again!*, The Official Report of the Human Rights Office, Archdiocese of Guatemala (Marynoll NY, Orbis Books, 1999).

[45] In 1999 Roberto Tepaz Lopez a member of the REMHI project visited Ardoyne and gave a talk as part of the launch and tour of Guatemala: *Nunca Mas*. In May 2000 three members of the ACP committee travelled to Guatemala, met with and interviewed activists and individuals involved in the Historical Clarification Commission (CEH), REMHI project and Centre for Human Rights Legal Action. The ACP committee seriously considered adopting the 'Never Again' title for the book it produced. The Ardoyne book is similar in style, focus and content to the *Nunca Mas* (Never Again!) publications. For a discussion of bottom-up initiatives in Guatemala beyond REMHI, see L Arriaza and N Roht-Arriaza (ch 7) in this collection.

[46] World Bank, *The World Bank Participation Sourcebook* (Washington DC, World Bank, 1996).

[47] M Rahman, 'Participatory Action Research: The Last Temptation of Saint Development' (1990) 15 *Alternatives* 199.

However, the apparently positive move toward the adoption of participatory approaches in mainstream development in general has been subject to severe criticism.[48] International institutions, it is argued, tend to engage in a problematic co-option of civil society and appropriate participatory discourse. The move towards participation strategies by the World Bank has been seen as a political move to neutralise resistance to Structural Adjustment Policies, a key feature of neo-liberal economic philosophy. In many underdeveloped countries this has involved drastic reductions in expenditure on social welfare provision and services in favour of the private sector, with devastating consequences for the most vulnerable groups in society.[49] One critic has pointed to the way in which international donors have been successful in influencing the current version of civil society in a number of African countries (for example, Ghana, South Africa and Uganda). In such situations a vocal, well-funded section of civil society, it is suggested, intervenes on key issues of national development strategy and acts not as a force for challenging the status quo, but for building societal consensus in its maintenance.[50] Others have argued that donors often bypass grassroots NGOs in favour of 'professionalised' NGOs, usually found in urban centres and capital cities. Human rights activists in Sri Lanka have referred disparagingly to such NGOs as 'grant eaters' and suggest that they represent a highly professionalised 'peace industry' that responds to donor agendas.[51] This, they argue, results in scarce resources being diverted away from worthy home-grown bottom-up projects that are considered important by local organisations. Reporting on the situation in Bosnia, one major report on civil society-building argued that the same 100–200 professionalised 'elite' NGOs, detached from the 'grassroots' problems and social reality, produce and attend hundreds of roundtables and workshops. As a result, one receives a fictitious view of local participation, which results in what is described as a 'virtual civil society'.[52] The same report goes on to say, 'it is a question whether these [NGOs] represent anyone else in addition to those who work in them'.[53] The legitimacy and credibility of such NGOs and the unintended results of

[48] J Hearn, 'The "Uses and Abuses" of Civil Society in Africa' (2001) 28 *Review of African Political Economy* 43.

[49] R Mani, *Beyond Retribution: Seeking Justice in the Shadows of War* (n 10 above) at 126.

[50] Hearn, 'The "Uses and Abuses" of Civil Society in Africa' (n 48 above).

[51] F Haniffa, 'In the Pursuit of Democracy in Post Colonial Sri Lanka: Local Human Rights Approaches to Transitional Justice' (Law and Trust Society (Sri Lanka), 2006).

[52] Z Papic, 'The General Situation in Bosnia-Herzegovina and International Support Policies' in *International Support Policies to South East European Countries—Lessons (Not) Learned in Bosnia-Herzegovina* (Sarajevo, Open Society Fund, Bosnia-Herzegovina, 2001) at 15.

[53] S Sali-Terzic 'Civil Society' in *International Support Policies to South East European Countries—Lessons (Not) Learned in Bosnia-Herzegovina* (n 52 above) at 153.

marginalising public participation are serious issues that donors need to reflect on. Certainly such critiques have raised questions about the actual meaning of 'participation' and 'empowerment' as concepts when applied in such circumstances. It would be wise if advocates of participatory approaches within the field of transitional justice kept such issues in mind.

There is also a substantial body of literature in development studies that cautions against romanticising participatory approaches and draws attention to potential abuses and what they might conceal.[54] While participation has the potential to challenge patterns of dominance, it may also be the means through which existing power relations are entrenched and reproduced.[55] For example, who are the 'locals' whose voices need to be heard and heeded, and how does a locally-empowering process overcome hierarchal differences (for example, of gender) within a local community that can otherwise preclude giving agency to the most marginalised?[56] As Mohan has argued, the rhetoric of participation often serves to conceal the operation of powerful interests *within* communities.[57] Such criticisms raise important points about the impact of international aid and intervention in general and the debate about who bears the cost of error.

VI THE ARDOYNE COMMEMORATION PROJECT: A CASE STUDY OF BOTTOM-UP TRANSITIONAL JUSTICE

A The Context, the Community and the Project

These critiques of participatory approaches to development, post-conflict transition and justice-making are clearly significant and should inform policy-making and practice. Nevertheless, given the apparent issues already examined that arise from 'top-down' mechanisms, there still appears to be a pressing need for the creation of genuine dialogue and grassroots ownership of transitional justice processes that will allow local people to be listened to and their needs and interests heeded. The adoption of bottom-up approaches designed to encourage participation and positive social change are directed precisely to this end. In order to illustrate the

[54] J Gaventa, 'Participatory Development or Participatory Democracy? Linking Participatory Approaches to Policy and Governance' (2004) 50 *Participatory Learning and Action* 150; S White, 'Depoliticising Development: The Uses and Abuses of Participation' (1996) 6 *Development in Practice* 6; Institute of Development Studies (IDS), Participation Group: www.ids.ac.uk/ids/particip.

[55] White, 'Depoliticising Development: The Uses and Abuses of Participation' (n 54 above). See also the chapters by Stanley and McGregor in this collection.

[56] Mobekk, '*After Intervention: Public Security Management in Post-Conflict Societies*' (n 34 above) at 384.

[57] G Mohan, 'Not so Distant, Not so Strange: the Personal and the Political in Participatory Research' (1999) 2 *Ethics, Place and the Environment* 41 at 46.

potential values (and limitations) of such perspectives and practices we will now focus on an example of an initiative with which the authors were closely involved in Northern Ireland. This was the Ardoyne Commemoration Project (ACP).[58]

The ACP was a grassroots 'truth-recovery' project set up in the Ardoyne area of North Belfast. Ardoyne is a small, Catholic, working class, republican community with a population of approximately 7,500. It is an enclave area, surrounded on three sides by neighbouring protestant working-class communities, with which it shares a series of 'interfaces'. As a whole, North Belfast was the site for roughly 20 per cent of all conflict-related deaths and between 1969 and 1998, 99 people from Ardoyne were killed by the various parties to the conflict; one of the highest rates of fatalities of any community in the North.[59] Many of the deaths occurred in highly contentious circumstances; some involved state forces and remain unresolved.

In Ardoyne, as elsewhere, political developments in the late 1990s ensured that the memory of such experiences would come to the fore, and provided the context for the setting-up of the ACP. The Irish peace process resulted in the signing of the Good Friday Agreement in April 1998. The emergence of this partial and uneasy 'peace' created a space for people to start to reflect and contemplate, possibly for the first time, on what they had lived through and endured over the past 30 years of conflict. Yet, such reflection was also taking place while little attention was being given to mechanisms to deal with the past within the formal political process.

Key to understanding what shapes and informs the transitional justice mechanisms adopted in any given situation are the specific political power dynamics at play. A focus on community-based approaches to transitional justice may, for example, be the result of a lack of interest amongst dominant political actors in developing formal mechanisms to deal with the legacy of the past as part of post-conflict transition. This was certainly an important factor in Northern Ireland. The Good Friday Agreement was a complex, multi-faceted document dealing with a wide range of issues. However, while the Agreement noted that there might be a need for a recognition and acknowledgement of the position of victims, it made no

[58] Ardoyne Commemoration Project, *Ardoyne: The Untold Truth* (n 6 above).

[59] Lundy and McGovern, *Community, 'Truth-telling' and Conflict Resolution* (n 6 above) at v; Ardoyne Commemoration Project, *Ardoyne: The Untold Truth* (n 6 above) at 6–7. Of these 50 were killed by loyalist paramilitaries, 26 by members of the security forces (ie British Army and Royal Ulster Constabulary) and 13 by various Irish republican groups. Another six were members of the Irish Republican Army (IRA) killed inadvertently while on active service, one died accidentally, and in three cases it is unclear who was responsible. The youngest victim was a young boy aged 12, and the oldest a woman aged 76, both shot dead by the British Army. The total of 99 deaths represents over 10 times the Northern Ireland conflict-related death rate average.

mention of what form this might take or any mechanism for dealing with the past.[60] This reflected the virtual absence of truth-recovery as an issue in the talks leading up to the signing of the Agreement and the political premium placed upon avoiding the potential divisiveness of 'dealing with the past'.

Certain transitional justice concerns (such as the reform of policing, aspects of the judicial system and the release of prisoners) were disaggregated from each other and the peace deal. Victims' issues were initially dealt with in the report of a Victims' Commissioner, retired senior civil servant Kenneth Bloomfield.[61] However, for many nationalists and the relatives of victims of state violence the Bloomfield Report represented a reinforcement of what they saw as a 'hierarchy of victimhood', in which the lives and experiences of certain victims were privileged over and above others. In addition, Bloomfield was primarily concerned with the creation of an administrative infrastructure for the delivery of practical services for victims while deferring any discussion of justice issues. That said, there had already been some steps towards the creation of past-focussed judicial processes. However, these were charged with examining particular incidents or facets of the conflict (for example, the Saville Inquiry set up in 1997 to re-examine the events of Bloody Sunday, January 1972). At the same time, public debate on these inquiries, victims and 'dealing with the past' had also become embroiled with the proposed early release of conflict-related prisoners, and the highly vocal opposition of a number of newly created (mainly unionist) victims' groups to those releases.

It was against this backdrop that an ad hoc group in Ardoyne of victims' relatives, interested individuals and community activists decided, after a series of public meetings, to produce a book that would contain the testimonies of the relatives, friends and eyewitnesses of the area's victims. This was designed to provide recognition to those who had been killed and (particularly in terms the victims of state violence) to challenge what was seen as a 'hierarchy of victims'. All (except one) of the committee members were from Ardoyne. From the outset the ACP was therefore an entirely community-inspired initiative. Literally dozens of Ardoyne people contributed to the project's work through their involvement with interviews, database collation, transcribing, returning edited interviews, proof reading and various other tasks. This created many difficulties but the advantages (ie of skills development and in gaining access) far outweighed these problems.

In fact community participation was always seen as the defining feature of the ACP. The idea of embeddedness underpinned the philosophy and

[60] *Agreement Reached In The Multi-Party Negotiations*, 10 April 1998.

[61] K Bloomfield, *We Will Remember Them: Report Of The Northern Ireland Victims Commissioner* (Belfast, Northern Ireland Office, 1997) at 20.

process to ensure that the community in effect took 'ownership' and control of the design, research process, editing, return phase and production of the book. In practical terms the grassroots nature of the project was crucial in order to gain trust, enable access and establish an empathetic relationship with the interviewees. The ACP saw itself as providing a means for individuals and the community to express itself and to place previously unrecorded experiences into the public domain. Local control was therefore seen as an absolute requirement for this to be achieved. This was particularly important because of the deep-seated distrust of 'outsiders' resulting from the long years of conflict and surveillance. To be an 'insider' in a place like Ardoyne meant that individuals had to have the full complement of credentials and/or life experiences (local background, family and friendship links, specific political history, etc) to achieve insider status.[62] The nature of the ACP allowed it access to groups, voices and knowledge that would otherwise have been inaccessible or 'out-of-bounds' for an 'outsider'. Alongside local participation and control, inclusivity was seen as a key principle of the project's ethos. The criterion for inclusion in the book was that the victim had to have been a resident of Ardoyne for at least some point in their life. It would have been easy for the project to deal solely with those cases that did not involve republican killings and to focus exclusively on deaths resulting from state and loyalist actions. Members of the project regarded their remit as an inclusive approach to 'truth-telling' in that it did not preclude anyone on the basis of their ethnic/religious identity, political affiliation and/or status as a victim.

B Doing Transitional Justice from the Bottom-Up

The work of the project took four years and resulted in the publication of a book (*Ardoyne: the Untold Truth*) in 2002 that was based around the edited testimonies of interviewees. The list of interviewees was arrived at in consultation with the families, and usually included a family member, close friend and, where possible, an eyewitness. All the interviews carried out for the project were recorded, transcribed and edited. As evidence of the desire to democratise the process (and to ensure that what went in the book was what the interviewee wanted), the initial edited version was then handed back to and discussed with the interviewee who was given a completely free hand to alter their testimony in any way they saw fit. This handing-back phase (while adding years to the workload of the project) was

[62] Lundy and McGovern, 'Participation, Truth and Partiality: Participatory Action Research, Community-based Truth-telling and Post-conflict Transition in Northern Ireland' (n 4 above) at 78–9.

regarded as a key element of its working process, ensuring that interviewees had a sense of control and ownership over what was written. Participants were also given pre-publication access to the *complete* case study, which included interviews with other family members, friends and eyewitnesses. Changes could only be made to one's own testimony but participants were encouraged to bring to the attention of the ACP any inaccuracies or issues of concern in the content of other testimonies. Families and friends often discussed these issues at great length amongst themselves and with members of the project. Providing a conduit of contact was often key to resolving differences of opinion. The work was undoubtedly difficult and challenging for all involved. Providing the full case study to the family of the victim helped ensure that any problems or issues could be resolved prior to publication. Given the highly personal and sensitive nature of the work, this was crucial.

There were also occasions when people sought further clarification about the incident from other groups or organisations in relation to the death, such as the republican movement. An obvious limitation of such a project, as discussed below, is that it does not have access to official records and all combatant groups involved in the conflict. Notwithstanding this, the ACP made every effort to get answers to questions and to resolve outstanding issues whenever possible. For this, the local character of the project was essential. Generating local agency as a means to empowering participants was a central aim in this; it was truth-recovery being played out at its most intimate level. That said, the problem of romanticising such notions as 'community' and 'empowerment' should always be kept in mind in order to counter the potential for manipulation and abuse masking marginalisation and exclusion. Otherwise, apparent 'participation' can entrench and reproduce rather than challenge power relations.[63]

Several community forums and public meetings were also organised, to which victims' relatives always received personal invitations. The meetings (generally well-attended by as many as 300 people) allowed people to be updated on the ACP's work but, perhaps more importantly, they were designed to create a public space for open dialogue about highly sensitive issues that in the past had been 'unspoken or taboo' subjects. For example, 13 local people had been killed by various republican organisations, some as alleged informers. These were among the most challenging cases the ACP had to deal with and feelings ran high when such issues were discussed. There is no doubt that the subject-matter was challenging for the ACP and community alike, stirring painful memories for many. For

[63] White, 'Depoliticising Development: The Uses and Abuses of Participation' (n 54 above) at 6.

others it provoked much soul searching and reflection. The goals of the ACP and the process it generated were therefore clearly more complex and deeper than collecting interviews for a book. By pushing the boundaries of what was 'acceptable' to articulate, the process was in many ways laying the foundation for a community-driven 'truth-telling' process.

C Strengths and Limitations

The authors carried out a follow-up study when the project ended to find out what was regarded as its strengths and weaknesses.[64] The discussion that follows draws upon the evaluation findings and provides insights into some of the ways in which engaging in the project impacted upon individuals, their families and the wider Ardoyne community and beyond. As noted in the introductory paragraph, this case study illustrates the ways in which a bottom-up 'truth-telling' process can make a significant contribution to transitional justice.

Recognition and acknowledgement were cited as an important outcome of the ACP. The process offered a space for individuals to tell their story and for previously excluded or marginalised voices to become part of public discourse. The restoration of dignity, through recognition and acknowledgement in the book—particularly to the families of alleged informers—was regarded as a significant outcome of the project. The relatives of victims of state violence were also provided the opportunity to challenge what they perceived as the 'denial of truth' in official accounts and given public recognition in the book, although the lack of state acknowledgment was a crucial limitation. However, the bottom-up approach of the ACP helped ensure that the process of gaining recognition and acknowledgement was one in which victims and relatives felt themselves to be active participants, rather than passive recipients of 'truth-telling'.

Community participation stood out as the single most important aspect of the ACP process for the majority of participants interviewed and indeed the wider community. The method of handing back edited testimonies created a sense of individual and collective ownership and was regarded as a fundamental strength and positive outcome of the project. It is in gaining direct control of the knowledge produced through such work that empowerment takes place. In just the same way, a victim-centred 'truth-telling'

[64] Lundy and McGovern, *Community, 'Truth-telling' and Conflict Resolution* (n 6 above). The research set out to critically assess the impact, value and limits of the work of the ACP as an example of community 'truth-telling'. A series of 52 in-depth interviews was carried out, designed to elicit the views and experiences of a sample of key respondent groups, including those who had participated in the project (ie gave testimony), residents of Ardoyne (non-participants), and the broader nationalist and unionist communities.

process needs to place the bearer of testimony at the heart of the decision-making process. Overwhelmingly it was felt that the sensitivities of the project necessitated the use of 'insiders' and individuals that were respected and rooted in the community. A key issue of concern when doing such sensitive work is the issue of trust. Undertaking work with 'insiders' trusted by local people created far greater possibilities and produced the sort of knowledge often 'hidden' from 'outsiders'. Any process devising wider strategies to deal with the legacy of the past needs to be conscious of the problems of accessing such experiences. The use of 'insiders could just as conceivably exclude certain 'voices' and lead to guarded and partial accounts and self-censorship. It is therefore imperative that those involved in such work are conscious of this tension and are fully reflective in their practice throughout.[65]

Intra-community conflict resolution was the most frequently mentioned positive outcome of the ACP process. A significant contribution of bottom-up participatory 'truth-telling' is its capacity to get to the nitty-gritty of intra-community conflict, understand the dynamics and be able to resolve certain unresolved issues. Ardoyne is not a homogenous community and there are very real and long-standing divisions, some of which are a by-product of the political conflict. The project created a process or mechanism to deal with difficult internal conflict-related issues and promoted resolution of what were often seen as 'taboo subjects' at a number of different levels. The experience of the ACP would suggest that a bottom-up participatory approach can make a significant contribution to creating dialogue at the community level.

One of the most serious limitations of unofficial bottom-up processes in general is their inability to uncover previously unknown information from outside agencies; obtaining some form of official recognition or recompense, or in pursuing accountability. That said, official truth-recovery initiatives can themselves face huge problems in this regard, not least through the continued opposition and lack of co-operation of state agencies in finding ways of dealing with past injustice.[66] Bottom-up unofficial processes can be more adept at uncovering previously 'hidden truths' that can lead on to other things. They can be highly effective in building a 'case to answer', playing a vital role in documenting human rights abuses and patterns of violations that make it increasingly difficult for the state to continue to deny culpability.

For some interviewees 'truth-telling' was regarded as part of, but not a substitute for, seeking justice. There was a sense for some in which the

[65] Lundy and McGovern, *Community, 'Truth-telling' and Conflict Resolution* (n 6 above) at 53–7.

[66] See, eg B Rolston and P Scraton, 'In the Full Glare of English Politics' (2005) 5 *British Journal of Criminology* 57 at 58.

recognition derived from their involvement in the project was itself a (sufficient) form of justice. In these circumstances 'truth' is used to denounce or challenge a perceived injustice. For others this was not the case and they saw a need for legal and judicial avenues to be pursued as thoroughly as possible. Finally, perhaps the most significant limitation of all for the ACP concerned the difficulties of conducting such sensitive research 'across the divide'. This certainly proved to be an issue for the ACP. Projects with a single identity focus call into question the validity of the 'untold truths' they are able to tell, though again, such criticisms can also be levelled at state-led processes.[67]

VII CONCLUSION

What we have sought to argue here is that the currently dominant conceptions of transition, justice and democracy, within the context of the prevailing post-conflict agenda, tend to delimit the potential of social and political change in post-conflict societies. In so doing they can act to deny the genuine exercise of rights and the promotion of active political agency on the part of their populations. This is a practical as well as a theoretical issue. Sustainability is key to the long-term success of any post-conflict justice program. Those conceived and imposed from the top down that do not have local ownership and genuine participation, are far less likely to have legitimacy andbe effective and therefore sustainable after the sponsors leave. We are not suggesting that bottom-up initiatives represent an alternative to the existing top-down approaches. What we are arguing, and have sought to illustrate with the Ardoyne case study, is that a bottom-up participatory 'truth-telling' approach has particular strengths and much to offer transitional justice strategies and conflict transformation in the long-term. A bottom-up participatory approach puts communities and those on the front line and receiving end of violent conflict at the very centre of transitional justice. As argued, a significant contribution of such an approach is its capacity to get to the nitty-gritty of intra-community conflict, understand the local dynamics, create dialogue and be context specific. Given appropriate resources, such initiatives have the potential to stimulate society-wide dialogue, something which is usually attributed to official 'truth-telling' processes. In general, however, transitional justice discourse has tended to undervalue a bottom-up participatory approach and it remains largely under-theorised and under-researched.

There is undeniably a range of difficult challenges involved in attempting to promote and establish locally-owned participatory transitional justice

[67] L Stanley, 'Truth Commissions and the Recognition of State Crime' (2005) 45 *British Journal of Criminology* 582.

approaches. There are valid questions around who the locals are, who speaks for whom and what exactly does local ownership and participation mean? Nor is the wholesale valorisation of 'insiders' to the exclusion of 'outsiders' either a sustainable or desirable approach. How, too, can proponents of participatory approaches ensure that they do not become mere window-dressing, or a means to inculcate external ideological projects under the guise of local control? The conundrum ultimately is one common to a range of other fields; how to combine the potentially laudable ends of a global human rights culture without the means of their introduction acting as the negation of those very rights.

Nevertheless, as the sphere of transitional justice appears to move ever more widely out into the realm of engendering social and political change, then the privileging of official agencies, international institutions, the law and legal 'expertise' over and above locally-generated embedded initiatives must be brought increasingly into question. An obvious source to inform such a rethink, as we discovered ourselves in carrying out work in Northern Ireland, is readily available. If transitional justice is to take participation seriously then perhaps a good starting place is to identify some of the key guiding principles that have been signalled in the substantial literature, experience and stock of knowledge derived from development and participatory theory and practice. There is a need to encourage agency by thinking imaginatively outside the 'prevailing transitional justice box'. However, the first step to developing strategies is to create spaces for people to determine, shape and develop solutions for themselves.

6

The Lost Agenda: Economic Crimes and Truth Commissions in Latin America and Beyond

JAMES L CAVALLARO, SEBASTIÁN ALBUJA*

I INTRODUCTION

INCREASINGLY, TRUTH COMMISSIONS (TRCs)[1] have taken centre-stage in transitional justice processes. Over the past 20 years, some two dozen such commissions have been created in states undergoing transitions from authoritarian or communist regimes to more democratic forms of government. These commissions have demonstrated remarkable adaptability along a number of dimensions. Thus, the commissions have varied as to the scope of abuses addressed[2]; the number, gender and affiliation of commissioners[3]; whether to include mechanisms to pardon violators in exchange for confession[4]; whether to name the names

* The authors wish to thank Dr. Siri Gloppen for her insightful comments on the draft, Patrick McNally and Habib Rahiab for research assistance, and the participants in the Harvard Human Rights Program colloquium series for their comments on an earlier version of this chapter.

[1] The initials 'TRC' come from the term 'Truth and Reconciliation Commission'. Not all such commissions include the term 'reconciliation' in their titles. Nonetheless, in the interest of simplicity, we use the term 'TRC' to refer to the class of commissions.

[2] The commissions established in Argentina and Chile focused on forced disappearances; later commissions have focused on other grave civil and political rights abuses. More recent commissions, such as the one created in East Timor, have included—albeit in a limited fashion—violations of economic, social, and cultural rights.

[3] For instance, Argentina's National Commission on the Disappeared had 16 members, while Chile's National Commission for Truth and Reconciliation had about half that number. Likewise, some TRCs have been chaired by non-political personalities, such as writers, while others have had seasoned politicians and congressmen at the helm. Yet other TRCs have included religious leaders as members, such as priests and rabbis.

[4] The South African Truth Commission pioneered this process, granting amnesty to persons who made full disclosure of all the relevant facts relating to acts associated with a political objective. See Promotion of National Unity and Reconciliation Act, 1995, available online at http://www.fas.org/irp/world/rsa/act95_034.htm.

of individuals responsible for abuse; whether to provide compensation and the measure of such compensation[5]; duration; and the scope of investigative powers.

Yet these truth commissions, despite their heterogeneity, have consistently adopted a set of parameters established by the conventional understanding of the scope of human rights law and practice at the time of the creation of the first such bodies in Latin America. These constraints led to a focus on gross violations of civil and political rights, especially forced disappearances, execution, and torture.[6] Because of this reliance on the human rights framework, we argue, state-sponsored TRCs have failed to include in their mandates economic crimes[7] and corruption[8]—issues only recently embraced by mainstream human rights organisations.[9] This is so, we contend, despite a marked grassroots condemnation of corruption and economic crimes and despite popular support for efforts to hold leaders accountable for economic crimes and corruption both in Latin America and Africa.[10] Apart from habit and the suspect notion that truth commissions should focus on human rights abuses (and then, only particular

[5] In Brazil, for example, Law 9.140/95 created a commission with limited investigatory powers but authorised relatively high levels of compensation—in excess of US$100,000 per victim of forced disappearance or political execution.

[6] The mandate of most TRCs in Latin America during the 1980s and 1990s reflects these priorities; TRCs (in chronological order) whose mandates (see Part III below) were linked to the human rights agenda are: Argentina, Uruguay, Chile, El Salvador, and Guatemala.

[7] By economic crimes we refer to acts by authorities in violation of generally applicable criminal law, such as large-scale embezzlement, fraud, and tax crimes such as evasion. However, it must be noted that specific definitions of what constitutes economic criminal behaviour vary between and among societies. In our analysis, we use a relatively broad definition such that the term encompasses any behaviour deemed to involve economic crime by the particular truth commission considered.

[8] Definitions of corruption vary dramatically. For a comprehensive analysis of the conceptualisation of corruption, see R Williams, 'New Concepts for Old' (1999) 20 *Third World Quarterly* 503. The definitions of corruption have shifted over time from the 'public office' view (eg S Nye, 'Corruption: A Cost-Benefit Analysis' (1967) 61 *American Political Science Review* 417), to the economic perspective (eg S Rose-Ackerman, *Corruption* (New Haven, Academic Press, 1978)), to agency theory (eg E Banfield, 'Corruption as a Feature of Government Organization' (1975) 8 *Journal of Law and Economics* 587). In this chapter, we draw on the 'public office' definition of corruption, which underscores the distinction between the public and the private spheres. We are interested in acts of corruption such as appropriation of public resources by military officials during dictatorships, especially high-ranking officials, even if they occur in collusion with private individuals and groups close to the government structure.

[9] Early TRCs operated in an environment that failed to prioritise economic, social, and cultural rights, which were marginal to mainstream human rights practice for much of the 1980s and early and mid-1990s. The idea that corruption and embezzlement might be related to human rights was even farther afield. It is thus understandable (though not necessarily defensible, even in hindsight) that economic crimes ordinarily would have been left off the transitional justice agenda.

[10] A recent civil society report on corruption during apartheid in Africa underscores the extent of corruption during the apartheid regime, the relevance given by members of civil society to the issue, and the negative effects of leaving the investigation of economic

abuses), there is no convincing a priori reason why economic crimes should be excluded from the ambit of transitional truth commissions.

Addressing corruption and economic crimes at the transition and, later, during democratic consolidation, is essential. We draw on recent political science literature, first to underscore the significant impact that corruption and economic crimes have on democratic transition and consolidation in Latin America and beyond, and secondly, to support the argument that the inclusion of corruption and economic crimes during the transition and, specifically, within truth commissions, is vital for the realisation of democratic objectives.

The chapter proceeds in three sections. Part II sets out the core of acculturation theory as a framework for understanding how 'top-down' transitional justice models have proliferated, dominating the discipline. Part III, the bulk of the chapter, starts by providing background on the creation of TRCs in Latin America, highlighting the exclusion of economic crimes and corruption from their mandates. Next, it considers the extent of corruption in authoritarian regimes in Latin America, as well as perceptions of this phenomenon. This part then addresses an issue central to the argument posed in this chapter, namely, that corruption and economic crimes are strongly rejected and condemned by the masses in Latin America. Consequently, the last section argues that, in light of this generalised, grassroots sentiment, including corruption and economic crimes in TRCs may be functional to de-legitimising authoritarian regimes and to democratic consolidation. Finally, Part IV includes a brief look at TRCs beyond Latin America, suggesting that the trends identified in Latin America have continued to shape and limit the field.

II TRUTH COMMISSIONS AND THE FRAMEWORK OF ACCULTURATION

Through an extensive body of comparative and longitudinal studies, sociology's neo-institutionalism advances the idea that the global institutional environment largely influences policy choices of nations around the world. Also dubbed the 'World Society' school, this theory posits that

> [w]orldwide models define and legitimate agendas for local action, shaping the structures and policies of nation-states and other national and local actors ...

malfeasance aside: See H Van Vuuren, 'Apartheid Grand Corruption: Assessing the Scale of Crimes of Profit In South Africa, 1976–1994: A Report Prepared by Civil Society at the Request of the Second National Anti-Corruption Summit' (2006), available online at http://www.ipocafrica.org/pubs/reports/apartheidgrandc.pdf (visited 25 July 2006).

> The institutionalization of world models helps explain many puzzling features of contemporary national societies, such as structural isomorphism.[11]

Isomorphism, in turn, may be defined as 'structural similarity across organizations'[12] based on the adoption of standard scripts despite the existence of differences between and among contexts, differences that should result in greater variety.

Ryan Goodman and Derek Jinks apply this framework to international relations scholarship, offering an account of state behaviour based on the socialisation of global models or scripts. Goodman and Jinks argue that state behaviour in human rights, as in other areas, is highly influenced by the surrounding environment, leading actors to follow the behaviour of others through mimicry, identification, and status maximisation,[13] a collective process termed 'acculturation'.

An important feature of this analysis is the recognition that, while a broad range of states may adopt certain norms or standards as a result of the influence of acculturation and associational processes, given the differences in domestic variables such as level of development, infrastructure, and local culture, the degree of implementation of these standards will vary widely. Thus, one finds significant 'decoupling,' that is, divergence between adopted norms and practice, a result to be expected when norms are imported.[14]

We posit here that top-down, transitional justice schemes based on international models have been adopted by states largely as a result of the process of acculturation, and not as a consequence of their suitability for context-specific needs. Thus, isomorphism and decoupling, characteristic of other aspects of state governance, are also present in transitional justice models adopted by nation-states.

As a result, the accepted range of options included in the transitional justice agenda, which has become widely adopted globally, may be insufficient because it ignores vital economic issues, specifically economic crimes and corruption.[15] As Goodman and Jinks write, when

> models [develop] universal authority and legitimacy, states follow the global scripts as members of world society despite the ineffectiveness (or even dysfunctionality) of resultant organizational forms.[16]

[11] JW Meyer, J Boli and GM Thomas, 'World Society and the Nation-State' (1997) 103 *American Journal of Sociology* 144 at 145.

[12] R Goodman and D Jinks, 'How to Influence States: Socialization and International Human Rights Law' (2004) 54 *Duke Law Journal* 621 at 647.

[13] *Ibid* at 626.

[14] Meyer, Boli and Thomas, 'World Society and the Nation-State' (n 11 above) at 154–6.

[15] For further discussion of the 'under-inclusiveness' of transitional justice mechanisms, see the contributions of Arriaza and Roht-Arriaza (ch 7); McConnachie and Morison (ch 4); and McGregor (ch 3) in this collection.

[16] Goodman and Jinks, 'How to Influence States' (n 12 above) at 652.

Transitional justice models—and the specific mechanisms that developed in connection to them—have been useful in denouncing and documenting gross violations of civil and political rights, and in allowing societies to consider and apply a range of solutions to past abuses. However, we suggest that they are insufficient because they exclude the problem of economic crimes and corruption. Applying the concept of acculturation to TRCs, we suggest that, once the model for TRCs as a vehicle for denouncing only a limited set of human rights violations developed legitimacy in world society, modifying the script to include economic crimes and corruption—and thus undoing the process of socialisation of the model—became extremely difficult.[17]

In practice, it is not difficult to identify the existence of personal and institutional links that have led to the development of this dominant script. While the first few truth commissions, such as the 1984 Argentine Commission, and the failed Bolivian commission of 1982, may have developed in relative isolation, subsequent TRCs have been the work of repeated information exchange and consultations with prior commission members and a cadre of international scholars and practitioners in the area. Thus, for example, Priscilla Hayner observes the genesis of the mandate of the truth commission in Burundi in the following terms:

> The terms of reference adopted for the commission closely followed the recommendation of the secretary general's special envoy to Burundi, Venezuelan lawyer Pedro Nikken, who had been part of the UN negotiating team in El Salvador several years earlier and had helped to draft the terms of the truth commission there. He recommended a very similar entity for Burundi.[18]

In her epilogue to her comprehensive study on truth commissions, Hayner herself notes that in the days and weeks approaching as she finished the text, she had been invited to consult on the development of commissions in Indonesia, Sierra Leone, East Timor and Cambodia. The organisation for which Hayner now works—the International Centre for Transitional Justice—has become the leading think-tank on issues of justice in transition. As such, it has been involved in the development and study of various TRCs in more than 30 countries.[19]

By no means do we suggest that this sort of international exchange should not occur, nor do we question the vital contributions that it has made to the field of transitional justice and to TRCs in particular. Quite the contrary: the free exchange of experiences, lessons learned, best and

[17] For a discussion on adopting a 'thicker' approach to transitional justice, moving away from dominant legalistic scripts, see McEvoy (ch 2) in this collection.

[18] P Hayner, *Unspeakable Truths: Facing the Challenge of Truth Commissions* (New York and London, Routledge, 2002) 67.

[19] For more on the work of the International Centre for Transitional Justice, see http://www.ictj.org/en/where/overview/.

worst practices, and historical and legal precedents, provide a vital basis for enhancing the strength, efficacy, and responsiveness of truth commissions. However, we hope to begin to unwrap in a preliminary fashion the processes that have led to the creation of a TRC script that, while fertile in many areas, has excluded economic crimes from its mandate. In so doing, we hope to promote more fully the development of an environment in which, as scholar Martha Minow writes,

> the variety of circumstances and contexts for each nation, and indeed each person ... inflect and inform purposes in dealing with the past and methods that work or can even be tried.[20]

We suggest that, increasingly, the dominant script has served to limit, at least in some ways, rather than expand possibilities, and to restrict, rather than encourage, full inclusion of grassroots preferences.

Further, there is good reason to believe that the forces leading to acculturation and adoption of 'world society' norms are present or perhaps intensified in situations of transition, in which states and their agents are particularly concerned, and their attention particularly focused, on the international community and its standards of legitimacy. Recent research on peace agreements and human rights (which were found to be similar in many respects across societies)[21] as well as work on issues such as incorporation of women's suffrage (which demonstrate similarities at the moment of adoption despite significant difference in local circumstances)[22] support this conclusion.[23]

[20] M Minow, *Between Vengeance and Forgiveness* (Boston MA, Beacon Press, 1998) 4.

[21] In the field of transition from civil war to peace, a similar trend towards the development of uniform standards has taken hold. To some extent, a recent report by the International Council on Human Rights Policy recognises that, 'the expertise built up within the international community, especially at the United Nations, may have contributed to a common approach to peace-making': *Negotiating Justice? Human Rights and Peace Agreements* (Geneva, International Council on Human Rights Policy, 2006) 12.

[22] See Goodman and Jinks, 'How to Influence States' (n 12 above) at 650.

[23] An interesting counter-example involving an effort to expand the truth commission format to respond to local circumstances comes from an unlikely source. The recent truth commission established in Morocco fails to conform to a common political feature of TRCs—their formation in periods of transition. The Moroccan commission, by contrast to most other TRCs, was established by the King after a relatively limited, top-down transition. For an excellent analysis of the Moroccan commission, see P Hazan, 'Morocco: Betting on a Truth Commission' (United Institute of Peace, Special Report, 2006) available online at: http://www.usip.org/pubs/specialreports/sr165.pdf.

III WHY INCLUDE ECONOMIC CRIMES IN TRANSITIONAL JUSTICE SCHEMES? THE CONTEXT AND SOME WORKING HYPOTHESES

During the course of the 1980s and 1990s, a host of Latin American nations engaged in transitions from authoritarian to civilian, more democratic rule. While these transitions occurred across a broad range of circumstances, the TRCs implemented during the transition were strikingly similar.

We may trace the beginning of the growth and development of truth commissions in Latin America to the Sábato Commission, established in Argentina after the fall of the military dictatorship and the election of Raúl Alfonsín to the presidency.[24] While the military junta had committed a range of civil and political rights abuses (and engaged in economic crimes and corruption), the single abuse most closely associated with the dirty war imposed on Argentina was forced disappearance.[25] Not surprisingly, then, this crime, and this crime alone, became the focus of the work of the Argentine truth commission,[26] the National Commission for the Investigation of Forced Disappearances (Comisión Nacional para la Investigación Sobre la Desaparición de Personas).

In 1985, shortly after a negotiated pact brought an end to 11 years of military rule in Uruguay, the newly-formed civilian government created a commission on disappearances. As in Argentina,[27] the investigatory body's mandate limited it to the crime of disappearance, despite the broad recognition that the Uruguayan dictatorship had made *relatively little* use of this horrendous practice.[28] Likewise, Chile's TRC, created after Pinochet's loss of the 1988 referendum and the 1989 victory by Patricio Aylwin and the Concertación, focused on forced disappearances.[29]

24 Two years before the establishment of the Sábato Commission in Argentina, a commission had been established in Bolivia by President Hernán Siles Suazo. That commission laboured from 1982 to 1984, collecting testimony on 155 disappearances that occurred between 1967 and 1982, but disbanded without producing a final report. See E Cuya, 'Las Comisiones de la Verdad en América Latina', *Dokumentations und Informationszentrum Menschenrechte in Lateinamerika Nürnberger Menschenrechtszentrum*, available online at http://www.derechos.org/koaga/iii/1/cuya.html.

25 The implementation of a plan by which people were systematically kidnapped and assassinated resulted in as many as 30,000 disappeared individuals during the '*guerra sucia*' or dirty war.

26 See Art 1 of Decreto Ley 187/83, creating the TRC.

27 This was also the case in Bolivia.

28 For the new Uruguayan leaders, following Argentina's lead would prove quite convenient: by avoiding investigation of torture, which had been practised massively in Uruguay, the transitional rulers could provide a minimal measure of accountability without provoking the wrath of the still powerful military. See, M Macedo, *Tiempos de Ida, Tiempos de Vuelta* (Montevideo, Ediciones Orbe Libros, 2002); L Weschler, *A Miracle, a Universe: Settling Accounts with Torturers* (Chicago, University of Chicago Press, 1998); D Gil, *El Terror y la Tortura* (Montevideo, EPPAL, 1990).

29 See Art 1 of Decreto Supremo No 355, creating the TRC.

In 1991, the United Nations brokered a peace deal to end the brutal 12-year civil war in El Salvador. The accord, negotiated over a period of three years (1989–92), included the intervention of a United Nations peace-keeping force and the establishment of a TRC. The mandate of that commission restricted it to investigating serious acts of violence only.[30] Shortly thereafter, Guatemala's protracted armed conflict also reached an end under the auspices of the United Nations, which established a peace-keeping mission, MINUGUA. Decisions about the powers and breadth of the commission were shaped by the conflicted context in which the TRC was created. In the end, the Commission focused exclusively on human rights violations and acts of violence.[31] In a similar vein, the Honduran National Commissioner for the Protection of Human Rights, Leo Valladares, also conducted an investigation into a similarly narrow set of violations that took place in the 1980s. With a familiar focus on forced disappearances, the Honduran Commission produced a report, *Los Hechos Hablan por Sí*, later translated into English by Human Rights Watch and the Centre for Justice and International Law (CEJIL).[32]

A Perception and Reality of Corruption in Recent Latin American Dictatorships

While we do not intend to provide a full account of corruption in recent Latin American dictatorships, in this section we draw upon examples from Chile, Argentina, Bolivia, Paraguay and Uruguay to illustrate and support the argument that economic crimes and corruption were common currency during military rule in Latin America, however, they have been largely ignored by truth commissions and, more generally, have received inadequate attention in post-transition Latin America.

As noted in the introduction, a dominant narrative exists in Latin America, namely, that corruption was limited during the many dictatorships throughout the region, and that it has increased with the advent of democratic rule. To some extent, this may be due to the fact that little investigation of corruption during authoritarian regimes was conducted

[30] See El Salvador: México Peace Agreement 1991 (27 April 1991) available online at http://www.usip.org/library/tc/doc/charters/tc_elsalvador.html.

[31] Agreement on the establishment of the Commission to clarify past human rights violations and acts of violence that have caused the Guatemalan population to suffer, 1994. Reproduced online at http://www.usip.org/library/pa/guatemala/guat_940623.html.

[32] See Centre for Justice and International Law (CEJIL) and Human Rights Watch, *The Facts Speak for Themselves: The Preliminary Report on Disappearances of the National Commissioner for the Protection of Human Rights in Honduras* (trans coordinator JL Cavallaro, Jr) (New York, Human Rights Watch, 1994).

during transitions.[33] As shown above, investigations of high-level corruption and economic crimes were excluded from the mandate of TRCs; this omission may have contributed to some extent to the unfortunate and largely inaccurate popular belief that Latin American dictatorships were not corrupt.[34]

Further, the omission of economic crimes and corruption from TRCs is especially striking because the vast social inequality, economic mismanagement, and abuse by elites were generally driving forces in the underlying conflicts whose resolution eventually led to the creation and implementation of transitional justice mechanisms.

Although evidence of these forms of abuse of power during authoritarian regimes is scarce—not surprisingly, for these matters were carefully concealed—some cases of serious acts of corruption involving high-ranking military officials, their family members, and economic groups to which they were linked, were denounced and reached the public. Some of them include direct embezzlement, fraud, and appropriation of assets; others concern fraudulent business agreements, especially in the process of privatisation of government enterprises.

The case of corruption in Chile under Pinochet is especially interesting because, historically, Chile has been a country with relatively limited corruption. As Patricio Orellana Vargas observes, Pinochet's dictatorship broke with this tradition (it was the '*punto de quiebre*'[35]). In other words, the dictatorship established a network of corrupt practices rarely seen before in Chile. The recently publicised case involving secret accounts at Riggs Bank in the United States is certainly the most visible.[36] However, several other forms of corruption existed that benefited Pinochet, his family, and friends.[37] Without a formal mechanism to investigate official

[33] Some studies find that an increase in corruption with new democratic regimes is more than just a perception. Montinola and Jackman find that corruption is likely to be higher in new or partially established democracies as compared to dictatorships. However, once democracies become more fully established, the level of corruption tends to decrease. See G Montinolla and R Jackman, 'Sources of Corruption: A Cross Country Study' (2002) 32 *British Journal of Political Science* 147.

[34] This narrative is not exclusive to Latin America; it also existed in South Africa: 'Public perception that a democratic South Africa is more corrupt than the apartheid regime dominated much of the public discourse for a number of years after 1994'. See Van Vuuren, 'Apartheid Grand Corruption' (n 10 above) at 12.

[35] P Orellana Vargas, 'Probidad y Corrupción en Chile' (2004) 3 *Polis Revista de la Universidad Bolivariana* 1 at 10, available online at http://redalyc.uaemex.mx/src/inicio/ArtPdfRed.jsp?iCve=30500818&iCveNum=0.

[36] A probe by the US Senate's Permanent Subcommittee on Investigations reported that from 1994 to 2002, Pinochet opened six accounts and issued several certificates of deposit while he was under house arrest in the UK and his assets were the subject of court proceedings. Deposits in Pinochet's accounts ranged from US$4 to US$8 million at a time.

[37] For several reports of corruption during the Pinochet Regime, including, inter alia, nepotism; fraud, which benefited the Pinochet family and close economic groups; illegal arms sales to Yugoslavia; undue benefits to high ranking officials; fraudulent deals in the

corruption during the Pinochet era, some individuals undertook efforts to examine abuses, often at significant personal risk.[38]

In Argentina, high-level officials, such as the Ministry of Economy under the dictatorship, José Martínez de Hoz, were also involved in corrupt affairs. Corruption took place in the form of protection to business groups that were close to the regime, as well as attacks against opposition business sectors ('desafectados'). In the case of SADECO, a cotton exports company, its owners were forced to give up export quotas when they were imprisoned.[39] On the other hand, some businesses were tightly linked to the regime:

> Business organizations such as the Coordinated Action of Free Business Institutions (ACIEL) and the Permanent Assembly of Entrepreneurial Entities (APEGE) were linked to the authoritarian regime. In many cases, key state bureaucrats during the authoritarian periods were members of these business organizations.[40]

Bolivia had a long history of authoritarian regimes. Luis García Meza, who held power from 1980 to 1982, was responsible for serious acts of corruption.

> In less than a year of de facto government, not only did he steal from the public moneys, but, from within the government, organized the most protected network of international trade of illegal drugs.[41]

Once his regime was ousted, he deposited in Citibank Argentina, on October 20 1982, US$15 million.[42]

Fraud and embezzlement were not unknown in Paraguay. During Stroessner's rule, millions of dollars were stolen through exchange hoaxes in the Central Bank, and were exported to international banks.[43] Uruguay,

privatisation of state enterprises; see M Brescia, *Manos Limpias: La Corrupción en las Empresas Públicas (de Todos los Chilenos)* (Santiago, Editorial Mare Nostrum, 2001) 147; B Pollack and A Matear, 'Dictatorship, Democracy, and Corruption in Chile' (1997) 25 *Crime, Law, and Social Change* 371 at 376; MA Monkeber, *El Saqueo de los Grupos Económicos al Estado Chileno* (Santiago, Ediciones B, 2001).

[38] Jorge Lavandero, who denounced some of the corruption acts described below, was beaten so severely that he nearly died. Independent periodicals that denounced corruption, like Revista Cauce, were censored or closed. See Orellana Vargas, 'Probidad y Corrupción en Chile' (n 35 above) at 15.

[39] P Miranda, *Terrorismo de Estado: Testimonio del Horror en Chile* (Santiago, Editorial Sextante, 1989).

[40] JW Freels, *El Sector Industrial en la política Nacional* (Buenos Aires, EUDEBA, 1970) 5. For more on the link between business sectors and government, see G O'Donnell, *Estado y Alianzas en la Argentina, 1956–1976* (Buenos Aires, CEDES/CLACSO, 1976) no 5; G O'Donnell, *Notas para el estudio de la burguesía local, con especial referencia a sus vinculaciones con el capital transnacional y el aparato estatal*, Estudios Sociales (Buenos Aires, CEDES, 1978) 12.

[41] P Miranda, *La Agonía del Dinero* (trans JL Cavallaro and S Albuja) (Santiago, Ediciones Sextante, 1990) 72.

[42] *Ibid.*

[43] Miranda, *La Agonía del Dinero* (n 41 above).

too, was no exception to this trend, but rather a country in which 'arbitrariness, theft, and illegal appropriation of public moneys took place at every level'.[44] Corruption took place, inter alia, in business deals like the sale of banks, privatisation of state businesses, and public works contracts.

B Grassroots Attitudes on Corruption in Latin America

Throughout Latin America, at the grassroots level, public opinion strongly rejects high-scale corruption and acts of economic malfeasance during democratic regimes. To an important extent, due to high perceived levels of corruption, broad segments of public opinion in Latin America have tenuous confidence in democratic institutions. Latinobarómetro reports, for example, that in all countries in the region, the public strongly distrusts governmental institutions: for 2004, on average, only 24 per cent of the population trusted legislatures and only 32 per cent trusted the judicial system.[45] Based on data from the Transparency International Corruption Percentage Index and the World Values Survey for 1995–97, other analyses establish an important nexus between citizen perceptions of official corruption and rejection levels for incumbent leaders, finding high levels of negative correlation between perception of corruption and support for those in power.[46]

> When citizens in Latin America perceive rampant political corruption, those views translate directly into downgrading of opinion for both incumbent officials and political institutions ... Citizens perceive corruption and they connect those perceptions to their judgments of incumbent leaders and political institutions.[47]

One of the motivations for the ousting of Ecuador's President Mahuad in 2000 focused on allegations of corruption, including one charge that he had received US$3 million from a banking and corporate group. Likewise, Abdalá Bucaram was ousted because of his famously corrupt practices

[44] M Carrió, *Pais Vaciado: Dictadura y Negociados* (Montevideo, Monte Sexto, 1987) at 7.

[45] Latinobarómetro, 'Informe Resumen Latinobarómetro 2004', Una Década De Mediciones (Santiago De Chile, Corporación Latinobarómetro, 13 August 2004). While the figures cited are aggregates, they show a general pattern of popular preference. See http://www.latinobarometro.org/.

[46] D Canache and ME Allison, 'Perceptions of Political Corruption in Latin American Democracies' (2005) 47 *Latin American Politics and Society* 91 at 103. Indeed, through another statistical analysis, Canache and Allison first determine that 'there is a high degree of correspondence between expert judgments and the views of the person on the street' when assessing corruption in the Americas. *Ibid* at 100.

[47] *Ibid* at 106. The Latin American Public Opinion Project also reports high degrees of rejection of corrupt behaviour.

throughout governmental institutions.[48] Grassroots unrest and mobilisation were the driving forces behind the removal of these corrupt leaders.[49] In all, from the early 1990s to 2005, 'nine Latin American presidents or former presidents have faced judicial proceedings or have been dismissed on corruption charges'.[50]

Against this tendency, there is a generalised feeling in Latin America that rejection for high-level corruption did not exist for authoritarian regimes. This idea may have its roots in a history of popular tolerance or even support for authoritarianism in the region. The co-existence of an authoritarian, personalistic culture in the political sphere and poorly developed democratic institutions has been the subject of much analysis by scholars studying Latin American political culture.[51] Historically, Latin Americans are less likely to condemn an authoritarian regime if it can achieve certain goals, such as order and predictability; in fact, they have systematically supported authoritarian figures. Not only does the region have a long-standing history of *caudillismo*, or strongmen with broad popular support, but this trend has continued well into the post-transitional period of the past two decades.[52]

Voting patterns corroborate this popular support for authoritarian figures. Hugo Chávez in Venezuela, Lucio Gutiérrez in Ecuador, and Ollanta Humala in Perú are cases in point. All of them violated the constitutional order and attempted to seize power by extra-legal means.

[48] Bucaram's networks of corruption involved the administration of customs, a national-scale housing project, and fundraising programmes for underprivileged children. See M Pallares and M Cevallos, 'Comedia de los Escándalos' in D Cornejo (ed), *Que se Vaya: Crónica del Bucaramato* (Quito, EDIMPRES, 1997) available online at http://www.hoy.com.ec/libro/indice.htm.

[49] The rejection of political corruption at the local level in Latin America has also motivated the organisation of grassroots, citizen-based bodies, known as *veedurías ciudadanas*, or *contralorías ciudadanas*, which have been implemented in nearly every Latin American country. These bodies focus on controlling political corruption by overseeing processes ranging from the appointment of judges to public contracts. See, eg Ecuador's *veedurías ciudadanas,* at *¿Qué son las veedurías ciudadanas?* available online at www.comisionanticorrupcion.com/paginas/veedurias.asp?idparam=s&idsubsec=23&idsec=10&idarea=2.

[50] Canache and Allison, 'Perceptions of Political Corruption in Latin American Democracies' (n 46 above) at 94. In addition to Bucaram, Mahuad and Collor de Mello, Canache and Allison include Alan García, Carlos Salinas de Gortari, Fabián Alarcón, Ernesto Samper, Carlos Menem and Alberto Fujimori.

[51] See, eg n 57 below.

[52] G O'Donnell, 'Battling the Undertow in Latin America' in Larry Diamond (ed), *Consolidating the Third Wave Democracies: Themes and Perspectives* (Baltimore MD, Johns Hopkins University Press, 1997); A Varas, 'Civil-Military Relations in a Democratic Framework' in L Goodman, JSR Mendelson and J Rial (eds), *The Military and Democracy: The Future of Civil-Military Relations in Latin America* (Lexington MA, Lexington Books, 1990); P Smith, *Democracy in Latin America* (New York, Oxford University Press, 2005); G O'Donnell, PC Schmitter and L Whitehead (eds), *Transitions from Authoritarian Rule: Comparative Perspectives* (Baltimore MD, Johns Hopkins University Press, 1986).

Yet a few years later, both Chávez and Gutiérrez won presidential elections. And Ollanta Humala, an ex-member of the military ranks who also attempted an insurrection, recently came very close to winning presidential elections in Peru. In fact, in Latin America, anti-democratic behaviour has proven to be a very efficient means of launching a political career and acquiring visibility.[53]

In the face of this widespread trend, we argue here that the generalised, widely documented public rejection of corruption in democratic regimes applies as well to authoritarian governments. While the public in Latin America may tolerate authoritarian behaviour under certain circumstances, it has shown low tolerance for high-profile corrupt practices of authoritarian rulers. Even though grassroots constituencies in Latin America may approve of authoritarian leaders through their vote, these same citizens often reject leaders once they have been demonstrated to be corrupt. For example, Lucio Gutiérrez, who won elections in Ecuador after he failed to take and hold power outside the electoral process, was driven from office when he granted amnesty to Bucaram, who at the time faced criminal charges for corruption. Today, social activists and rights groups have recognised that corruption and economic crimes constitute strong foundations to challenge authoritarian rule.[54]

Despite high levels of popular rejection of corruption and acts of economic malfeasance in both democratic and authoritarian regimes, 'bottom-up', citizen-based TRCs have also regularly excluded economic crimes and corruption from their investigations.[55] While other causes may also explain this phenomenon, we suggest that the transfer and institutionalisation of a standard script from above accounts for the exclusion of corruption-related concerns. In other words, it should be expected that these commissions might omit economic crimes and corruption from their investigations in response to the institutionalised, widespread model established and fostered by official commissions.

A more pedestrian rationale is that citizen-based commissions are typically constrained by limited resources and basic technical capabilities.

[53] Interview with Osvaldo Hurtado, scholar and ex-president of Ecuador, Quito, Ecuador, (June 7 2006).

[54] A recent manifestation of this is found in a December 2005 Human Rights Watch report calling for the extradition of former Peruvian head of state, Alberto Fujimori, based largely on economic crimes involving malfeasance, indirectly related to rights violations. See Human Rights Watch, 'Probable Cause: Evidence Implicating Fujimori' (HRW, vol 17, No 6(B), 21 December 2005) In September, the Chilean Supreme Court authorised Fujimori's extradition on human rights and corruption charges. S Romero, 'Court Approves Extradition of Fujimori', *New York Times*, 21 September 2007.

[55] Examples of such TRCs include: Paraguay's *Comité de Iglesias para Ayuda de Emergencia* (CIPAE); Brazil's *Proyecto Nunca Más*, based at the Archdiocese of São Paulo; Guatemala's *Proyecto Interdiocesano de Recuperación de la Memoria Histórica*; and Bolivia's *Comisión Nacional de Investigación de Desaparecidos Forzados.*

Investigating acts of high-level fraud and embezzlement, which normally take place through complex and highly technical procedures, is beyond the capacity of community-based TRCs. In practice then, even though the grassroots and community-based TRCs may be concerned by acts of financial malfeasance, investigating these crimes may be beyond their resources.[56]

The problems faced by community-based TRCs in dealing with economic crimes and corruption, described above, are equally applicable to state-sponsored TRCs. However, community-based TRCs may hold the potential to pressure officials to overcome some of these impediments—especially those technical in nature—in a way that state-sponsored commissions may not, precisely because they are not part of the state apparatus. This detachment from the objects of their investigations is certainly an asset of community-based TRCs. Admittedly, to investigate economic crimes and corruption effectively, citizen-based TRCs would have to be given investigatory powers, and privileges to access classified information.

C De-legitimising Dictatorial Regimes, Attaining Consolidation

Under the functionalist view that dominated the political science literature for several decades, corruption was considered useful to political organisation and performance; it was seen as even more relevant during authoritarian times, as it provided 'zones of freedom and of free movement' and helped 'redistribute public resources by parallel means accessible to groups that would otherwise be excluded'.[57] More recently, strong challenges to the functionalist view have been advanced. These challenges, supported by empirical evidence, contend that both the experience and perception of corruption undermine regime legitimacy.[58] The argument that corruption's prevalence in many societies and its status as a parallel set of rules and

[56] However, even if community-based TRCs are not able to conduct such investigations on their own, they could exert pressure on government officials and state-based TRCs to include the issues within their mandates. Admittedly, breaking the standard script would require a high degree of local mobilisation and political momentum. However, community-based organisations may be the best advocates for expanding the scope of transitional efforts; in other words, challenging and ultimately modifying the standard top-down script is an effort that may be best attained from below.

[57] J Becquart-Leclerq, 'Paradoxes of Political Corruption: A French View' in AJ Heidenheimer, VT LeVine, and M Johnston (eds), *Political Corruption: A Handbook* (New Brunswick NJ, Transaction, 1989) 193, cited in M Seligson, 'The Impact of Corruption on Regime Legitimacy: A Study of Four Latin American Countries' (2002) 64 *The Journal of Politics* 408.

[58] Some of these studies are: SR Ackerman, *Corruption and Government: Causes, Consequences, and Reform* (Cambridge, Cambridge University Press, 1999); W Mishler and R Rose, 'What are the Origins of Political Trust?' (2001) 34 *Comparative Political Studies* 30.

accepted behaviours render it salutary to social processes is no longer dominant. Contemporary research on experience with corruption (not only perception) shows that those who experience corruption lose trust in the legitimacy of their regimes, and also lose interpersonal trust.[59]

Likewise, corruption and economic crimes are highly corrosive of confidence in the justice system.[60] One of the fundamental goals of transitional justice is to put an end to widespread impunity and to establish the rule of law. Impunity for economic crimes and corruption undermines this goal.[61]

Therefore, even in countries in which corruption is not deeply pervasive, addressing these issues within the context of truth commissions may be necessary to the consolidation of new democratic regimes, especially because

> [s]ituations of transition offer unique windows of opportunity to address issues of impunity which are of crucial importance in a society's development.[62]

If this is true—and we believe it is—investigating and documenting cases of economic crimes and corruption under military rule could help de-legitimise authoritarian regimes even more than investigations of human rights violations. If, as Seligson puts it,

> one of the major limitations that authoritarian regimes have in establishing their own legitimacy is that more often than not they operate as cleptocracies, in which the state is corrupt to its core, and citizens know it,[63]

making corruption during authoritarian regimes more visible through investigations during transitional periods would help erode their legitimacy. This is particularly true in cases in which dictatorships enjoy high degrees of legitimacy and popular support. Otherwise,

> citizens can seek alternatives to democracy through support for the return of military rule, or through support for populist but anti-democratic figures.[64]

[59] M Seligson, 'The Measure and Impact of Corruption Victimization: Survey Evidence from Latin America' (2006) 34 *World Development* 381.

[60] A United Nations Congress on Criminal Justice found that 'economic crimes affect people's sense of society's fairness, creating feelings of resentment'. Eleventh UN congress on Crime Prevention and Criminal Justice, held in Bangkok, Thailand (18–25 April 2005). Available online at http://www.un.org/events/11thcongress/docs/bkkcp08e.pdf.

[61] Van Vuuren, 'Apartheid Grand Corruption' (n 10 above) at 14 stresses this point, arguing that corruption entrenched in authoritarian rule does not vanish with the advent of democracy, but rather, 'inevitably serve[s] to corrode the new order'.

[62] Transparency International Kenya, (March 2006) 76 'Adili' News service Editorial 1, Nairobi. Available online at http://www.tikenya.org/documents/adili76.pdf .

[63] M Seligson, 'The Political Culture of Democracy in Mexico, Central America, and Colombia, 2004', Latin American Public Opinion Project (2004) at 43. Available online at http://www.vanderbilt.edu/americas/Docs/The%20Political%20Culture%20of%20 Democracy%20in%20Mexico%20Central%20America%20and%20Colombia%202004.pdf.

[64] Seligson, 'The Measure and Impact of Corruption Victimization' (n 59 above) at 382.

The case of Augusto Pinochet illustrates the idea that corruption and economic crimes hold vast potential for de-legitimisation. At the same time, it corroborates the position that popular condemnation for economic malfeasance is significant and a potentially powerful political force. During the 17 years in which it ruled Chile, the Pinochet regime committed widespread and horrendous human rights abuses. Despite this, for nearly a decade, Pinochet and almost all of those in the chain of command avoided serious threat of prosecution at home, until the 1998 London arrest, pursuant to Spanish judge Baltazar Garzón's request. The London arrest led to indictments for rights abuses against many others during Pinochet's rule.[65]

Notwithstanding the enormous global, symbolic, and domino effect of the October 1998 London arrest, the greatest threat to the recently deceased Pinochet was not necessarily related to the human rights charges in Spain, England or Chile, but instead, to the discovery of secret bank accounts in Riggs Bank in Washington, DC. The Riggs case led not only to Pinochet's November 2005 arrest, but also the detention of 10 of his family members[66] and to further loss of stature and respect in Chile.

When on 23 November 2005, Chilean authorities placed General Augusto Pinochet under arrest on tax fraud charges in connection with recently discovered bank accounts holding millions of dollars, the New York Times reported the following day that

> Since returning to Chile after being freed from detention in Britain in March 2000 on Spanish court accusations of human rights violations and genocide, General Pinochet has twice been formally accused of human rights violations during the 17 years he was in power. But this is the first time he has been charged with other crimes, *and lawyers said the likelihood of a trial and conviction was greater on these charges* (emphasis added).[67]

Sebastian Brett, Chile researcher for Human Rights Watch and long-time analyst of Chilean politics, told the *Boston Globe* in early 2005 that the Riggs case affected Pinochet's image in Chile more than all the human

[65] See, eg N Roht-Arriaza, *The Pinochet Effect: Transnational Justice in the Age of Human Rights* (Philadelphia PA, University of Pennsylvania Press, 2005). Pinochet's wife and son were also charged with tax evasion (see P Abramovich, 'Pinochet son arrested in case of US bank accounts', *Agence France-Presse*, 29 July 2004; 'Pinochet's wife, son arrested on tax evasion charges', *Deutsche Presse-Agentur*, 8 August 2005.) Pinochet was also investigated for his role in authorising 15 summary executions that took place within Operación Colombo in 1974 and 1975 ('Ponen Bajo Arresto Domiciliario a Pinochet por sus Cuentas Ilegales', *Diario El Clarín*, Santiago, 24 November 2005).

[66] PJ McDonnell, 'Pinochet Family Members Arrested', *Los Angeles Times*, 24 January 2006.

[67] L Rohter, 'Pinochet Held on Charges Linked to Bank Accounts', *New York Times*, 24 November 2005. Due to Pinochet's death in late 2006, neither pending human rights nor corruption charges could be concluded.

rights allegations. In a colourful yet powerful fashion, Lakshmanan wrote for the Boston Globe that

> there were many people who thought [abuses] may have happened, but that was the price they had to pay to get rid of a crazy socialist government, and at least [Pinochet] didn't line his pockets. Now the myth of Pinochet as the honest citizen has been shattered.[68]

While many in Chile today still tolerate and even justify violations of civil and political rights to achieve greater goods—for instance, security and economic development—those same Chileans categorically reject corruption and economic crimes.

IV LOOKING BEYOND LATIN AMERICA

Over the past 15 years, a second wave of states, primarily outside Latin America, has undergone transition from authoritarian and democratic rule. These states, much like those Latin American nations discussed above, have implemented transitional justice measures consistent with the growing international consensus, which provides a privileged place for truth commissions. As in Latin America, these states have, with some important exceptions, followed the dominant script with regard to economic crimes, even when this has differed significantly from indigenous demands. While TRC mandates have involved significant modifications and adaptations—such as naming perpetrators, expanding the range of civil and political rights covered, and providing pardon in exchange for confessions—they have consistently excluded economic crimes.

The most important and closely followed truth commission outside of Latin America has been the institution established to reckon with the crimes of the Apartheid state in South Africa. This TRC was created by the Promotion of National Unity and Reconciliation Act in 1995, an extensive and detailed enabling Act. Commentators have generally recognised the role of the South African TRC in the regional and global debate on truth commissions. In a recent text, John Daniel and Marisha Ramdeen analyse the impact of the South African TRC on other commissions in Africa. Daniel and Ramdeen note that

[68] IAR Lakshmanan, 'Old Allies' Support for Pinochet Wanes', *Boston Globe*, 13 February 005.

> for academics and NGOs concerned with transitional justice, the South African truth commission process has become the model by which all other such commissions are evaluated.[69]

In Africa, they continue,

> [t]he attention that the South African truth-commission process attracted and its widespread international acclaim have seen this particular instrument come, in the last ten years, to form a part of the settlement packages in a number of African conflict situations.

Since the beginning of South Africa's transition, there have been over a dozen TRCs in Africa and Asia. A quick look at the mandates of the following TRCs reveals that they have followed the model of focus on gross violations of civil and political rights: Burundi (1995–96); Chad (1990); Germany (1992); Ghana (2001–04); Uganda (1986–94); Sri Lanka (1994–97); Zimbabwe (1985); South Korea (2002); Liberia (2006); Nigeria (1999); Haiti (1994–96); Sierra Leone (2002–04); East Timor (2001–05); Morocco (2004–06); Togo (2000); Fiji (2005). There have, however, been some exceptions. In East Timor, for example, the truth commission considered economic, social and cultural rights. That report, however, does not include economic crimes nor does it seek to identify individuals and high-level authorities responsible.[70]

Chad is the only other country in which the investigation of economic crimes was conducted by a Commission at the transition. The president, elected in 1990, created a 'Commission of Inquiry into the Crimes and Misappropriations Committed by ex-President Habré, his Accomplices and/or Accessories'. Even though this commission's recommendations were never implemented, it successfully investigated economic crimes of the Habré regime. The fact that this commission was implemented before a period in which the acculturation and expansion of an international standard model was widespread may confirm our preliminary hypothesis, namely, that local TRCs might include economic crimes if they are not highly influenced by the international script.

Two countries originally considered including corruption and economic crimes within the mandate of their official TRC, but ultimately did not. The first is Kenya. After the end of the Moi regime, democratically elected

[69] J Daniel and M Ramdeen, 'Dealing with Africa's Post-Independence Past: Truth Commissions, Special Courts, War Crimes Trials, and Other Methods' in R Southall (ed), *South Africa's Role in Conflict Resolution and Peacemaking in Africa* (Cape Town, HSRC Press, 2006).

[70] See Commission for Reception, Truth and Reconciliation Timor Leste (CAVR), 'Chega! The Report of the Commission for Reception, Truth, and Reconciliation Timor-Leste, Executive Summary' (2005), available online at http://www.etan.org/news/2006/cavr.htm. For a discussion of the range of transitional justice mechanisms pursued in Timor-Leste, see Stanley in ch 8 of this collection.

President Mwai Kibaki favoured establishing a truth commission. A Task Force on the Establishment of a Truth, Justice and Reconciliation Commission was created which discussed and ultimately provided the Kenyan Government with the mandate for the TRC. Although the inclusion of economic crimes was seriously considered by the Task Force, they were ultimately left aside.[71]

Makau wa Mutua, the chairperson for the Task Force, saw permanent judicial bodies as highly incapable of dealing with economic crimes because, added to the high levels of corruption within them, people who commit economic crimes are usually in a position to hire good lawyers and circumvent legal boundaries.[72] Further, he acknowledged that

> there is no one formula for a Commission. A Truth Commission is an instrument for producing transitional justice, so one would have to look at various models and Kenya's history when deciding on what the Truth Commission should look like.[73]

Still, the mandate of the TRC excluded corruption and economic crimes, incorporating 'international best practices', and was drafted with the advice and support of international NGOs, notably, the ICTJ.[74] The influence of other notable TRCs such as South Africa's has also been acknowledged.[75]

Ghana also excluded corruption and economic crimes. Although the original legislation creating the National Reconciliation Commission included a provision for the investigation of corruption, it was ultimately dropped. Instead, the investigation of these abuses was entrusted to the Serious Fraud Office (SFO), an institution that had earlier been used to repress opponents. In the end,

> the public hearings in Ghana have included a fair share of 'economic crime' hearings, partly because there was a significant amount of politically motivated property seizure that was accompanied by harassment and unfair arrest. It looks likely that one of the key recommendations of the commission will be restitution of property.[76]

[71] See Task Force on the Establishment of a Truth, Justice, and Reconciliation Commission, Makau Mutua, Chairperson, *Report of the Task Force on the Establishment of a Truth, Justice, and Reconciliation Commission* (Nairobi, Kenya: The Government Printer, 2003).

[72] Transparency International Kenya, *Adili* News service (n 62 above) at 6.

[73] Transparency International Kenya, *Adili* News service (n 62 above) at 3.

[74] Priscilla Hayner of the ICTJ provided advice at the invitation of the Task Force. Hayner, *Unspeakable Truths: Facing the Challenge of Truth Commissions* (n 18 above).

[75] 'We have learned a lot from the Truth and Reconciliation Commission of South Africa and other commissions in Latin America', said Kiraitu Murungi, the new justice and constitutional affairs minister of Kenya. Cited in Fredrick Nzwili, 'Kenya: Churches Back Truth Commission' in *Christianity Today*, 1 April 2003.

[76] P Hayner and L Bosire, 'Should Truth Commissions Address Economic Crimes? Considering the Case of Kenya' (New York, International Centre for Transitional Justice, 26 March 2003). Available online at www.tikenya.org/documents/TruthComm.doc.

The report, released by the Ghanaian government in April 2004, does include a section—albeit limited in scope—on restitution of property, which declares that

> those who suffered unlawful confiscation of property, such as lands and buildings should, in principle, have their properties restored to them.[77]

The mandate of the Liberian TRC includes economic crimes. As that Commission progresses, it will remain to be seen whether, and to what extent, these crimes and corruption are in fact documented.[78]

V CONCLUSION

This chapter has argued that, despite significant flexibility in certain aspects, TRCs have consistently excluded economic crimes and corruption from their mandates, focusing primarily on the priorities of the human rights movement as defined nearly two decades ago. The repeated exclusion of these issues across temporal and geographic boundaries, we suggest, may be caused by the international transfer of models and norms at the international, state level.

TRCs face a variety of constraints, related to political pressures, as well as limits on time, resources, and professional staff. Admittedly, the inclusion of corruption and economic crimes might serve to heighten these challenges. Nevertheless, investigating acts of economic malfeasance committed by authoritarian regimes may serve a variety of functions, rendering it a net gain for TRCs. First, investigation may provide a mechanism to address popular demands for accountability in an effective manner. Secondly, it may be highly functional to de-legitimising authoritarian regimes—even more so than denouncing violations of civil and political rights. Finally, investigating this class of crimes may prove highly useful to the consolidation of burgeoning democracies.

The time may have come to re-think, at least in part, the prevailing TRC paradigm. The human rights movement has undergone a relatively recent shift towards greater emphasis on economic, social and cultural rights. As a result, refocusing TRCs in accordance with this mandate expansion might well lead to greater inclusion of economic crimes and corruption as violations of economic, social and cultural rights. Yet, rather than waiting for the impetus to change from within human rights organisations, those

[77] See National Reconciliation Commission Report, *Recommendations for Reconciliation and Institutional Reforms*, vol 1 ch 8, October 2004. Available online at http://ictj.com/downloads/ghana/Ghana.NRC.V1.C8.Reforms.pdf.

[78] See 'An Act to Create the Truth and Reconciliation Commission (TRC) of Liberia', approved June 10 2005, Art IV, s 4(a), Mandate of the Commission (specifically enumerating 'economic crimes' within the scope of matters to be investigated.

considering TRCs in the future might arrive at the same goal by considering the origins, social function and goals of these bodies. In this vein, we would hope that the concerns outlined in this chapter related to grassroots demand to investigate economic crimes and corruption, as well as the other bottom-up issues raised throughout this volume, are afforded adequate weight.

7

Social Repair at the Local Level: The Case of Guatemala

LAURA ARRIAZA AND NAOMI ROHT-ARRIAZA*

I INTRODUCTION

FROM 1960 TO 1996, some 200,000 people were killed in Guatemala in the course of waves of government repression and armed conflict. In 1996 peace accords were signed promising extensive reforms. Efforts have been made to establish a historical record of the nature and consequences of the conflict. A UN-sponsored Commission for Historical Clarification (CEH or 'Truth Commission') heard some 8,000 testimonies and compiled an extensive record of the historical causes, nature and consequences of the conflict. A second, unofficial report sponsored by the Catholic Church published a large number of testimonies of horrendous crimes, most from the primarily Mayan mountainous areas of Western and Northern Guatemala.[1] Currently, an ambitious although troubled National Reparations Programme has distributed some cheques to widows and other victims of the conflict. A few trials in notorious cases have resulted in convictions, although the justice system remains compromised and ineffective. In sum, despite limitations and halfway measures, Guatemala has enacted many pieces of the 'transitional justice' agenda. Yet, it is not clear how much, and how, these efforts—while necessary—have impacted upon peoples' daily experience. Ten years after the peace accords, Guatemala remains a deeply wounded society.

We argue that there are two main reasons why these efforts have not translated more fully into changes in lived experience and perception. The

* A version of this article was first printed in the International Journal of Transitional Justice, vol 2(2) of 2008.

[1] Recovery of Historical Memory Project (*Recuperación de la Memoria Histórica* ('REHMI')), *Guatemala Nunca Mas* (Guatemala, Office of Human Rights of the Archbishop, 1998).

first, which is largely beyond the scope of this chapter,[2] is the continuing lack of social and economic justice. People are poorer than ever; the formal political system continues to be dominated by *ladino*[3] elites; racism and discrimination against the Mayan majority is rampant and the economy is largely dominated by large landholders, drug dealers and various types of smugglers. The second, which is our focus here, is that national-level initiatives by themselves are insufficient to capture the meaning of the conflict for people living in specific villages, towns, 'hills', or other local spaces, whose experience may vary widely from that of people elsewhere in the country. When it comes to post-conflict interventions aimed at reconstructing a shattered society, international and national policy-makers have treated countries as an undifferentiated whole. This has its uses in terms of establishing global norms and creating a national (re)founding mythology[4]; certain kinds of tasks[5] can only be carried out on a uniform basis, by a national state. But such efforts ignore existing local dynamics aimed at reinforcing or transforming the power relations that are often most relevant to peoples' lives, especially given the perennial weakness of the central state. In transitional justice as elsewhere, all politics is local.

We are not simply arguing that national-level initiatives should have a regional aspect or component—something that has been done[6]—but that those assessing past efforts and contemplating new ones should look at independent initiatives arising from the local level as an integral part of the post-conflict justice landscape, incorporating a perspective that encompasses bottom-up local efforts as well as top-down state or internationally-driven ones. Such local-level efforts often precede formal national-level programmes, and they can also follow on or extend such programs, making them more locally relevant. They are particularly important to unravel the complexities of local power dynamics, and may also more

[2] See J Cavallaro and S Albuja, 'The Lost Agenda: Economic Crimes and Transitional Justice in Latin America and Beyond' in this collection.

[3] In Guatemala, *ladino* refers to people who self-identify as non-Indian through their use of the Spanish language, non-use of traditional dress and the like. A majority of the Guatemalan population belongs to indigenous groups descended from the pre-Columbian inhabitants of the region. Although these groups identify themselves largely based on their languages and places of origin (eg Ki'che, Kequ'chi, K'achiquel, Achí, etc), in the last few years, they have begun to also self-identify as Maya, and that word will be used here to refer to the indigenous population as a whole.

[4] See R Wilson, *The Politics of Truth and Reconciliation in South Africa: Legitimizing the Post-Apartheid State* (Cambridge, Cambridge University Press, 2001).

[5] These include, but are not limited to, national court systems, truth commissions, infrastructure repairs, national education campaigns, etc.

[6] See, eg the work program of the Peruvian Commission for Truth and Reconciliation. Volume IV, ch 1 of the Commission's Final Report is entitled 'Violence in the Regions' and divides the country into several distinct regions with distinct histories of violence and repression. Commission for Truth and Reconciliation, *Final Report* (Lima, 2003), available online at http://www.cverdad.org.pe/ifinal (visited 16 June 2006).

easily tap into the agency of survivors and be less prone to large-scale patronage and corruption. At the very least, national and international initiatives should strive to be aware of, and not to undermine, local-level processes.

Part II of this chapter describes the nature of the conflict in Guatemala. Part III explores the possible advantages, and roles, of a focus on local-level efforts at social reconstruction and transformation.[7] Part IV looks at examples of local-level efforts in different parts of the country, including 'houses of memory', community-sponsored psycho-social interventions and community-generated exhumations, and mediation based on Mayan 'cosmovision'. Part V concludes that such efforts should be more systematically identified and supported in a post-conflict setting, both as building blocks and complements to a national approach, and that assessments of the reach of post-conflict justice efforts should include these types of initiatives within their parameters.

II THE COMPLEX NATURE OF THE ARMED CONFLICT AND THE POST-ARMED CONFLICT LANDSCAPE

The conflict in Guatemala began, depending on who is counting, with the Spanish invasion in the 16th century, with the overthrow of the democratically-elected Arbenz government by CIA-backed mercenaries in 1954, or with the rebellion of young army officers against the resulting dictatorship in 1960. In practice, most of the violence at issue today stems from selective state repression of outlawed opposition parties, trade unions, peasant leagues, student organisations and similar groups in the 1970s. In the 1980s the violence escalated, as the army put down armed revolutionary movements that had grown roots among the indigenous population of the western highlands, through bombings, massacres, scorched-earth policies, hunting down of refugees and concentration of survivors in army-controlled 'model villages'. Most of the victims were Mayan peasants: according to the UN truth commission, the Commission on Historical Clarification (CEH), acts of genocide against Mayans were carried out in at least four areas of the country.[8] Of the killings,

[7] These efforts are sometimes referred to as 'reconciliation'. While we understand this to mean the complex process by which individuals, families, communities and polities come to terms with past atrocities, conflicts and state repression, we are not convinced that the overtones of forgiveness and atonement implied by the term are necessarily applicable in every case. We prefer the term 'social reconstruction', although we add that this implies a transformative element, not simply a return to an unjust status quo. See also L Fletcher and H Weinstein, 'Violence and Social Repair: Rethinking the Contribution of Justice to Reconciliation' (2002) 24 *Human Rights Quarterly* 573.

[8] CEH, *Memoria del Silencio (Memory of Silence)* vol III. For accounts of the destruction of Mayan communities, see, eg R Carmack (ed), *Harvest of Violence: The Mayan Indians and*

disappearances, torture and destruction, the CEH found the army responsible for 93 per cent. Over 600 villages were completely destroyed, sometimes with no survivors. Women were raped on a massive scale; children and old people were targeted as bearers of culture; and crops, forests and animals were destroyed. The effects were devastating throughout a broad swathe of the country.

Layered on top of this violence committed by the organised state against its own people are a host of complexities. The country is divided into over 20 language groups that inhabit different (although overlapping) regions, mountainous valleys with little communication between them, and different histories, social composition and cultural practices. In some areas, Mayan communities lived next to *ladino* ones, while in others a *ladino* minority held local economic and/or political power within a largely Mayan town and in still others there were no *ladinos*. In some areas, land or water disputes were at issue, as were rising tensions between Catholics and Evangelical Christians. In fact, the contours of the conflict varied widely throughout the country, with some regions, such as the largely *ladino* eastern region of the country, remaining practically untouched by the 1980s political violence. Other areas were massively attacked or wiped out entirely and still others experienced more selective state attacks on community leaders.

The army played on and exacerbated these pre-existing divisions as well as personal feuds, for example, by issuing ID cards allowing freedom of movement to Evangelicals but not Catholics (who were widely viewed as supporting the insurgency). Army repression was aimed at replacing traditional religious and civic authorities with people aligned with the military, who benefited by their association, obtaining the lands (and sometimes widows) of those killed. Most importantly, the army created paramilitary forces known as Civil Defence Patrols (*Patrullas de Autodefensa Civil* (PAC). These forces served as the eyes and ears of the military in their villages, and were used as cannon fodder to sweep areas where the army believed there was guerrilla activity. They also committed many of the atrocities of the period, including some of the worst massacres. Some PAC members voluntarily took advantage of army sponsorship to settle old scores with neighbours or neighbouring villages, or to amass wealth and local power. However, substantial numbers of civil patrollers were made up of Mayan men who were intimidated or forced to join on pain of death. Most PACs were indigenous while their commanding officers were *ladino*, often local military commissioners. Thus,

the Guatemalan Crisis (Norman OK, University of Oklahoma Press, 1988); V Sanford, *Buried Secrets: Truth and Human Rights in Guatemala* (New York, Palgrave Macmillan, 2003).

> society was transformed by the army's coerced integration of the rural indigenous majority into its counter-insurgency design, with negative effects for indigenous and religious practices.[9]

Like most armed conflicts, the Guatemalan had both 'vertical' (state/citizenry) and 'horizontal' (neighbour/neighbour) aspects, with the relative weight of each varying among localities. Adding to this complexity is the net of complicities, betrayals, and duress designed by the army to tear apart the bonds holding communities together. Many families had members in both the guerrillas and the PAC, and many were forced to collaborate or to betray family and friends. PAC members were told that if they did not adequately repress the local population they themselves would be killed as presumptive insurgent sympathisers. Worse, the army in a number of cases forced PAC members to publicly kill other PAC members as supposed guerrilla collaborators.[10] In still other cases, PAC and army together forced villagers, and sometimes an entire village, to participate in the public killing or torture of community members or in desecration of their bodies.[11] These events continue to divide and traumatise communities even years later.

In the post-war period, conflicts within and between communities continue, exacerbated by the newly exalted position of some ex-PAC members as compared to the almost uniform destitution of their victims. Populations are heterogeneous: certain regions are now heavily populated by communities in which residents never left, while other regions house refugees who returned to their old communities or were forced to make their homes in new places, creating tensions with existing residents.[12] Sometimes, returning refugees found others in their homes and lands.[13] In some communities, everyone is a massacre survivor. Local structures of power are also heterogeneous: in some communities local power is held by ex-PAC members; in others some traditional authorities have been reconstituted; and in others new political forces, including Evangelical pastors, justices of the peace, or activists linked to national Mayan organisations

[9] R Sieder, 'War, Peace, Memory Politics in Central America' in A Barahona de Brito, C González-Enríquez and P Aguilar (eds), *The Politics of Memory: Transitional Justice in Democratizing Societies* (New York, Oxford University Press, 2001) 165.

[10] See the discussion of such events in Cucabaj and Zacualpa, Quiché in CEH, *Memoria del Silencio (Memory of Silence)* (n 8 above) at 43, 53.

[11] See, for example, Illustrative case 107 (the Acul massacre) in CEH, *Memoria del Silencio (Memory of Silence)* (n 8 above); see also REHMI, *Guatemala Nunca Mas*, vol 1 (n 1 above) at 35 (forced collaboration as a way of promoting collective complicity and the normalisation of violence). Of course, such practices are not limited to Guatemala, but have been a feature of many recent conflicts.

[12] ML Cabrera, *Violencia e Impunidad en Comunidades Mayas de Guatemala: La massacre de Xamán desde una perspectiva psicosocial* (Guatemala, ECAP, 2006) 85–91.

[13] For a description of one such community, see B Manz, *Paradise in Ashes: A Guatemalan Journey of Courage, Terror & Hope* (Berkeley CA, University of California, 2004).

have emerged. Fear of continued violence contributes to silence about the past, sometimes even within families, and has been manifest in myriad types of social disfunctionality, from lynchings to somatic illnesses. It is this degree of variation and complexity that makes international and national-level responses inadequate and, to some degree, irrelevant at the local level, and that requires further exploration of local-level responses.

III LOCAL, NATIONAL AND INTERNATIONAL RESPONSES TO ARMED CONFLICT AND SOCIAL BREAKDOWN

Relevance requires ownership. One common attribute of all kinds of local-level responses to past atrocities is that they are best able to ensure 'a comprehensive community-based approach that includes the opinions and ideas of those whose lives have been most directly affected'.[14] In addition, such responses tend to be more agile than national or international efforts, which because of their scope and complexity may come after local communities have engaged in their own form of—just or unjust—re-composition.[15] Such local responses can help compensate for some of the limits of other forms of post-armed conflict or transitional measures.

A Truth-Telling

In this context of variation and complexity, national-level fact-finding exercises must necessarily, by themselves, fall short. As mentioned, Guatemala had not one but two major investigative commissions. The first, organised by the Catholic Church, used some 700 bilingual lay Catholic statement-takers to interview people throughout the highlands around a number of open-ended themes. They collected over 5,000 testimonies and produced a four-volume report, *Guatemala Nunca Mas* ('Guatemala Never Again'), that detailed the kinds of violence, the effects, the history and, where possible, the names of both victims and perpetrators. The 1998 REHMI report was intended to both feed into, and set a standard for, what was expected to be a much weaker official truth commission.

The official commission, composed of German law professor Christian Tomuschat and Guatemalans Alfredo Balsells Tojo (a lawyer) and Otilia

[14] Fletcher and Weinstein, 'Violence and Social Repair' (n 7 above) at 638.

[15] For example, in Guatemala the worst period of violations took place in the early 1980s, yet because of the drawn-out peace negotiations and funding issues, the Truth Commission did not begin work until over a decade later, and presented its findings in 1998. See also the work of R Shaw, 'Remembering to Forget: Unmaking War for Child Ex-Combatants in Northern Sierra Leone', presented to the Nordic Africa Institute, Uppsala, May 21 2003 (on file with authors); and K Theidon, 'Justice in Transition: The Micropolitics of Reconciliation in Postwar Peru' (2006) 50 *Journal of Conflict Resolution* 1.

Lux (a Mayan educator), had a very short period in which to document and analyse 36 years of conflict, and a mandate that required the Commission not to individualise responsibilities. From this weak and much-criticised start,[16] the recommendations and conclusions turned out to be far stronger than had been expected by most human rights organisations, in part due to pressure from civil society groups and the existence of the REHMI report. The CEH also, importantly, found that in at least four areas of the country genocide had been committed.

Nonetheless, although the reports were extensive and alluded to the magnitude of the effects of *la violencia*, they do not—could not—cover all the victimised communities, nor all the local experiences. A truth commission must, due to its inherent time and space limitations, pick and choose illustrative and exemplary cases; not everyone will see their experience reflected in the report. At most, there will be a listing of their community, or of the names of the known victims. What is more, the Commission must, by necessity, pick its illustrative cases based on the amount of evidence available, with the result that they will not be the cases involving the worst violations, where there may be no survivors to bear witness or even to list the dead. Nor will they be the most common types of violations, since a search for illustrative cases may fail to consider all the places where broad patterns repeat again and again. Thus, in cases of massive violations, a truth commission report, no matter how well researched, will provide only a general, not a personal 'truth' to many.

Moreover, a short-term truth-seeking endeavour cannot hope to garner widespread trust among people of a deeply traumatised society, and thus the testimonies taken may be from those less affected, or more articulate, or from members of organised groups. Furthermore, without reaching all sectors of society, a partial, fictionalised or exaggerated past of a few may become the official narrative through the truth commission process.[17] Even under the best of circumstances, a truth commission can only hope to portray a snapshot of memory at a particular moment, and cannot capture the processes of memory changing over time.[18] Nor can a single opportunity to give testimony (whether public or privately) substitute for long-term rehabilitation of survivors. For these things, longer term, local-level processes are needed.

[16] See especially, R Wilson, 'The Politics of Remembering and Forgetting in Guatemala' in R Sieder (ed), *Guatemala After the Peace Accords* (London, Institute of Latin American Studies, University of London, 1998). See also R Sieder, 'Conclusions' in R Sieder (ed), *Guatemala After the Peace Accords* (London, Institute of Latin American Studies, University of London, 1998).

[17] J Zur, *Violent Memories: Mayan War Widows in Guatemala* (Boulder CO, Westview Press, 1998) 179.

[18] M Halbwachs, *The Collective Memory* (New York, Harper and Row, 1980) (French original *La Mémoire Collective* published in Paris in 1950). For more recent work on the

B Justice

A key demand of human rights advocates in the wake of massive atrocities is for those who are responsible to be individually brought to justice. In the last decade or so, an array of international and hybrid courts have been set up as national justice was judged unavailable or untrustworthy. At the same time, millions of dollars have been spent reforming, modernising, streamlining and otherwise attempting to change domestic judiciaries, prosecutors' offices and police forces. Although improvements have been made, in most post-armed conflict countries, including Guatemala, the justice system remains a poor venue for those seeking justice.

Years of repression and armed conflict drain legitimacy as well as resources from judicial systems. Judges, prosecutors and lawyers are killed, forced into exile, or survive through complicity with the regime. After the conflict, judges and lawyers involved in human rights-related cases continue to be subject to threats as well as tempted by corruption and bureaucratic inertia. These are problems that cannot obviously be solved at a local level.

There are deeper problems with judicial systems, however. Even before the years of armed conflict, the majority of poor, rural, Mayan Guatemalans did not see the justice system as a source of rights vindication. Instead, they saw it as at best irrelevant and at worst an incarnation of the discrimination and oppression to which they had been (and are) subject since colonial times. Even now, proceedings are opaque, held in a language that most speak imperfectly, and Maya are treated with disrespect and contempt throughout the system. Only the poor go to jail, but when crimes are committed against them suspects are hardly ever found. Variants on this situation are common to many post-armed conflict countries. What is more, it is unrealistic to expect even the best set of anti-impunity and judicial reform measures to reverse the centuries of warranted distrust of formal legal systems.

In societies where formal legal systems do not work for the majority, other forms of dispute resolution exist. These forms, under the names of 'traditional justice' or 'customary law', vary among regions, and often from place to place. Guatemala's Mayan communities, for example, have long had minor disputes settled by their own authorities, be they religious or secular (*cofrades*, Mayan priests or 'indigenous mayors'). The survival or revitalisation of these traditional authorities, or their replacement by other kinds of authority, varies from one municipality to another (see Part IV of this chapter). A focus on local-level justice can take into account

same subject, see, eg E Jelin, *State Repression and the Labors of Memory* (trans J Rein and M Godoy-Anativia) (Minneapolis, University of Minnesota Press, 2003).

these cultural variations, and can tailor dispute resolution mechanisms to forms that resonate with local populations and are recognised as their own.[19]

Recent trials involving serious crimes under international law exemplify the range of difficulty in using the justice system for such a complex and layered case as Guatemala. In 1995, a group of soldiers opened fire on recently-returned refugees in the village of Xamán, Chisec, Alta Verapaz, killing 11 people. A first trial resulted not only in the acquittal of the soldiers but, according to a case study, was a harrowing and hugely disappointing experience for the survivors, who felt mistreated and alienated by the tone of the legal proceedings.[20] It was only in 2004, after intense national and international pressure, that a lieutenant and 13 soldiers were sentenced to 40 years in prison for the killings. In another well-known case, it took 17 years and three attempts at prosecution for a local court to convict notorious PAC leader, Cándido Noriega of several killings, due in part to threats to judges and prosecutors.[21] And in Colotenango, a town in the far north of the country, a judge convicted PAC leaders in a massacre case, only to have a mob of ex-PAC members surround the jail and forcibly free the defendants, who have still not been found.[22] The national level justice system, which utilises national courts and domestic judges with all their shortcomings, does not work well for these cases.

One option might be to turn to international justice, assuming the political will could be found to do so (a dubious proposition). Even so, hybrid and international mechanisms create their own dilemmas. They have been roundly criticised for irrelevance to the local communities, lack of outreach, and problematic practices towards witnesses.[23] Problems of

[19] It is important not to romanticise traditional justice systems. Such systems generally do not deal well with serious (ie homicidal) crime; they can be patriarchal and exclusionary toward women and minorities; they can be coercive and create pressures on individuals to subsume their own needs in those of the 'community'; and they generally rely on a high degree of case-by-case discretion that can easily become arbitrariness. See L Waldorf, 'Mass Justice for Mass Atrocity: Rethinking Local Justice as Transitional Justice' (2006) 79 *Temple Law Review* 1; R Terris and V Inoue-Terris, 'A Case Study of Third World Jurisprudence—Palestine: Conflict Resolution and Customary Law in a Neopatrimonial Society' (2002) 20 *Berkeley Journal of International Law* 462 at 487.

[20] Cabrera, *Violencia e Impunidad en Comunidades Mayas de Guatemala* (n 12 above).

[21] Amnesty International, 'Guatemala's lethal legacy: Past impunity and renewed human rights violations', 28 February 2002 (AI Index: AMR 34/001/2002). Available online at http://www.amnesty.org/en/library/info/AMR34/001/2002/en.

[22] US State Department (Bureau of Democracy, Human Rights and Labor), 'Guatemala—Country Report on Human Rights Practices' 23 February 2001, available online at http://www.state.gov/g/drl/rls/hrrpt/2000/wha/775.htm.

[23] E Stover and HM Weinstein (eds), *My Neighbor, My Enemy: Justice and Community in the Aftermath of Mass Atrocity* (Cambridge, Cambridge University Press, 2004) and E Stover, *The Witnesses: War Crimes and the Promise of Justice at the Hague* (Philadelphia PA, University of Pennsylvania Press, 2005).

distance and lack of ownership may be exacerbated by the emerging practice which posits a division of labour between the national and international justice systems. The latter are to focus on the leaders and organisers—'those who bear the greatest responsibility'—leaving the 'little fish' to national actions.[24]

Given this emerging practice, and given the dysfunction of national prosecutorial and judicial systems, the 'impunity gap' in places like Guatemala is likely to be particularly large. Although focusing on leaders and organisers makes sense from a standpoint of both limited resources and moral culpability, it is often quite unsatisfying for victims. The army high command, even though survivors recognise its ultimate responsibility, may be as much of an abstraction as the state itself from a ground-level perspective.[25] Rather, people are interested in seeing in the dock those they saw and heard giving orders and committing atrocities: only then does justice take on a real face. Moreover, those who participated in and organised terror at the local level and who continue to enjoy impunity are often still 'the most powerful local members of the local apparatus of repression'.[26] It is galling and disturbing to have to live among such people, to see them flaunt their power (and often, wealth) and to feel permanently silenced and threatened by their very presence. For people to perceive a change in their daily lives, those people need to be removed from the scene.

An example of the complexities of justice at the local level comes from the attempts to prosecute those responsible for several 1982 massacres in the village of Río Negro near Rabinal. A group of soldiers commanded by Captain José Antonio Solares led some 40 civil patrollers from the nearby village of Xococ in the massacres. Several hundred villagers were killed (including at least 107 children), houses and possessions were burned, and 18 children were selected as 'war booty' to be slaves in the homes of PAC members. Unlike other cases, here apparently the Xococ civil patrollers acted knowingly and voluntarily, in part because of pre-existing tensions over land in the area. After many years, survivors asked for exhumation of the bones of those killed, and filed a criminal complaint against the military and against 12 PAC members, including the three Xococ PAC leaders. Their 1998 convictions were overturned by the regional appeals court, which also ordered the cases closed. A second trial, involving judges imported from outside the region, eventually resulted in a murder verdict

[24] See, eg the 'completion strategy' of the ICTY and ICTR: UNSC Res 1329 (30 November 2000) UN Doc S/RES/1329; UNSC Res 1503 (28 August 2003) UN Doc S/RES/1503; also UNSC Res 1534 (26 March 2004) UN Doc S/RES/1534.

[25] This is not to argue that survivors are uninterested in seeing the army high command and others of that ilk brought to justice, simply that doing so may be insufficient for many people. It is also true that prosecution of *only* subordinate officials, even if providing a face to survivors, may result in scapegoating those who are less responsible.

[26] Sanford, *Buried Secrets: Truth and Human Rights in Guatemala* (n 8 above) at 269.

against the three PAC leaders and a decision to reopen the remaining cases. An initial death sentence was commuted to life imprisonment.[27]

As Kathleen Dill points out, the local trial proved problematic for sorting out the relationship between national and local justice. National groups were more interested in focusing on the national military leaders—those most responsible—and had insufficient resources to support both local and national investigations. Community organisations, on the other hand, were far more interested in prosecuting the local PAC leaders, both because they were the visible face of repression and because of their continuing threats to communities in the region. Also, talking about the role of the PAC might open up a conversation about the different levels of coercion and complicity in Xococ and other nearby villages.

The focus on national-level prosecutions may make justice advocates miss important opportunities. In the Rio Negro case, for example, once it became clear that arrest orders would be issued against the PAC leaders, they reportedly entered into negotiations with a local victims' group. The PAC leaders wanted the victims group to support leniency in sentencing; in exchange, the victims' group wanted the men to admit their role and to testify as to who had given the orders to massacre the villages. In effect, the PAC leaders named Captain Solares, and the victims supported commutation of the sentences. A focus simply on high-level prosecutions would miss opportunities like this not only to build cases from the bottom up, but also to meet other important community objectives.

Finally, it is hard to see how formal justice systems, either criminal or civil, can adequately grapple with the ambiguities, mixed motives and shades of grey that colour most conflicts. Criminal justice requires categorisation as perpetrator, accomplice or innocent witness. It does not deal adequately with bystanders,[28] and even less well with the kinds of forced complicity described above. As discussed, the dynamics of the victim-perpetrator relationship varied greatly in Guatemala; in some places the roles were blurred while in others crimes were clearly committed by outsiders in uniform. Moreover, the roles varied over time; shifting allegiances were common. While the few cases involving PAC leaders that have come to trial so far seem to target individuals who acted voluntarily and intentionally, neither trials focused on the military high command nor those of PAC leaders would necessarily bring out the perverse dynamics of

[27] This account is taken from Kathleen Dill's detailed observations of the trials. K Dill, 'International Human Rights and Local Justice in Guatemala: The Rio Negro (Pak'oxom) and Agua Fría Trials' (2005) 17 *Cultural Dynamics* 323.

[28] See L Fletcher, 'From Indifference to Engagement: Bystanders and International Criminal Justice' (2005) 26 *Michigan Journal of International Law* 1014.

the PAC system or allow discussion in places where roles were blurred and complicated. But local-level trials of local perpetrators are more likely to do so.

C Reparations

In the wake of large-scale violence or repression, reparations can provide one of the most tangible manifestations of a government's recognition of victims' dignity and rights, and of its commitment not to repeat past wrongs. In an extremely poor country, reparations also have a chance to make a real difference in the lives of those who lost everything. Reparations can be material or symbolic, individual or collective.[29] According to the 2005 UN Principles on the subject, reparations can include restitution (of property, jobs, pensions, good name, etc), physical and mental rehabilitation, economic compensation, and a wide range of guarantees of non-repetition, including commemoration, legal and political reforms, and access to justice.[30]

In practice, however, when faced with poor societies, a weak state, and many victims, reparations programmes confront a great many challenges. For one, the state may not be in a position to efficiently and fairly administer programmes involving a great deal of money. After a prolonged conflict, societies are in some degree of disarray; government is either dysfunctional or overwhelmed or both; and past patterns of patronage or group-based politics may persist. There may be, as in Guatemala, little or no tradition of a democratic process and still less administrative capacity, along with a long history of self-dealing, capture of popular organisations, corruption, influence-peddling and the like, now exacerbated by the transformation of criminal and intelligence networks into organised crime rings.[31] Into this scenario comes a short-term burst of foreign aid money for both government and NGOs, one that after a few years will subside in favour of the next troubled post-conflict country. There is also an unhealthy tradition of centralisation[32]: by working mostly from the capital,

[29] See N Roht-Arriaza, 'Reparations Decisions and Dilemmas' (2004) 27 *Hastings International and Comparative Law Review* 157.

[30] UNGA Res 60/147 of 16 December 2005 adopting by consensus/without a vote the 'Basic Principles and Guidelines on the Right to a Remedy and Reparation for Victims of Gross Violations of International Human Rights Law and Serious Violations of International Humanitarian Law,' UN Doc A/C.3/60/L.24.

[31] SC Peacock and A Beltrán, *Hidden Powers in Post-Conflict Guatemala: Illegal Armed Groups and the Forces behind Them* (Washington Office on Latin America, Sept 2003) 43, 44, available online at http://cgrs.uchastings.edu/pdfs/HiddenPowersFull.pdf (visited 16 February 2008).

[32] This is a tradition common to Latin American countries. See RL Harris, 'Centralization and Decentralization in Latin America' in G Shabbir Cheema and DA Rondinelli (ed

organisations run the risk of misunderstanding community needs and realities as well as of stretching limited resources too thin. Trying to create large-scale social reconstruction projects in this context risks having them collapse into in-fighting over patronage and spoils, administrative disarray and cynicism.

Guatemala's considerable efforts at reparations illustrate some of the difficulties. The CEH recommended a national reparations programme, but while one was conceived in 2002, political opposition stalled its implementation until 2004. On paper, the National Reparations Programme (*Programa Nacional de Resarcimiento* (PNR)) sounds impressive. It has a 10-year mandate, with a planned annual budget of 300 million *Quetzales* (about US$37.5 million). The categories of violations to be repaired include forced disappearances, summary executions, physical or mental torture, forced displacement, forced recruiting of child soldiers, sexual violence and crimes against children, and massacres. Massacres and forced displacement can give rise to collective victims who can claim reparations as such.[33]

In practice, difficulties arose. The civil society organisations fought bitterly among themselves. Some Mayan representatives argued that if the reparations were for the victims of the genocide, they should be given directly to Mayan communities. Others wanted everyone who was a victim of human rights violations to be covered, pointing out that non-Mayans also suffered greatly from disappearances and killings. Although never ultimately resolved, the debate degenerated into charges and countercharges of racism and race baiting.[34] Furthermore, each constituency of the Commission fought for the patronage opportunities, and opportunities to [re]organise their political base, engendered by access to funds through the programme.

To compound matters, the reparations issue became conflated with the question of payments to former PAC members for services rendered to the military. Organised and vocal groups of ex-PACs claimed that the state owed them millions of dollars in unpaid wages and reparations for their own suffering during the internal armed conflict. Former President Portillo agreed to pay but only partially did so. With the creation of the PNR, many ex-PACs saw it as an opportunity to pressure the government to include them as a group to which the PNR should provide reparations. This outraged the victims' groups, and the government finally agreed to

Decentralization and Development: Policy Implementation in Developing Countries (Beverly Hills/London/New Delhi, Sage Publications, 1983).

[33] Acuerdo Gubernativo 258–2003, May 7 2003; Acuerdo Gubernativo 188–2004, July 7 2004 contain the basic structure and definitions of the programme.

[34] See, eg the press communiqué emitted by a number of Mayan organisations on July 15 2005, calling for the resignation of the programme's executive director on charges of racism.

exclude PACs from the PNR but pay them from a separate fund. From a grounds-eye view, it looked to many people like the government was distributing cheques right and left; all efforts to use reparations as a means of dignification of victims rather than a simple handout were lost in the in-fighting and confusion over who constitutes a 'victim' and why.

Smaller amounts distributed to a lot of different groups at the local level, with adequate training and accountability, stand a better chance of avoiding these problems. By staying smaller, or at least having decentralised offices and budgets, agencies and groups are less likely to fall victim to the inter-organisational problems that access to large amounts of money can reap. Decentralisation is now recognised as a component of responsive, responsible public administration.[35] On the other hand, localised reparations projects do mean that uniformity will be sacrificed, and that resources may flow to the most organised or most compelling places but not to others. We suggest that, given the conditions we describe, this will happen even under a nationally-administered scheme, with the difference that communities will have less ownership of the process and middle-men (be they bureaucrats or consultants) will take a greater cut.

D Reconciliation or Community Rebuilding

In addition to truth-telling, justice and reparations, the transitional justice literature has begun to grapple with the independent need to focus on creating some kind of dialogue, mutual recognition or other processes to knit back together the fabric of communities deliberately destroyed or damaged by armed conflict. This is especially important where communities turned on each other or on themselves ('horizontal' conflicts), where the wealth and power disparities between the two sides are less salient, and where former enemies need to continue to live side by side. Community healing, it seems, is not an automatic consequence of truth-telling, or even justice, although both might be components of it. Rather, it is a very context-specific exercise, which may involve ritual, religious practices, public discussion, apology, vetting, punishment and/or reparations.

A number of experiences have provided new impetus to thinking about community rebuilding. In East Timor, the Truth, Reception and Reconciliation Commission organised Community Reconciliation Processes that incorporated traditional *adat* dispute resolution, including a public airing of facts, apology and/or reparation and acceptance of responsibility, in

[35] See, eg WB Stöhr, JS Edralin and D Mani (eds), *Decentralization, Governance, and the New Planning for Local-Level Development* (Westport CT, Greenwood Press, 2001); P Bardhan, 'Decentralization of Governance and Development' available online at http://www.globetrotter.berkeley.edu/macarthur/inequality/papers/BardhanGovt.pdf.

exchange for conditional amnesty for low-level offenders.[36] The water rituals of Mozambique and Sierra Leone cleansed the child soldiers of their crimes and reincorporated them into their communities with a cool, non-violent, heart.[37] In Peru, local communities found ways first to dehumanise, and then to rehumanise—through public reincorporation ceremonies involving truth-telling, apology and symbolic punishment—those who had joined *Sendero Luminoso*.[38] In Cambodia, religious as well as local civic authorities staged ceremonies to welcome back Khmer Rouge soldiers who laid down their arms in the 1980s.[39] Although Rwandan *gacaca* traditional dispute resolution has now been appropriated by the government and substantially modified, in the wake of the 1994 genocide some communities spontaneously employed *gacaca* techniques to resolve land and other disputes.[40]

These experiences are, almost by definition, local, since they rely heavily on specific cultural traditions and mass community involvement. They arise generally without central government or international intervention, through local religious or community actors. In Guatemala, the continuing stranglehold on local power by those who committed the atrocities has limited the extent of these initiatives, although, going forward, they may become more important, as detailed below.

IV GUATEMALAN POST-ARMED CONFLICT LOCAL INITIATIVES

Guatemala's post-armed conflict experiences with local-level initiatives encompass a wide range of activities. These combine elements of truth-telling, local justice, commemoration, and the creation of new spaces for dialogue. Almost all share certain characteristics: an emphasis on Mayan practice, a connection to present-day issues and tailoring to the specific needs of the place and people.

[36] P Burgess, 'East Timor's Community Reconciliation Process: A New Tool for Reconciliation?' in Roht-Arriaza and J Mariezcurrena (eds), *Transitional Justice in the Twenty-First Century: Beyond Truth vs. Justice* (Cambridge, Cambridge University Press 2006).

[37] P Hayner, Unspeakable Truths: Confronting State Terror and Atrocity (New York, Routledge, 2001); Shaw, 'Remembering to Forget: Unmaking War for Child Ex-Combatants in Northern Sierra Leone' (n 15 above). For an account of similar experiences in Uganda with the reintegration of Lords Resistance Army fighters, see M Lacey, 'Atrocity Victims in Uganda Choose to Forgive, *NewYork Times*, April 18 2005.

[38] Theidon, 'Justice in Transition: The Micropolitics of Reconciliation in Postwar Peru' (n 15 above).

[39] J Iverson, 'Center Stage: The Contributions of Non-State Actors to Accountability and Reconciliation in Cambodia' (December 2005), unpublished paper on file with author.

[40] Waldorf, 'Mass Justice for Mass Atrocity: Rethinking Local Justice as Transitional Justice' (n 19 above).

A 'Houses of Memory'

In several communities hard-hit by massacres, community members and supporters have developed variations on community museums. These community museums, designed by local groups and including the local customs and history as well as references to the massacres and destruction, exist in Panzós (Alta Verapaz), Rabinal (Baja Verapaz) and Santiago Atitlán (Sololá), all sites of extensive massacres and repression and local areas where survivors have been particularly well organised and proactive. These museums continue and deepen the documentation work begun by the truth commissions, and combine that work with compilation of oral histories and other commemorative techniques.

The community museum in Panzós commemorates of one of the first large-scale rural massacres, in 1978. Working with ideas of community museums and collective healing, the *Historial* for Peace includes three elements: compiling and publishing records of local cultural practices and traditions and local experiences of *la violencia* up until the signing of the Peace Accords; building physical memorials; and erecting community peace museums.

The central element of this project was based on community participation and direction. Thus, respected leaders of the community—two from each village, elected by the community elders according to Mayan tradition—participated closely with *Historial* employees through every facet of the *Historial*'s work. These 'historical promoters' volunteered to meet weekly to discuss the progress of the *Historial* and attend multiple workshops on memorialisation. Community participation was especially important with regard to the collection of personal narratives and memories of local traditions and their changes over time. Through individual and collective interviews the *Historial* aimed to publish a book in Spanish and *Q'eqchi'* which documents local customs and traditions, such as midwifery and religious groups, and how they changed during and since the internal armed conflict. A second publication was based on hundreds of testimonies about local experiences during *la violencia*. This document is intended as a supplement to the CEH and REMHI reports, bringing to light the specifics of the regional experience, which was impossible to do at the time of the nationwide truth-seeking endeavours. Furthermore, the *Historial* was able to record more testimonies, not only because they concentrate their efforts on a smaller region than the CEH or REMHI reports, but also because they are connected to the community and therefore trusted by it. Being integrated into the Panzós area, it is more likely that individuals will open up and contribute to the *Historial*'s project.

Through its unique 'historical promoters' component, the *Historial* has also made the development of a commemorative museum a truly communal project. Through consistent collaboration over a period of time, community outsiders were able to incorporate themselves into the community and grasp the memorialisation needs in the Panzós area. The promoters were brought to the nation's capital early in the process of the *Historial* in order for them to better understand the layout of a museum, and later they participated in numerous workshops about the creation of commemorative rooms. The promoters act as liaisons between *Historial* employees and community members, and thereby increase community input and participation in *Historial* activities.

Originally, the *Historial* planned to work with all communities in the Panzós area, each with its own commemorative room, and ultimately to build the actual community museum in the town of Panzós proper. But almost from the project's inception there were problems regarding working simultaneously with communities that were composed primarily of survivors and communities that were made up in large part of former PACs. Many survivors refuse to work with former PACs; the wounds of the conflict are just too fresh. By this time the local government of Cahoboncito, a former-PAC dominated village, had donated a one-room building intended for a commemorative room. The *Historial*'s peace museum project and commemorative rooms depend on these donations for the space needed to install them, thereby necessitating the continued partnership with the Cahoboncito community. So they accepted the donation, and the building is used as a community centre for Cahoboncito. Although a dialogue between the ex-PACs and the survivors has not yet resulted from the *Historial*'s project, both groups have the space to express and come to terms with their memories, and the *Historial*'s organisers hope some dialogue will eventually result. It is not clear how far this project can progress, but variants on it are being developed in many communities around the country.

B Exhumations, Memorials and Psycho-Social Community Interventions

Guatemala is riddled with clandestine and unmarked graves. Part of the military's strategy of terror was to leave bodies in town squares and along the sides of roads, and to prohibit family members from recovering or properly burying those killed. As is true in other places, the lack of appropriate burial ceremonies and of a place to mourn and remember the dead has been a source of anguish,[41] especially since the local culture posits a continuing relationship between the dead and the living that requires proper attention to the dead. As elsewhere, one of the most common needs

[41] See E Stover and R Shigekane, 'Exhumation of Mass Graves: balancing legal and humanitarian needs' in Stover and Weinstein, *My Neighbor, My Enemy* (n 23 above) at 95.

of survivors is to recover the body and rebury it with the appropriate (Catholic, Mayan, Protestant or a combination) ceremonies.

Since the early 1990s, two groups of forensic anthropologists have been hard at work exhuming clandestine gravesites; over 700 have been discovered so far, with years more work to go.[42] These exhumations are not simply technical affairs, but have deep connections to community mental health and commemoration efforts as well as to local justice processes. The process requires extensive preparation of family members (both for finding the remains and for the risk of not finding them) and has often become the collective task of a community. Community members provide food for forensic anthropology teams, and help with digging and erecting the temporary structures needed for a major exhumation.

Exhumation of a clandestine grave cannot proceed without the presence of the Public Prosecutor's office or a judge, and the identification of bodies, by law, triggers a criminal investigation. (In practice few identifications actually lead to a criminal complaint being filed, much less pursued). For local communities where PACs were involved in the crimes, the tie-in to the criminal justice system raises the stakes, since the judicial authorities are there to take statements from witnesses who may well implicate individuals still living in or near the area. A pending exhumation often leads to renewed threats against victims' families and local social activists. On the other hand, the presence of judicial authorities may impede the ability of communities to use the exhumations as a moment for acknowledgement of wrongdoing. While there have been several anecdotal accounts of former PAC members and supporters helping out at, or even showing remorse towards victims' families in the course of exhumations, any public acknowledgement of responsibility for the crimes would lead to an automatic duty on the part of the Public Prosecutor or judge to file a criminal complaint against the individual(s) involved. So PAC members generally hold their peace.

Once bodies have been exhumed and, where possible, identified, many local communities have organised massive public reburial ceremonies.[43] These have been moving, impressive affairs, where hundreds of people turn out to accompany the coffins of the dead to the burial ground, prayers are said, food and memories are shared, and a marker or memorial has been erected to mark the names of those buried there. Where no bodies have been recovered, plaques, markers or memorials have been set up at the massacre sites. These memorials, sometimes with large crosses, others with Mayan altars but always listing the names of the dead, can become quite

42 See Sanford, *Buried Secrets: Truth and Human Rights in Guatemala* (n 8 above).

43 The use of public reburials as a way of creating public memory spaces is not unique to Guatemala. See, eg KP Benziger, 'The Funeral of Imre Nagy: Contested History and the Power of Memory Culture' (2000) 12 *History and Memory* 142.

elaborate as well as contested. For example, outside Rabinal, the Rio Negro memorials involve a series of murals depicting the massacres (described above) and several different markers with victims' names. After a first, modest memorial was pulled down by civil patrollers from Xococ, the village associations rebuilt a bigger concrete memorial, and again inscribed it with the names of murdered villagers, adding that they were 'killed by the civil patrollers from Xococ'. Similar murals exist in Comalapa and other towns of the Chimaltenango area. These often constitute the first community recognition of local history.

With the support of local civil society, including the Human Rights Consortium, the *Historial* for Peace spearheaded an initiative to create a community memorial for the victims of the 1978 Panzós massacre. Designed by community members to be a functional space and a 'living monument', the *Monument for Peace and Tolerance* sits adjacent to the site of the massacre victims' mass grave. The site was exhumed in 1997; the victims reburied by their families in a mass interment ceremony a year later. The monument is an open-air chapel, thus incorporating both the Mayan tradition of connecting with the natural world and the Christian tradition of praying inside a chapel. Furthermore, the monument has one Christian cross in the front and an offerings altar, which was specially designed in a truncated elliptical form to represent the interrupted lives of the slaughtered men, women and children. Adjacent to the Christian altar, directly over the site of the former clandestine grave, is a second altar for Mayan ceremonies. Community members who sacrificed workdays in order to participate carried out the bulk of the monument's construction. The altar's common use demonstrates how a memorialisation effort can genuinely become integrated into a community.

These initiatives arise from, and are organised and financed at, the local level, sometimes with support from national NGOs, local community organisations or religious authorities. Because they arise from local, deeply felt initiatives, they are protected and 'owned' by community members. They stand in stark contrast to the lack of any kind of national memorial relating to the armed conflict—although individual plaques marking where victims were killed dot Guatemala City, there is no central cemetery marker or memorial, and a planned museum has not yet opened its doors.

Exhumations and reburials are stressful for survivors, reviving old memories and traumas. In some communities, people have never spoken of what happened to them even within their own families; this is especially true of women victims of sexual violence. A culture of fear is one in which trauma-associated stresses become exacerbated, making daily life more difficult by affecting emotional stability and a person's sense of worth. A number of groups have developed methodologies for working with communities before, during and after exhumations to combat the culture of fear developed over years of terror and to allow people to begin to speak of, and make sense of, their experiences. Accompaniment programmes and individual and group mental health programmes emerged as a response to the shifts in culture that followed the 36 years of conflict in Guatemala. Although each programme uses its own techniques for alleviating some of the psychological stresses and engaging communities in dialogues about their past and the difficulties of living in a culture of violence, fear and silence, all use a long-term approach in their work. Much of the success of these programmes lies with how much the community trusts them. Trust in Guatemala is built by demonstrating that the organisation will not abandon the community—as the government and the guerrillas both did during the internal armed conflict—thereby making the programme an enduring one. For this, the organisation must be embedded in a local area.

A number of psycho-social intervention programmes are firmly grounded in Mayan *cosmovision*, an abstract term that incorporates philosophy, ideology and history. Each community interprets the specificities of Mayan *cosmovision* differently, and in some places more memory exists of the old ways of doing things than in others where specific rituals need to be reinvented. In the context of exhumations, fire-based ceremonies are often used to cleanse survivors of guilt and to communicate with those who were killed.[44] Key elements to Mayan *cosmovision* include the belief in place-based spirituality related to the local landscape, the interconnectedness of nature and people, and deference to elders. By incorporating Mayan traditions into their work, these organisations are more accessible to community members who might otherwise be sceptical of a programme that relates back to the internal armed conflict. Moreover, attempting to demystify *cosmovision* to a larger Guatemalan public, including *ladinos*, is one of the first steps necessary in a rehumanisation process of all those affected by, and involved in, a perennially racist and exclusionary society. At the same time, most organisations working with Mayan rituals do not work solely on post-conflict trauma, but also incorporate either a focus on new forms of dispute resolution (see below) or a focus on health, education and empowerment. The focus is not solely on survivors as victims, but as bearers of a valuable history and culture.

The Mayan organisations as well as non-Mayan psycho-social programs have focused their energies on working with survivors of the conflict, deliberately choosing to concentrate on working with this group rather than both survivors and perceived victimisers. Given that many survivors are neighbours with people who actively served as agents of the state, psycho-social intervention workers understand that this is not a permanent strategy. Focusing on one group was a conscious decision, however, in

[44] Interviews, Domingo Hernández, who has worked with a number of groups using Mayan customs as part of exhumation-related accompaniment (2004 and 2006).

order to concentrate the bulk of the psycho-social intervention organisation's attention on those most traumatised, so as to allow them the time needed to at least partially heal before they would be willing to face and work with their victimisers in rebuilding their society. The idea is that eventually these organisations will be able 'to provide a psychologically safe space'[45] for exchange and the reconstruction of community trust.

C Dispute Resolution

A number of locally-based organisations are attempting to use old, revived and reformed Mayan practices for resolution of present-day disputes. In part, this work is driven by the persistence of tensions around land and resources, and in part by burgeoning domestic violence and common criminality, which has in turn spawned incidents of lynching.[46] It is also driven by the continuing dysfunction and discriminatory practices of the formal justice system, which has never recovered the trust of most Mayans. By tailoring their mediation and dispute resolution techniques to both the culture and the underlying issues and history of each zone, these *Defensoría* groups[47] are setting the stage for a new relationship within communities, where disputes are settled peacefully. They are also beginning to redefine the relationship between justice and the state in a multicultural society, through methods which have not yet—but may eventually—play a role in resolving disputes over the past.

Some of the conflict resolution work involves dealing with individuals accused of stealing, wife beating and other crimes (although generally not homicide or rape). With regard to justice, Mayan beliefs stress that the goal in dealing with those who have committed crimes is getting them to understand their mistakes and reintegrating them into the community, not punishment. The goal is to make the individual recognise that they have done something unwarranted[48] and that they need to develop 'shame' or a social conscience. This usually involves a public meeting including the family, victim(s) and whoever else may be affected. Punishments may include public discussion and acknowledgement by the wrongdoer, or, in serious cases, whipping with a tree switch (explained as releasing positive

[45] D Ajdukovic and D Corkalo, 'Trust and Betrayal in War' in Stover and Weinstein, *My Neighbor, My Enemy* (n 23 above) at 295.

[46] It is also perhaps an attempt to re-appropriate and revert the use of Mayan symbols and beliefs by the military, which tried to create the belief that the military embodied the spirits of the mountains. See R Wilson, *Maya Resurgence In Guatemala: Q'Eqchi Experiences* (Norman OK, University of Oklahoma Press, 1999)

[47] There are a number of such groups, including *Defensoría Maya*, *Defensoría Indígena Ki'che*, *Saq'be* and *Ukux'be* in Chimaltenango, etc.

[48] The K'iche word 'awas' means both crime and sin, and refers to something that should not be done: Interview, Domingo Hernández (2006).

energies rather than as a punitive measure) or temporary or permanent banishment or ostracism. Such methods, while highly controversial from the standpoint of international human rights law, are considered highly effective by some traditional community leaders. In cases of conflicts between communities, dialogue and mediation takes place in mass meetings of both communities, preceded by careful preparation with religious (Mayan and Christian) and secular leaders.

We found little evidence that these Mayan *cosmovisión*-based dispute resolution practices have been applied to tensions arising from the legacy of the armed conflict itself, rather than current disputes. In part, this is a timing issue: after more than 20 years from the worst massacres, people in many places no longer base their identity solely on their status as victim or perpetrator, and although those tensions persist they have been joined by newer sources of tension—economic, familial or political—that often involve different groupings. Paradoxically, while in some senses 'too late', in another it may be 'too soon', as the local power relationships between former perpetrators and their victims continue largely to favour the first group. Ex-PAC members and army representatives continue to wield economic, political and military power at the local level, and to be able to threaten others. These people have no interest in reintegration into a community or in acknowledging their past acts, so there are no grounds for invoking any local dispute resolution process. The potential is there: we were told of a recent case in which a Ki'che widow invoked the help of a *Defensoría Indígena* to claim the return of land stolen by a PAC member years before. But whether the techniques of dialogue and mediation used to deal with thievery and thuggishness can deal with the sequelae of plunder and massacre is still an unknown.

V CONCLUSIONS

These local-level initiatives can tailor their strategies to the unique experiences of each geographic region and community. They can foster the integration of cultural practices, and promote participation and a sense of ownership, making such initiatives sustainable beyond the short window of external project financing. They can begin to bring about a cultural shift. Still, certain problems emerge from working at the local level, especially for those trying to design post-conflict social reconstruction policies.

First, there is a question of whether the kinds of spontaneous, culturally-specific commemoration seen in Guatemala, and the local dialogue and reincorporation ceremonies seen elsewhere, lose their value if 'programmed' or even encouraged by governments or international actors. After all, part of the strength of such initiatives is that they are insider-driven and a product of local initiative. In other words, the kinds of local-level initiatives that seem to work best do so without any formalisation in Western systems of aid and consultation, much less in legal commitments, and may be so place-and time-specific that they cannot be duplicated. While this may be so—and indeed, the absolute specificity of such initiatives and practices may be one of their strengths—at the least transitional justice practitioners need to look carefully and take into account such local dynamics. The existence and nature of such local practices may provide important clues as to what will, or will not resonate at a national level, what kinds of 'reconciliation' have already happened and what remains to be done. The careful documentation and study of such practices is also important to assess the success or failure of a 'transition', as well as to understand what people understand to be justice.

Secondly, while the actual development of local-level practices may need to be left to the local population, at the least governments, international agencies and transitional justice practitioners can aim to 'do no harm'. For example, an amnesty law or de facto amnesty may give one side of the conflict an impunity that allows them to avoid engaging in any recognition of their acts or dialogue with their victims, since there is no incentive to do so.[49] In Guatemala, lack of a law allowing some benefit to accrue to ex-perpetrators who provided valuable information and were even sometimes prepared to acknowledge their role also impeded local dialogue efforts.

Thirdly, in designing national post-armed conflict initiatives space can be left for local precursors or follow-ons. Thus, for example, a truth commission can plan on working through regional offices not only to obtain and collate testimony, but also to take advantage to identify and support efforts to deepen local understandings of what happened through community mapping or community museums. Many times the chance to speak to an official commission will provide a mobilising spark for communities, whether it takes the form of gathering or rehearsing their testimony or of organising hearings or statement-taking. Those efforts should not be seen simply in function of the overall national report, but also as starting points for ongoing local initiatives.

Similarly, exhumations are not simply about recovering bodies, or even about preparing judicial cases, but can be starting points both for commemorative activities and for local-level psycho-social intervention work. The presence of sympathetic, trained outsiders over a sustained period of time may also provide a neutral party to help community organisations begin thinking about what a fruitful dialogue with ex-adversaries might

[49] See Theidon, 'Justice in Transition: The Micropolitics of Reconciliation in Postwar Peru' (n 15 above). For example, in Peru an amnesty law for some ex-*Senderistas* immunised them from having to participate in community-based public reintegration of those who had supported Sendero.

entail. In some areas, local power disparities may impede such dialogue, but in others the creation of a safe space and a neutral arbiter steeped in local culture may provide an opening. This is especially true in areas where many of those who collaborated with the military did so under duress, as with PAC members in parts (but not all) of Guatemala.

Attention to the local level will mean thinking specifically about a rebalancing of local power away from victimisers, and about how to create new and more equitable relationships between those who played more ambivalent roles as PAC members and those who bore the brunt of the violence. In part, this involves recalibration of the balance between support for trials of the leaders and organisers and support for those of local-level operatives who continue to exercise power at the municipal and village levels. This is not just a question of criminal trials, but of land and household goods restitution and vetting of local military, police and political office-holders. It may be that, given the shortcomings of the formal justice system, some of these issues can be better worked out through alternative systems of dispute resolution.

Finally, a local-level focus might prompt some re-evaluation of funding for transitional justice initiatives. The time frame would have to be considerably longer—thought of in terms of decades. Decentralisation and responsiveness to bottom-up initiatives with small quantities of funds, rather than large-scale mega-programmes, would align post-armed conflict initiatives with much thinking in the development area. On the other hand, a focus on the local might lead merely to increased funding for local NGOs, perpetuating the weakness of the state as well as the project-driven dynamic that now transforms all social activism into an NGO seeking external project funding, a dynamic that hobbles the re-emergence of viable social movements in Guatemala. Keeping things small might more easily create opportunities for local residents (even very poor ones) to contribute part or all of the financing of 'their' projects.

Thus, we are not arguing that national or international initiatives should be abandoned, simply enriched and more carefully calibrated. The lessons learned regarding the importance of a localised approach to social reconstruction underscore the role of local communities as cornerstones of wider-scale human organisations, and the ways in which different post-armed conflict strategies work together. Without the building blocks carefully understood and differentiated, larger-scale attempts at social reconstruction will surely crumble.

8

The Political Economy of Transitional Justice in Timor-Leste

ELIZABETH STANLEY

I INTRODUCTION

THIS CHAPTER EXAMINES the mechanisms that have emerged to provide transitional justice for the people of Timor-Leste (formerly East Timor)—principally, the 'Ad Hoc Human Rights Court', the 'Special Panels for Serious Crimes', the 'Commission on Reception, Truth and Reconciliation' and the 'Commission on Truth and Friendship'. Through this study,[1] it is argued that there is a 'political economy' of transitional justice. The term 'political economy' is taken here to describe the changing ways in which local, national and international political systems connect with economic forces. Thus, a specific focus is developed on how economic and political agendas have, in practice, impacted on the potential of these bodies to establish 'truth' or to do 'justice'.

The chapter shows that there is a political economy of transitional justice that has inhibited opportunities to discover the 'truth' or to bring perpetrators to account. This issue is most explicit in the operations of the courts, the Panels and the 'Friendship' Commission that have been implemented 'from above', by international institutions and national governments. These initiatives have a number of flaws—they have embedded impunity, engaged in 'othering' and exclusionary practices, and consolidated inequalities at global, regional and national levels—which have ensured that neither the 'truth' nor 'justice' has been fully pursued. However, the issue of political economy is also apparent in the methods of the 'Truth and Reconciliation' Commission that was inspired from the 'bottom up'. While this venture offers a more hopeful vision of transitional justice, it has also practised in ways that have re-iterated inequalities of

[1] The author's research project examined torture and transitional justice in Timor-Leste. During 2004 and 2005, she undertook three in-depth research visits, interviewing torture survivors and transitional justice workers.

power and economy at the local and regional levels. As a result, some groups have experienced less 'truth' or 'justice' than others. These failures have served to create further conflict within a country struggling to deal with a violent and repressive past.

II THE BACKDROP OF REPRESSION

The situation of Timor-Leste irredeemably changed on 25 April 1974, following the Portuguese decision to leave colonial posts; the result was a power vacuum in East Timor. Three principal parties, 'Fretilin' (the Front for an Independent East Timor), 'UDT' (Timorese Democratic Union) and 'Apodeti' (Timorese Popular Democratic Association), emerged and a short civil war ensued. Fretilin took popular support yet, for economic, political and ideological reasons, the Indonesian government proposed that an independent Timor could not exist.[2]

On 28 November 1975, Fretilin declared East Timor's independence at the United Nations (UN). Nine days later, the Indonesian government invaded, and the subsequent occupation lasted almost 25 years. The Timorese truth commission estimates that up to 183,000 people were killed as a result of conflict. People died in massacres, bombing raids or other military operations. Tens of thousands were starved to death in the 'resettlement camps' established by the Indonesian military to move people from the mountains to closely surveilled, low-lying villages. Timorese people were routinely forcibly removed from their homes and land, 'disappeared', raped, detained without trial and tortured.[3]

The Timorese people were finally given a vote on 30 August 1999 and, despite severe intimidation, they voted for independence. The Indonesian response was swift—over 1,400 people were murdered, thousands were raped, beaten and tortured, over 75 per cent of the country's infrastructure was destroyed, over 60,000 homes burnt down and approximately 550,000 civilians fled into the mountains for safety or were forced across the border into West Timor.[4] A UN military force eventually landed on 20 September 1999 and, as Indonesian troops and militias left, peace was established. In May 2002, the country gained independence. Xanana Gusmão, the new President, rejoiced, 'Today we are a people standing on

2 See A Nairn, 'Foreword' in C Pinto and M Jardine, *East Timor's Unfinished Struggle: Inside the Timorese Resistance* (Boston, South End Press, 1997); J Taylor, *Indonesia's Forgotten War: The Hidden History of East Timor* (London, Zed Books, 1991).

3 *Comissão de Acolhimento, Verdade e Reconciliacão de Timor-Leste* (CAVR), 'Chega! The Report of the Commission for Reception, Truth, and Reconciliation in Timor-Leste' (Dili, CAVR, 2005).

4 *Ibid* at pt 3.21.625.

equal footing with the rest of the world'.[5] These spirited words reflected the stance of a Timorese population that demanded international recognition, and which viewed the UN and powerful states as having a moral obligation to pursue acknowledgement, legal accountability and redress for violation.

III THE FLAWS OF TRANSITIONAL JUSTICE 'FROM ABOVE'

These Timorese aspirations were quickly acknowledged by the UN's 'International Commission of Inquiry', established to ascertain the situation in 1999. In their report, Commissioners argued that Timorese victims 'must not be forgotten in the rush of events to redefine relations in the region' and they recommended an international tribunal.[6] Given the seriousness of the crimes as well as the 'trusteeship' relationship the UN had developed with Timor, they reasoned that the responsibility for addressing international justice fell on the UN.[7] Kofi Annan, then UN Secretary-General, provided a more muted response, detailing that, while the UN had 'an important role to play', he was particularly 'encouraged by the commitment shown by President Abdurrahman Wahid to uphold the law'.[8] He proposed that the Indonesian government should be supported in prosecuting those responsible themselves[9]—these efforts would be 'closely monitor[ed] to ensure that they were both credible and reflected human rights standards.[10]

In place of an international tribunal for Timor-Leste, a range of transitional justice initiatives has subsequently been implemented. These include: (i) the Jakarta-based 'Ad Hoc Human Rights Court', established

[5] J Nevins, *A Not-So-Distant Horror: Mass Violence in East Timor* (Ithaca NJ, Cornell University Press, 2005) 154.

[6] Report of the International Commission of Inquiry on East Timor to the Secretary-General (31 January 2000) UN doc A/54/726, para 146.

[7] *Ibid*. Three UN Special Rapporteurs visited the region in 1999. Their report also recommends the creation of an international tribunal. See 'Situation of Human Rights in East Timor' (10 December 1999) UN doc A/54/660.

[8] Identical Letters Dated 31 January 2000 from the Secretary-General addressed to the President of the General Assembly, the President of the Security Council and the Chairperson of the Commission on Human Rights (31 January 2000) UN doc A/54/726.

[9] *Ibid*. Explanations for this include: (i) the high costs and slow progress of the ICTR and ICTY had decreased support for a similar body; (ii) there was optimism for a new 'human-rights conscious' Indonesia; and (iii) Security Council members wanted to re-establish good relations with Indonesia as soon as possible. See M Hirst and H Varney, *Justice Abandoned? An Assessment of the Serious Crimes Process in East Timor* (New York, International Criminal Tribunal for Jakarta, 2005); Komnas HAM, *Report of the Indonesian Commission of Investigation into Human Rights Violations in East Timor* (Jakarta, Komnas Ham, 2000).

[10] UN letters (n 8 above). See P Burgess, 'Justice and Reconciliation in East Timor. The Relationship between the Commission for Reception, Truth and Reconciliation and the Courts' (2004) 15 *Criminal Law Forum* 135.

by the Indonesian government in 2000; (ii) the 'hybrid' serious crimes process created in 2000—incorporating the 'Special Panels for Serious Crimes' (SPSC, the courts), the 'Serious Crimes Unit' (SCU, the prosecution unit) and the Defence Lawyers Unit; (iii) the Commission for Reception, Truth and Reconciliation (known by its Portuguese acronym, 'CAVR'[11]) that operated from 2002; and (iv) the 'Commission of Truth and Friendship' (CTF), formed by the governments of Indonesia and Timor-Leste in 2005.

With the exception of the CAVR (that is identified, here, as a mechanism that encourages transitional justice 'from below'), these schemes have each been condemned for being 'controversial' and implemented without 'sufficient or meaningful consultation with the East Timorese' people.[12] These 'top-down' transitional justice initiatives may be critiqued on a number of grounds. First, they have been used to provide 'political cover' or immunity for certain types of perpetrators, particularly Indonesian officials; secondly, they have often engaged in the exclusion and 'othering' of Timorese people; and thirdly, they have failed to make a challenge to the regional power and structural relations that underpinned violations in the first instance.

A Entrenching Political Cover and Impunity

In the UN Security Council's Report on transitional justice, the 'rule of law' is stated to be at the heart of the UN's mission.[13] This means that

> all persons . . . and entities . . . including the State itself, are accountable to laws that are publicly promulgated, equally enforced and independently adjudicated, and which are consistent with international human rights norms and standards.

Despite this, such principles have not always been vigorously pursued by the transitional justice initiatives for Timor-Leste. While these mechanisms 'from above' have provided 'political cover' (that is, they have given the appearance that something has been done to attain justice) they have often entrenched impunity, particularly for Indonesian officials. As detailed below, this situation has emerged through: an intense lack of political and judicial will in Indonesia to prosecute or convict perpetrators; the limited resources, poor management and planning afforded to transitional justice measures by the UN; and the Timorese government's decision to halt

[11] *Comissão de Acolhimento, Verdade e Reconciliacão de Timor-Leste.*

[12] S Linton, 'New Approaches to International Justice in Cambodia and East Timor' (2002) 845 *International Review of the Red Cross* 93 at 106.

[13] UNSC, Report of the Secretary-General to the Security Council, 'The Rule of Law and Transitional Justice in Conflict and Post-Conflict Societies' (23 August 2004) UN doc S/2004/616 at para 6.

prosecutions in favour of positive bilateral relations with its economically powerful neighbour.

It appears that the Ad Hoc Human Rights Court was established to quell criticism against the Indonesian government and to discourage the UN from establishing an international tribunal. While declaring that they would 'ensure full accountability', Indonesian officials managed to protect their personnel through a legal process that was 'intended to fail'.[14] The Jakarta trials consistently illustrated the deep 'lack of political will to prosecute and accept the outcome of the legal process' within the Attorney General's office and the Indonesian government.[15]

Commencing work on 14 March 2002, the Court's jurisdictional mandate ensured that investigations excluded most violations—it examined just three (Liquiça, Suai and Dili) of Timor-Leste's 13 districts, for events that occurred during two months, April and September 1999. The political and judicial disregard for the process of justice was, however, exemplified in numerous other operational standards. As the UN Commission on Human Rights[16] notes, prosecution staff failed to undertake thorough investigations despite the extensive information available to them; they lodged weak indictments that did not sustain arguments regarding crimes against humanity; there were limited numbers of experienced court personnel; there was consistent intimidation of and hostility to witnesses by judges, court staff and defendants; and judges failed to punish individuals in a way that reflected the seriousness of the violations. Of the 18 defendants brought to trial, 12 were initially acquitted and six convicted.[17] Following appeals, five had their convictions overturned. In the end, only one (Eurico Guterres, the Timorese leader of the Aitarak militia) was convicted—he was handed down a 10-year sentence at his 13 March 2006 Supreme Court hearing. Overall, the Court has demonstrated a willful avoidance by the

[14] D Cohen, *Intended to Fail: The Trials before the Ad Hoc Human Rights Court in Jakarta* (New York, International Center for Transitional Justice, 2003).

[15] *Ibid* at vii.

[16] UNHRC, 'Question of the Violation of Human Rights and Fundamental Freedoms in any Part of the World: Situation of Human Rights in Timor-Leste' (4 March 2003) UN doc E/CN.4/2003/37 at para 52. These arguments are also reflected in Cohen, *Intended to Fail* (n 14 above).

[17] The following defendants were acquitted: Timbul Silaen, Herman Sedyono, Liliek Kushadianto, Ahmad Syamsudin, Lieutenant Sugito, Col. Gatot Subiyaktoro, Asep Kuswani, Adios Salora, Leoneto Martins, Endar Priyanto, Tono Suratman and Yayat Sudrajat. The following defendants were convicted (with the sentence indicated in brackets) and then acquitted on appeal: Abilio Soares (three years), Lieutenant Col. Soedjarwo (five years), Adam Damiri (three years), Nuer Muis (five years) and Hulman Gultom (five years). Eurico Guterres was sentenced to 10 years, a judgment upheld on appeal.

Indonesian government and judiciary of the matter of bringing Indonesian officials to account.[18]

The Dili-based Special Panels for Serious Crimes (SPSC) have consolidated this Indonesian impunity. Serious crimes investigators initially focused their attentions on those accused of crimes that did not invoke international law.[19] For almost two years, there was no prosecution strategy in place to 'maximize limited resources' into investigations on high-ranking Indonesian officials responsible for crimes against humanity.[20] While the final trial figures seem healthy,[21] those processed through the courts have overwhelmingly been low-ranking Timorese militia members—illiterate farmers who often became involved through coercion or payment. 339 indictees, including all high-ranking perpetrators, remain out of reach, with many continuing to serve within the Indonesian military.

This situation has caused widespread consternation, not least among some UN workers who argue that their work was used as a smoke-screen. As one SCU employee explained, when the UN knew that they could not prosecute Indonesian officials, 'things should have been stopped ... instead, we continued and provided a cover—a sense that something was being done'.[22] For this worker, the continuing court process made the situation worse as it allowed Indonesian officials to reconfigure their international identity as a 'good global citizen'. A further critique can be levelled at the serious crimes process regarding its failure to undertake investigative, prosecutorial and judicial proceedings in a manner consistent with international standards of fairness and due process.[23]

It is evident, for example, that the serious crimes process was 'funded at a level . . . insufficient to meet [its] minimum requirements'.[24] Funding was low compared to other international tribunals: the annual budget of the Special Panels stood at about US$5 million.[25] In comparison, the annual cost of the Extraordinary Courts in Cambodia is budgeted at just under

[18] Cohen, *Intended to Fail* (n 14 above). Amnesty International and Judicial System Monitoring Programme (JSMP), Indonesia, *Justice for Timor-Leste: The Way Forward* (AI Index: ASA 21/006/2004).

[19] D Cohen, 'Seeking Justice on the Cheap: Is the East Timor Tribunal Really a Model for the Future?' (2002) 61 *Asia Pacific Issues: Analysis from the East-West Center* 5–6.

[20] Report to the Secretary-General of the Commission of Experts to Review the Prosecution of Serious Violations of Human Rights in Timor-Leste (then East Timor) in 1999 (26 May 2005), UN doc S/2005/458 at 22. Also Linton, 'New Approaches to International Justice in Cambodia and East Timor' (n 12 above) at 93.

[21] 95 indictments, representing 440 defendants, were issued; 55 cases were tried; 84 defendants were convicted; three acquitted and one defendant ruled unfit to stand trial.

[22] SCU worker in interview, 23 November 2004, Dili.

[23] UN Commission of Experts' Report (n 20 above) at 28.

[24] UN Commission of Experts' Report (n 20 above) at 104.

[25] Judicial System Monitoring Programme (JSMP), *Unfulfilled Expectations: Community Views on CAVR's Community Reconciliation Process* (Dili, JSMP, 2004).

US$19 million per year,[26] the Special Court in Sierra Leone is costed at US$16 million per year[27] and the International Criminal Tribunals for Rwanda and the Former Yugoslavia have a combined 'annual budget of over a quarter of a billion dollars'.[28] This lack of funds has had an extensive impact. In 2003, at the peak of its organisational powers, the SCU operated with between six to eight investigators, each with a responsibility for more than 300 murders.[29] Similarly, the Defence Lawyers Unit team was impossibly small; few staff members had previous experience in international law; and the team struggled to provide 'equality of arms' against the better resourced prosecution unit.[30] Until 2004, the judges on the Special Panels could not always access legal documentation or basic electricity, telephone or computer services and they did not have assistants or stenographers—which means that there are no reliable case transcripts.[31] In addition, translation staff—an essential component in a court operating across four languages—were not always available and it was not so unusual for judges to translate themselves or for participants to just not understand proceedings.[32]

The failure of the legal processes in Jakarta and Dili, to effectively prosecute any senior Indonesian officials or to attain international standards of due process, has led to negative perceptions of formal criminal justice processes within local populations.[33] The procedures have been, as the UN Commission of Experts (CoE) argued in 2005, 'manifestly inadequate'.[34] In light of these failings, the CoE recommended that the UN 'create an ad hoc international criminal tribunal'.[35] This position, reflecting the claims of Timorese grassroots organisations, did not meet a warm reception with high-ranking Timorese leaders. In response, ex-President

[26] UN Commission of Experts' Report (n 20 above).

[27] UNSC, Report of the Secretary-General to the Security Council (n 13 above) at para 42.

[28] UNSC, Report of the Secretary-General to the Security Council (n 13 above).

[29] SCU worker in interview, 21 November 2004, Dili.

[30] Open Society and Coalition for International Justice, *Unfulfilled Promises: Achieving Justice for Crimes against Humanity in East Timor* (New York, Open Society and CIJ, 2004).

[31] *Ibid* at 41–2; Judicial Systems Monitoring Programme, *Overview of the Justice Sector: March 2005* (Dili, JSMP, 2005).

[32] E Stanley, 'Towards a Criminology for Human Rights' in A Barton, K Corteen, D Scott and D Whyte (eds), *Expanding the Criminological Imagination: Critical Readings in Criminology* (Cullompton, Willan Publishing, 2007).

[33] Such negative perceptions have been a consistent feature of the author's interviews in Timor-Leste.

[34] Summary of the Report to the Secretary-General of the Commission of Experts to Review the Prosecution of Serious Violations of Human Rights in Timor-Leste (then East Timor) in 1999, UN doc S/2005/458 at paras 8–17. The CAVR Report (n 3 above) also recommends an international tribunal, if justice measures continue to face obstructions.

[35] *Ibid* at para 29.

Gusmão wrote to the UN arguing that 'jail terms for senior [Indonesian] military officers would ... undermine stability'.[36]

The distancing of this Timorese President from further prosecutorial provisions reflects a governmental turn in favour of friendly bilateral relations with Indonesia, a stance illustrated in the establishment of the Commission of Truth and Friendship (CTF) by the two governments. Following previous transitional justice measures, the main objective of the CTF is to 'establish the conclusive truth in regard to the events prior to and immediately after the popular consultation in 1999'.[37] The most controversial aspect of this Commission lies in its proposed 'measures to heal the wounds of the past' through the recommendation of 'amnesty for those involved in human rights violations who cooperate fully in revealing the truth'.[38] While, the CTF can only 'recommend' amnesty, the Catholic Church and victims' groups in Timor-Leste vehemently argue that this amounts to an official immunity for the prosecutions.[39] It is widely observed that the CTF is an attempt to encourage the UN to abandon any future plans to implement an international tribunal.

In summary, these transitional justice 'from above' initiatives have fundamentally failed to fulfil a crucial role—to bring serious human rights violators to account.[40] The impunity for Indonesian officials has emerged out of willful avoidance on the part of the Indonesian government. However, it has been further entrenched by both the UN's failure to provide adequate resources or good management for court proceedings as well as the Timorese government's decision to pursue political and economic imperatives at the expense of prosecutions. At the ground level, these transitional justice bodies have led to further feelings of injustice. While many Timorese have been relatively forgiving with the actions of their government—after all, as Casimiro[41] details, 'what can they, who have nothing, do against these big powers?'—there is a common view that the UN and the Indonesian government have not fulfilled their legal and moral obligations to provide redress.

[36] Letter dated 14 July 2005 from the Secretary-General addressed to the President of the Security Council (15 July 2005) UN doc S/2005/459.

[37] The CTF is a 10-person Commission, with equal representation from Timor-Leste and Indonesia. It is pertinent to note that three Commissioners from the CAVR (Aniceto Guterres, Jacinto Alves and Olandina Caeiro) have been appointed to the CTF. CTF, 'Terms of Reference for The Commission of Truth and Friendship Established by The Republic of Indonesia and The Democratic Republic of Timor-Leste', available online at http://www.ctf-ri-tl.org/ at s 12.

[38] *Ibid* at s 14c.i.

[39] The UN Commission of Experts argued that such terms 'contradict international standards on denial of impunity for serious crimes' and contain no 'mechanism compelling witnesses to tell the truth' (n 34 above) at s 20.

[40] The possibility of pursuing accountability has been made more difficult by the May 2006 destruction and looting of SCU records and evidence in Dili.

[41] In discussion, 28 November 2005, Dili.

B Creating 'Othering' and Exclusion

It is also evident that these transitional justice initiatives have engaged strategies of 'othering' and excluded local populations from fundamental decision-making and practices. Jamieson and McEvoy[42] have detailed how states may hide their responsibility for violations through a range of 'othering' techniques, in which state involvement is either minimised (states are presented as being distant from direct involvement[43]) or in which victims are downgraded (for example, their status is hidden, or they are represented in ways that attribute guilt to them or they are placed outside of legal protection altogether). One common objective of transitional justice mechanisms is to work against these 'othering' techniques in a way that can illustrate the 'truth' of responsibility for violations and to acknowledge victims *as* victims.[44] However, in some instances, the transitional justice mechanisms for Timor-Leste have reproduced these 'othering' strategies.

This criticism is apparent within the operations of the Ad Hoc Human Rights Court. During these proceedings, both defence and prosecution teams presented the argument that Indonesia acted as a neutral arbiter between opposing local groups. This position, that the violence erupted without any 'organized support or participation by Indonesian military, police, or security units', was a myth perpetuated by the regime during occupation.[45] The acceptance of this myth in the Court recreated the popular view—widely held in Indonesia—that Indonesian forces were not involved in Timorese violence. Thus, the culpability of the Timorese was maximised. This technique was also illustrated in the general treatment of witnesses in the courtroom. Most witnesses were members of the Indonesian army, police or government, who all stressed the responsibility of Timorese actors in violence. The small number of Timorese witnesses were not given an opportunity to contest this version of events as, lacking interpreters, they could not always understand the proceedings and they were frequently subjected to hostile treatment from all Court members. In many instances, these victim witnesses felt like they were personally on trial.[46]

[42] R Jamieson and K McEvoy, 'State Crime by Proxy and Juridical Othering' (2005) 45 *British Journal of Criminology* 504.

[43] *Ibid*. For example, state officials may resort to perfidy (hiding their affiliations), engage in collusion with paramilitary groups, hire private mercenaries or military firms and give special favour to specialist units that operate outside the usual rules of combat.

[44] E Stanley, 'What Next? The Aftermath of Organised Truth Telling' (2002) 44 *Race and Class* 1.

[45] Cohen, *Intended to Fail* (n 14 above) at viii.

[46] Amnesty International and JSMP, *Justice for Timor-Leste: The Way Forward* (n 18 above).

Forms of 'othering' were also apparent in the SPSC. These judicial practices were not so aggressive in their techniques, yet one might conclude that the end-result (which presented Timorese people as perpetrators and which placed some victims outside of legal protection altogether) may well enhance Indonesian claims that the Timorese population was fundamentally responsible for violence.

Although the SPSC took universal jurisdiction over charges of genocide, war crimes and crimes against humanity,[47] and prosecutors initially assumed a remit to consider serious crimes from 1975, the SCU subsequently changed policy to focus all attention on cases from January–October 1999, a period that covers less than one per cent of killings.[48] The UN, therefore, established a process to prosecute serious crimes that occurred over 24 years but then retracted the scope to just 10 months. This policy change illustrates the lack of planning and limited resources (discussed above), yet it also demonstrates the concerns of the UN with regard to its own status. During 1999, the UN felt that its own authority had been attacked and that accountability was fundamental to 'ensuring that future Security Council decisions are respected'.[49] This primary response to the problem of accountability signifies an organisation that is perhaps guided by the lack of respect shown to the institution, not just to the defence of human rights in Timor-Leste. The ultimate impact is that the majority of victims have not enjoyed any investigation or prosecution of their cases.

These techniques, that have minimised Timorese access to justice, have also been linked with practices of exclusion. All the top-down transitional justice mechanisms have been criticised for having been imposed without sufficient consultation—the Ad Hoc Court, for instance, operated almost entirely without Timorese participation and the CTF has faced bitter challenges from local groups on the basis that it has been implemented without consideration of victims' needs. Even the serious crimes process in Dili, a mechanism that has perhaps enjoyed the most local support, has been seen as an impositional force. Many Timorese people simply did not know that the SPSC existed[50] and serious crimes workers have been challenged for their distant approach to communities (in their common

[47] UNTAET Regulation 2000/15 provides the SPSC with universal jurisdiction over war crimes, crimes against humanity, genocide and torture as well as murder and sexual offences committed between 1 January and 25 October 1999.

[48] The Deputy General Prosecutor, Nicholas Koumjian, argued that this position was supported by the UN Security Council and the UN Secretary General. In interview, 23 November 2004, Dili.

[49] Report of the International Commission of Inquiry (n 6 above) at 147.

[50] For instance, I met hundreds of taxi drivers in Dili during my research yet very few knew about the UN's serious crimes process. This situation was intensified in the districts, where access to radios and televisions was limited.

practice of taking statements and then not returning to provide information on outcomes).[51] In addition, international staff have also been charged with excluding capable Timorese actors from investigations. A number of local organisations have a wealth of knowledge regarding violations. However, these capacities tended to be ignored by some serious crimes workers who saw themselves as 'the experts' in the field.[52] This approach created feelings of exclusion in local human rights groups. The modes of working undertaken by many international staff, that reflected Western cultures and priorities, served to dismiss local populations. While impairing the ability of serious crimes workers to efficiently conduct investigations, it further damaged public perceptions of this transitional justice process.

C Consolidating Unequal Power Relations

The dominance of Indonesia, as a state that holds economic and strategic power, has been consolidated through the processes and end-results of these transitional justice measures. This situation has been maintained by the way in which relevant actors have appeared unable or unwilling to commit themselves to, or to 'own' the prosecutorial process. Indeed, key prosecuting parties have actively sought to distance themselves from court proceedings.

For example, consider the SPSC case against General Wiranto, six senior TNI (army) members and the former governor of East Timor, Abilio Soares. The SCU issued this high-level indictment on 24 February 2003 and Indonesia immediately argued that the UN had pushed a politically-motivated case.[53] In response, the UN issued a declaration insisting that the indictment was the work of Timor-Leste's prosecution service.[54] While this was technically correct,[55] it was rather disingenuous, as the UN had set up the judicial process and the SCU was staffed by UN workers. Following this, senior Timorese politicians also discredited the indictment and argued that it was not of their doing. Subsequently, Xanana Gusmão met President Megawati Sukarnoputri and undertook a photo-shoot where he hugged Wiranto and stated that the proceedings of the Ad Hoc Human Rights

[51] Explained by a Serious Crimes investigator, in interview, 21 February 2004, Dili.

[52] In interview with Serious Crimes worker, 21 November 2004, Dili.

[53] Hirst and Varney, *Justice Abandoned?* (n 9 above).

[54] T Järvinen, *Human Rights and Post-Conflict Transitional Justice in East Timor* (UPI Working Paper 47, Finnish Institute of International Affairs, 2004).

[55] The SCU operated under the Office of the General Prosecutor in Timor-Leste.

Court showed 'determination' and an 'attitude of political courage'.[56] Thus, the major 'players' distanced themselves from the process.

The political leaders in Timor-Leste have begun the process of sacrificing justice for ties with its larger, economically stronger neighbour, Indonesia. Survival has become the main concern. The UN has consistently failed to provide firm support for transitional justice initiatives and other relevant powerful states (eg the United States, United Kingdom and Australia) have not pressed for further action. Added to this, Timor-Leste continues to face significant issues with regard to poverty and development. It is one of the poorest countries in the world and the UN Development Programme claims that it is getting poorer.[57] Around 40 per cent of the population lives on less than 55 US cents a day, which means that the reality for many is that even basic needs go unmet. There is high food insecurity, limited access to safe drinking water, high unemployment, poor education standards and individuals struggle to receive health care.[58] For some, particularly those in rural areas, the transitional period has brought a deterioration in living situations. In this context, the Timorese government's promotion of economic development, trade and bilateral reconciliation over the provision of justice is more understandable.

Moreover, it must be acknowledged that the government and local institutions continue to be almost completely dependent on external sources and, consequently, have often been at the mercy of the standards and priorities of external donors.[59] The consequences of non-conformity to international expectations can be devastating. For instance, there are examples of human rights groups losing vital international funding following their criticism of the Australian government's negotiations regarding the oil in the Timor Sea.[60] The necessity of Timorese organisations, including the government, to conform to international demands for action (including the dismissal of troublesome claims for justice) is clarified in this economic context.

In sum, the flaws of the top-down international and national initiatives have been wide-ranging. Through these mechanisms, transitional justice has been used as a way to entrench impunity, while giving the appearance

[56] Järvinen, *Human Rights and Post-Conflict Transitional Justice in East Timor* (n 54 above) at 25–6.

[57] United Nations Development Programme (UNDP), *The Path out of Poverty: Timor-Leste* (Dili, UNDP, 2006).

[58] *Ibid.*

[59] In the wake of the 2006 conflict, the involvement of internationals (particularly Australia, New Zealand, Portugal and Malaysia) has been further intensified.

[60] In particular, 'Forum Tau Matan', a prison monitoring and legal rights project, lost its AUS$65,000 funding from Ausaid after it signed a press release (along with 13 other NGOs) calling for the maritime boundary to be set fairly, according to international legal principles. The withdrawal of funding, in 2005, was attributed to the organisation's criticism of the Australian government.

that justice is being done. These forms of transitional justice have consolidated the 'othering' techniques employed by the Indonesian regime and have simultaneously placed Timorese victims outside of legal protection. Further, they have often excluded Timorese groups from making a vital contribution to their future. Ultimately, as the 'owners' of these mechanisms have distanced themselves from the processes when they became politically difficult, they have failed to provide redress or challenge the power imbalances within the region. In these respects, these top-down initiatives have placed dominant political and economic agendas ahead of providing for the 'basics' of transitional justice—'to punish perpetrators, establish the truth, repair or address damages, pay respect to victims, and prevent future abuse'.[61] Yet, can mechanisms that encourage transitional justice 'from below' offer more positive strategies to deal with human rights violations? This question is the subject of the following section.

IV THE POTENTIAL AND PITFALLS OF TRANSITIONAL JUSTICE FROM BELOW

The Commission for Reception, Truth and Reconciliation (CAVR) garnered wide public approval and was supported by Timorese political leaders as well as the UN. It is argued, here, that this mechanism has provided a more inclusive and participatory approach to transitional justice, and has provided a challenge to the 'othering' techniques of the previous regime by exposing complex truths. However, this initiative has not been able to challenge the structured disparities that continue to pervade life in Timor-Leste and some CAVR practices have re-iterated the unequal divisions that exist within Timorese communities. These latter aspects have weakened the CAVR's potential while illustrating, once more, that transitional justice bodies have to find new ways to establish truth and 'do' justice in a manner that does not reinforce political and status inequalities.

A A Participatory Approach

The CAVR started work on 21 January 2002 and, over four years, employed hundreds of people to facilitate its programmes[62]: to establish the truth regarding human rights violations committed between 25 April

[61] P Hayner, *Unspeakable Truths: Confronting State Terror and Atrocity* (London, Routledge, 2001) 11.

[62] At the peak of CAVR's operations, there were 278 staff. CAVR, 'Chega!' (n 3 above) at pt 1.6.

1974 and 25 October 1999[63]; to assist in restoring the dignity of victims; to support the reception and reintegration of individuals who have caused harm to their communities; to promote human rights and reconciliation; to make recommendations; and to refer matters, where applicable, to the serious crimes process.

The CAVR's final report, entitled '*Chega!*' (meaning 'no more, stop or enough'), was released onto the internet in December 2005.[64] Stretching over 2,500 pages, it details the level of participation by the Timorese population in the proceedings: 7,669 victims and 1,541 perpetrators gave statements and 1,000 others provided further information; in every sub-district, individuals engaged in public victims hearings and, in Dili, people participated in national hearings as well as healing workshops; households across the country assisted in surveys and mortality 'mapping' exercises; and an estimated 40,000 people attended Community Reconciliation Process (CRP) hearings.[65] Overall, the process had good 'buy-in' from perpetrators, victims and communities.

B A (Partial) Challenge to 'Othering'

The CAVR report details that Timorese people did perpetrate violence. During 1975, Fretilin and some UDT members killed 'between 1,500 and 3,000' fellow Timorese[66] and Fretilin engaged in violations against suspected enemies until 1979.[67] Moreover, thousands of East Timorese benefited, politically and economically, by participating in the Indonesian Armed Forces and the militias, as well as in community 'civil defence forces'. This violence, inflicted by Timorese on Timorese, has left deep wounds and, as shown in the recent unrest in Timor-Leste, it has fuelled further conflict.[68]

Yet, the CAVR presents a strong challenge to the 'othering' techniques of the previous regime by showing that the 'conflict . . . was . . . primarily . . .

[63] The former date refers to the Lisbon coup that gave rise to Portuguese decolonisation practices while the latter is when the UN took control of the territory.

[64] It can be found at: http://www.ictj.org/en/news/features/846.html and http://etan.org/news/2006/cavr.htm.

[65] There were 216 reconciliation hearings, involving 1,371 perpetrators. CAVR, 'Chega!' (n 3 above) at pt 1.5.126.

[66] CAVR, 'Chega!' (n 3 above) at pt 3.7.153.

[67] CAVR, 'Chega!' (n 3 above) at pt 8.2.1.

[68] The recent violence illustrates the continuing divisions between independence and pro-Indonesia fighters. However, the rise of violence has resulted from a range of divisions. In particular, conflicts within the army, between the army and the police, within governmental departments, and between powerful parties and internationals all seem to provide reasons for the new disturbances.

one of foreign intervention, invasion and occupation'.[69] The CAVR concluded that, despite the UN's criticism of the Indonesian invasion and occupation, most UN members failed to stop Indonesian activities or provide support to East Timor. Furthermore, the US, UK and Australian administrations provided significant aid and trade as well as military and political support to Indonesia.[70] Australia also profited considerably by signing the 'Timor Gap Treaty' with Indonesia in 1989. In return for de jure recognition of Indonesia's sovereignty over the territory, Australia gained access to the oil and mineral reserves located in Timorese marine territories—estimates indicate that the Australian government has taken over US$2 billion from these oil reserves since 1999.[71] Finally, multinational companies, such as Goodyear, General Electric and Caltex, have also been implicated in lobbying for Indonesian interests while international financial institutions provided significant monies to the Indonesian government for repressive policies.[72]

This 'truth', of how violations resulted from groups pursuing their own strategic goals, is a helpful reminder in a period in which more powerful actors have started to 'whitewash' the past. Helped along by weak media coverage,[73] some states have begun to downplay their involvement and to frame the past in a way that hides their previous political and economic gains from Timor-Leste's repression.[74] The CAVR report may be a useful tool to counter such 'othering' narratives that operate to de-contextualise violations away from their foundations of global economic and political relations.

Yet, the CAVR has not been effective in highlighting all significant truths in the region. In a study of the coffee industry, Nevins[75] argues that the CAVR has not given sufficient weight to structural or systemic forms of violence. Coffee growing has dominated the Timor-Leste economy. During the occupation, an Indonesian military-owned company, PT Denok, took

[69] CAVR, 'Chega!' (n 3 above) at pt 11.1.

[70] The US approved over US$1 billion of arms sales during the occupation and in 1996, UK arms sales to Indonesia were valued at £438 million. Stanley, 'Towards a Criminology for Human Rights' (n 32 above).

[71] Timor Sea Justice Campaign, Briefing Paper (28 July 2005), available online at www.timorseajustice.org.

[72] Stanley, 'Towards a Criminology for Human Rights' (n 32 above). The CAVR Report, 'Chega!' (n 3 above) recommends that those states and companies who profited from arms sales and military training should provide reparations to the Timorese people.

[73] J Klaehn, 'Corporate Hegemony: A Critical Assessment of the Globe and Mail's News Coverage of Near-Genocide in Occupied East Timor 1975–1980' (2002) 64 *Gazette: The International Journal for Communication Studies* 301.

[74] Nevins, *A Not-So-Distant Horror* (n 5 above) shows how UK, Australian and US politicians have focused on their 'humanitarian assistance', neglecting to detail their involvement in creating violence in the first place.

[75] J Nevins, 'Restitution over Coffee: Truth, Reconciliation and Environmental Violence in East Timor' (2003) 22 *Political Geography* 677.

ownership of most plantations and slashed sales prices, leading to extreme income loss for growers and increased military profits. Following the breakdown of the 'International Coffee Accord' system, coffee prices fell dramatically and the situation of farmers, facing fierce competition, has deteriorated. These global, structural concerns live on—today, about 25 per cent of the Timorese population are dependent on coffee production and the average six-member family makes an annual income of just US$200 for their efforts. The decreased coffee income has resulted in increased malnutrition, preventable-disease deaths and a decline in 'primary school enrolment because families cannot afford the modest school fees'.[76] However, this kind of continuing 'violence', which results from a global political-economic system, is not illustrated or challenged by the CAVR. The CAVR's focus on individual acts of violence, and individual state involvement (that is, the who did what, when, to whom and why), pays little attention to the conditions that will perpetuate injustices and potentially create further conflict in the future. This minimisation could also be viewed as a technique of 'othering', as it hides the responsibility of structural systems in the maintenance of violence and places victims of such conditions outside consideration.

C Accepting Immunity in Exchange for Reconciliation

The Community Reconciliation Process (CRP) focused on the reintegration of low-level offenders into their communities. This process was vital in addressing the conflicts which emerged following Timorese participation in house-burnings, intimidation, lootings, minor assaults, crop destruction or the theft of livestock and property during the militia violence in 1998–99.

The CRP was a voluntary process, started at the request of a perpetrator who submitted a written statement. The statement, which included a full description of specific 'political' crimes, an admission of responsibility, the identities of those involved, a renunciation of violence and a request to participate in a hearing, was reviewed by the CAVR and then forwarded to the Office of the General Prosecutor (OGP), that determined whether the matter should be dealt with by the CAVR or through the courts. CRP hearings were conducted in the affected community and led by a panel of local leaders and a Commissioner. Following discussions, the panel determined a Community Reconciliation Agreement (CRA), through which the perpetrator agreed to undertake certain actions such as making an apology, paying a fine or undertaking community work. Having performed these acts, the perpetrator gained immunity, via the district courts, from civil or

[76] *Ibid* at 694.

criminal action. If the perpetrator defaulted, they could be liable to a sentence of a year in prison or a US$3000 fine.[77]

The acceptance of judicial immunity in exchange for perpetrator participation in reconciliation hearings was relatively widespread. In this regard, local populations emphasised the need for communities to hear the 'truth' and to live peacefully together. However, the rationale for accepting immunity for 'less serious' offences was based on the almost universally held view that high-level offenders would face prosecution.[78] To this end, the CAVR actively encouraged low-level perpetrators to participate in the CRP on the basis that serious offenders would be prosecuted, and Commissioners would regularly remind audiences that if they hid their involvement, the formal system would 'catch-up' with them.[79] In light of the limited legal attention paid to serious crimes, there is a considerable amount of 'unfinished business'—a significant caseload that falls in between the transitional justice processes, 'more serious than those dealt with by CRP's and yet . . . not dealt with at all'.[80] Consequently, the status of the CAVR as a facilitator of justice has been downgraded.

D Reconciliation . . . at the Expense of Those Less Powerful?

In contrast to the 'thin' reconciliation inspired by the CTF, in its emphasis on political priorities that have meant relatively little to many local people, the CAVR processes promoted a 'thick' reconciliation[81] by sharing narratives in ways that have drawn on customs and spiritual leaders. The CRP, for instance, was built on the traditional practices of 'lisan' or 'adat', to bring opposing parties together and gain consensus. These practices are based on historical knowledge, ceremony and customary belief. In the CRP context, hearings incorporated the chewing of betel-nut, the drinking of wine or blood, the rolling of the biti (the traditional mat used in local conflict resolution), chanting and dancing, the sprinkling of coconut water, the sacrifice of animals or a celebratory feast.[82]

[77] CAVR, 'Chega!' (n 3 above) at pt 9.1.1. There have not been any formal punitive actions against those that did not comply.

[78] CAVR, 'Chega!' (n 3 above) at pt 9.1.1.

[79] CAVR, 'Chega!' (n 3 above) at 37.

[80] Burgess, 'Justice and Reconciliation in East Timor' (n 10 above) at 155. In 'serious crimes' cases, the SCU was to investigate and, potentially, indict perpetrators. However, this has not happened.

[81] These ideas of 'thin' and 'thick' reconciliation are from R Wilson, *The Politics of Truth and Reconciliation in South Africa: Legitimizing the Post-Apartheid State* (Cambridge, Cambridge University Press, 2001).

[82] See CAVR, 'Chega!' (n 3 above) at pt 9.1.2; D Soares, 'Nahe Biti: The Philosophy and Process of Grassroots Reconciliation (and Justice) in East Timor' (2004) 5 *The Asia Pacific Journal of Anthropology* 15–33.

The incorporation of spiritual customs gave meaning to an institutionalised event and encouraged wider community participation. And reconciliatory acts emerged in various ways—many low-level perpetrators revealed their truths, others asked for forgiveness while, in highly publicised events, politicians made emotional statements to their previous opponents. Notwithstanding these 'successes', as a result of the CAVR's limited mandate and the Commission's inability to challenge relations of power at the personal and community levels, the promotion of reconciliation has remained a partial achievement.

For example, in terms of mandate, the Commission focused on intra-village reconciliation. While this was needed, the CAVR missed the opportunity to build reconciliation between villages or between Timorese and Indonesian populations. This issue may be reflected upon in light of the recent violence between groups from the East and from the West of Timor-Leste as well as the ongoing issue of inter-national reconciliation.[83]

Participation in CRP hearings was also subject to networks of power—for instance, many victims participated out of a sense of duty to the CAVR and the local community. There was a tendency for victims to defer to the CAVR panel or to the *Chefe de Suco* (village head) for discussions and some victims were reticent to speak or to choose harsh punishments for fear of retribution.[84] Victims did not always engage freely with the process.

Added to this, CAVR personnel were not always seen as efficient or neutral arbiters. In Baucau, only 19 perpetrator statements were taken—an issue associated with the 'personality clashes' and lack of cohesion between CAVR workers.[85] In other circumstances, it was felt that 'the employment selection process had not been rigorous enough' and that certain CAVR workers were associated with wrongdoings.[86] Staff members have also been blamed for manipulating hearings in ways that facilitated positive outcomes by 'manoeuvring victims and community members towards "peace and reconciliation"'[87] and by setting CRAs that only involved a perpetrator apology. While this resulted from lack of time[88] it also emerged from situations in which the family members of CAVR staff were present as perpetrators.

[83] In 2005 'La'o Hamutuk', a Timorese NGO, started a project to bring Timorese and Indonesian victims of violations together in an effort to build understanding between the two groups.

[84] JSMP, *Unfulfilled Expectations* (n 25 above).

[85] CAVR, 'Chega!' (n 3 above) at pt 4.1.106.

[86] P Pigou, *Crying without Tears: In Pursuit of Justice and Reconciliation in Timor-Leste: Community Perspectives and Expectations* (New York, International Center for Transitional Justice, 2003) 36.

[87] JSMP, *Unfulfilled Expectations* (n 25 above) at 37.

[88] Having processed about 600 cases between October 2002–December 2003, the Commission undertook 887 cases in just three months, between January and March 2004.

These circumstances, in which those with political power shielded certain perpetrators, created a barrier to reconciliation. These processes were further weakened when victims experienced financial hardships. Most victims have not enjoyed economic assistance[89] and there is a common view, among victims, that they live poorer lives compared to perpetrators, many of whom have secured positions in the civil service or state administration.[90] These conditions have led to feelings of injustice and resentment,[91] and have made reconciliatory processes more difficult.

The power networks which facilitated truth-telling and reconciliation processes were also defined by gender. In June–July 2002, there was only one woman working for the CRP hearings. Following a United Nations Development Programme appraisal, a further 13 female workers were recruited; starting in September 2003, they worked until March 2004.[92] Female staff sometimes found it difficult to build trust with community leaders and some struggled to fully participate in the hearings.[93] Alongside this, it is evident that the majority of victims and perpetrators within the CRP have been male. Men were more likely to have undertaken or suffered from acts of violence and politically-inspired harm. However, male perpetrators, who guided the hearing through their initial statement, would tend to focus on male victims. Women also found that their husbands or male family members did not always want them to participate in hearings.[94] And, given that hearings 'could continue all day and into the night',[95] women regularly faced difficulties in participation due to their home duties and childcare.[96] For such reasons, women were sidelined in truth-telling and reconciliation activities.

It is apparent that the CAVR, as a transitional justice 'from below' process, has consolidated inequalities at personal, social and structural levels. CRP processes reconstituted the dominant relations of power within villages. Part of the problem, here, could be attributed to certain Commission staff who used their position for private ends. However, the CAVR has not been able to challenge the status inequalities experienced by victims. As a result, some groups—such as women, victims who experience relative deprivation and victims who hold little political sway—have not always experienced the levels of 'truth', 'justice' or reconciliation enjoyed by other more powerful actors. This latter problem raises the issue of whether these

89 A very small group were provided with urgent reparations and given a one-off sum of US$200.

90 JSMP, *Unfulfilled Expectations* (n 25 above) at 27.

91 From author's interviews.

92 Interview with CAVR worker, 19 November 2004, Dili.

93 Pigou, *Crying without Tears* (n 86 above) at 83–4.

94 JSMP, *Unfulfilled Expectations* (n 25 above).

95 CAVR, 'Chega!' (n 3 above) at pt 9.1.1.5.

96 JSMP, *Unfulfilled Expectations* (n 25 above) at 40.

types of 'ground-up' initiatives might actually create more harm than good for significant groups of people—a point that connects to the question, 'can future ground-up initiatives work against structural inequalities or social disadvantage?'

In summary, the CAVR provided the Timorese population with a culturally-resonant opportunity to relate their experiences of violence during Indonesian occupation. This accounting provides a complex exposure, which can serve as a useful antidote to the techniques of 'othering' that have been employed by powerful groups. However, certain 'truths'—such as those that relate to how global political and economic relations underpin violations, or those that exemplify how politics, the economy or gender continue to structure life in Timor-Leste—are yet to be fully explored. A further aspect that will persist, of course, is the issue of 'justice'; while Timorese communities often accepted 'truth' and reconciliation in exchange for prosecutions for less serious perpetrators, they continue to claim that those involved in 'serious crimes' must proceed through the criminal justice system. The weaknesses of other mechanisms in this respect presents a useful reminder that transitional justice initiatives are often assessed by the public 'in the round'—the failures of one mechanism can easily impact on the success or otherwise of another.

V CONCLUSION

The political economy of transitional justice has been exposed through each of the mechanisms under examination in this chapter. The top-down transitional justice measures for Timor-Leste have repeatedly illustrated the dominance of politics and the economy over the provisions of 'truth' and 'justice'. While providing a 'political cover' that 'justice' was being done, these initiatives have maintained immunity for Indonesian officials who continue to hold strategic sway. This fundamental failure, underpinned by a distinct lack of political will by powerful parties together with poor administration by the UN, have reinstalled Indonesia as the 'untouchable state'. Moreover, these mechanisms have also worked to reproduce the ideological management of events and identities, pursued by the Indonesian regime through techniques of 'othering' and exclusion. Thus, the historical, regional power relations that underpinned repression in the first instance have largely been re-iterated through these transitional justice measures.

This legacy of transitional justice 'from above' has been given legitimacy by a Timorese government that struggles to carve a secure, independent economic future. In many respects, the Timorese population understand the political and economic imperatives that guide such decisions. However, many remain resolute that powerful bodies, like the UN, have failed to fulfil their legal, moral and political obligations to see 'truth' and 'justice' done. While many communities will accept immunity for less serious perpetrators, in exchange for 'truth' and reconciliation, a distinction is made for serious perpetrators. From the experiences of other transitional states, it is clear that these claims for 'justice' will persist, they will 'not necessarily diminish' with time.[97]

Initiatives that have encouraged transitional justice 'from below' in Timor-Leste have presented, in some respects, a more hopeful vision. The CAVR demonstrates that transitional justice can be conducted in culturally-resonant and participatory ways. This Commission has served as a useful antidote to the techniques of 'othering' employed by powerful groups, during and in the aftermath of repression. However, this transitional justice 'from below' initiative has also shown how, at the local and regional level, the collation of 'truth' and practices of 'justice' remain routed through established networks of power that are contextualised by the economy, politics and other status disparities. Hence, as a result of personnel and practices that did not always work beyond dominant local social structures, the unequal divisions that exist within Timorese communities have been re-established. The consequence has been that less powerful groups have had a different experience of transitional justice than their more powerful counterparts.

The suggestion that Timor-Leste represented 'a people standing on equal footing with the rest of the world' has not been borne out by transitional justice realities. The aspirations of the population have been drastically inhibited by 'top-down' mechanisms, that have prioritised the needs of perpetrating states and international institutions, and by 'bottom-up' initiatives that have sometimes struggled to work against mainstream traditions and social relations. These realities raise the issues of whether, and how, future initiatives might place 'truth' and 'justice' ahead of status, economic and political agendas.

[97] R Teitel, *Transitional Justice* (Oxford, Oxford University Press, 2000) 227.

9

Challenging Impunity from Below: The Contested Ownership of Transitional Justice in Colombia

CATALINA DIAZ*

I INTRODUCTION

THE EXTENT TO which Colombia is undergoing a political transition is a matter of considerable debate among international, national and local commentators. Nowhere is this more apparent than in the demobilisation process of the paramilitary coalition *Autodefensas Unidas de Colombia* (AUC).[1] This process, operating under the auspices of the controversial Justice and Peace Law discussed throughout this chapter, is presented by the national government, certain political elites and the paramilitary leadership as a peace process requiring new and explicit 'restorative' understandings of justice.[2]

* I would like to thank the anonymous reviewers for their comments on previous drafts. I would also like to acknowledge the work of Kieran McEvoy and Lorna McGregor for their excellent comments and assistance in the editing of this chapter. I would also particularly like to thank Professor McEvoy whose interventions in Colombia inspired me to begin reflecting and writing on this topic—his encouragement, guidance and patience is appreciated. This piece was mostly written in early spring of 2007. More recent developments in the implementation of the Peace and Justice arrangement in Colombia are discussed in the case study 'Colombia's Bid for Peace and Justice' that I prepared for the Conference *Building a Future on Peace and Justice*, held in Nuremberg (Germany) from 25–27 June 2007. A revised version of the paper will be published in K Ambos, J Large and M Wierda (eds) (Springer, 2009)

[1] Translated in English as 'United Self-Defence Forces of Colombia'. Notably, the demobilisation process is primarily directed at right-wing paramilitary forces and does not include the Marxist guerrillas such as *Fuerzas Armadas Revolucionarias de Colombia-Ejército del Pueblo* (FARC-EP).

[2] Ministry of Interior and Justice, 'Exposición de Motivos al proyecto de ley estatutaria número 85 de 2003-Senado', 436 *Gaceta del Congreso* (27 August 2003) at 3 (explaining that the reintegration of armed groups is provided in order to enable them to effectively contribute to national peace.)

Yet, the position of what might be termed the 'from below' actors—meaning peasant, indigenous, African-Colombian and urban peripheral organised groups; community-based organisations and their networks; grassroots initiatives; victim's organisations; local non-governmental organisations (NGOs); and trade-unions—differs markedly. Alongside the international human rights community, many such groupings claim that the paramilitary demobilisation process legitimises de facto authoritarian regimes operating in several regions of the country. These regions have been controlled by paramilitary fronts through resort to terror and brutal violence perpetrated against the civilian population, by tactics such as large-scale massacres, selective killings, 'disappearances', sexual violence and forced displacement.[3] Many of those involved in work on the ground in Colombia are deeply suspicious of the claim, primarily advanced by the state and the paramilitaries themselves, that the demobilisation process reflects a radical political transformation that has either widened or deepened democracy. Indeed, they question whether Colombia is undergoing a transition at all.

At the same time, certain communities to which the ex-combatants are returning, local governments, and NGOs confronted with the changing power dynamics in their communities have started to involve rank and file ex-combatants in diverse communal activities with a view to promoting reconciliation.

The purpose of this chapter is to trace how various 'actors from below' have engaged with and used transitional justice discourses in the Colombia context. The chapter focuses on the power dynamics surrounding the various usages of transitional justice terminology and the ensuing contestations over the meaning, requirements and ownership of transitional justice processes. In this respect, the chapter seeks to explore the contribution of critiques and initiatives generated 'from below' to the broader transitional justice debate.

Part II describes the official understanding of the Colombian transition and the basis upon which the national government, political elites and the paramilitary leadership justify the adoption of transitional justice measures. The chapter argues that the official use of the transitional justice rhetoric corresponds to a *thin* understanding of transition. Part III outlines why the projected transition is contested, focusing in particular on the

[3] See Office of the United Nations High Commissioner for Human Rights (OHCHR), 'Report of the United Nations High Commissioner for Human Rights on the Situation of Human Rights in Colombia' (16 May 2006) UN Doc E/CN.4/2006/9; US Department of State, Bureau of Democracy, 'Country Reports on Human Rights Practices' (Released 8 March 2006) (see section on Colombia); United Nations Development Programme (UNDP), 'National Human Development Report for Colombia: The Conflict, a Cul-de-Sac with Ways Out' (2003) (INDH Report); Human Rights Watch, 'The "Sixth Division"—Military-Paramilitary Ties and U.S. Policy in Colombia' (4 October 2001).

perceptions and experiences of the transition by 'actors from below'. Part IV discusses the drafting process of the 'Justice and Peace' law. In this section, the chapter focuses on the use of language relating to truth, justice and the right to reparation and its potential to contest formulas advanced at the official level. Finally, in Part V two case studies are explored to demonstrate how 'players from below' have confronted changing local power dynamics, moving beyond criticism and opposition towards institutional engagement which is opening up transitional sites beyond the criminal justice system. The first deals with recognition of victims, truth-telling and property restitution by local government actors in the city of Medellín. The second addresses the empowerment of victims through grassroots reconciliation initiatives in Eastern Antioquia Province.

II THE OFFICIAL IMAGE OF TRANSITION IN COLOMBIA

A Background to the Conflict

On conservative estimates, Colombia has been involved in an internal armed conflict for somewhere between 40 and 56 years. Traditionally, the conflict has been seen by local elites, sectors of the population and some international actors, in a very simplistic way. It is view by these constituencies as a war against left-wing guerrillas who have been trying (unsuccessfully) to take national power but who have achieved some control over some of the least accessible parts of the country. Other equally simplistic understandings, often encouraged by the US government in particular, have framed the Colombian conflict as a war against drugs and drug-trafficking. More recently, it has also been described as part of the global 'War on Terror'.

However, as the United Nations Development Programme (UNDP) 2003 Human Development Report on Colombia (the INDH Report) demonstrates that such explanations are simplistic and inadequate. The INDH Report argues that 'Colombia's war is particularly complex,' portraying it as an 'eight-faced monster' which can be attributed to three specific circumstances.[4] First, the multiplicity of actors involved: guerrillas with diverse forms of Marxist allegiances; paramilitary groups with different origins; drug lords as well as smaller and medium-sized traffickers; and an array of different state actors. Secondly, the variety of geographical, historical, cultural and ethnic settings in which the war is being waged.[5] And thirdly, the exceptionally long duration of the various confrontations.

[4] INDH Report (n 3above) at 5.
[5] INDH Report (n 3 above) at 5.

The three main illegal armed groups are the *Fuerzas Armadas Revolucionarias de Colombia-Ejército del Pueblo* (FARC-EP),[6] the *Ejército de Liberación Nacional* (ELN)[7] and the AUC, a coalition of anti-subversive/paramilitary groups, which was formed in 1997. The older anti-subversive/paramilitary groups emerged throughout the 1980s and early 1990s, initially as legal self-defence groups under the auspices of the official military forces, to defend the persons and properties of landowners, wealthy ranchers and merchants from the action of the Marxist guerrillas.[8] In the late 1980s, the self-defence groups had already turned into powerful private armies, controlling by force and terror large regions of the country. Although the legal framework that authorised their creation and their sponsorship by the official military forces were declared unconstitutional in 1989,[9] the Colombian government has never adopted serious measures to combat the self-defence groups or to dismantle their economic and political networks.[10] The origins of the self-defence/paramilitary groups are also linked to the expansion and protection of the drug-trafficking business in the country: it is public knowledge that certain paramilitary commanders were major leaders of drug-trafficking cartels and that a significant portion of paramilitary funding comes from the armed front's participation in the various links of the drug-trafficking business chain.[11]

The paramilitary federation did not confront the state and its armed forces; on the contrary, it defended the status quo. In many cases, the paramilitary fronts conducted joint operations with official military battalions or counted on the open or implicit cooperation of military, police and intelligence forces.[12] Indeed, the Inter-American Court of Human Rights

[6] Translated as 'Revolutionary Armed Forces of Colombia—People's Army'.

[7] Translated as 'National Liberation Army'.

[8] For comprehensive and detailed accounts of the origins and expansion of the different paramilitary groups see INDH Report (n 3 above); Human Rights Watch, 'Colombia's Checkbook Impunity: A Human Rights Watch Briefing Paper' (2003); M Romero, *Paramilitares y Autodefensas—1982–2003* (Bogotá, Instituto de Estudios Políticos y Relaciones Internacionales, Universidad Nacional de Colombia y Editorial Planeta, 2003).

[9] República de Colombia, Supreme Court of Justice (Judgment of 25 May 1989). Various executive decrees authorised civilians to bear combat weapons and the military forces to support communal committees to buy weaponry and organise defence strategies. For an interesting and detailed account of the legal history of the provisions authorising the creation of self-defence groups in Colombia see *Case of the 19 Tradesmen v Colombia*, Inter-American Court of Human Rights Series C No 109 (5 July 2004) paras 84.a–84.h.

[10] OHCHR, 'Report of the United Nations High Commissioner for Human Rights on the Human Rights Situation in Colombia' (10 March, 2004) UN Doc E/CN.4/2004/13 (highlighting ongoing violations by these groups in spite of the unilateral ceasefire declared by the AUC in December 2002 and 'its political commitment to demobilisation and ceasefire').

[11] For a detailed account of the relationship between paramilitary groups and narco-trafficking, see F Cubides, 'Narcotráfico y paramilitarismo:matrimonio indissoluble?' in A Rangel (ed), *El Poder Paramilitar* (Bogotá, Fundación Seguridad y Democracia y Editorial Planeta, 2005).

[12] See OHCHR, 'Report of the United Nations High Commissioner for Human Rights on the Situation of Human Rights in Colombia' (16 May 2006) UN Doc E/CN.4/2006/9; US

has recently addressed allegations of collusion between paramilitary fronts and state security forces. In five cases, the Court declared the state of Colombia responsible for human rights violations involving paramilitary and state actors.[13]

B A 'Thin' Transition

After a failed three-year peace process with the FARC-EP Marxist guerrillas, the then Governor of the province of Antioquia, Alvaro Uribe Velez, won the presidential election in 2002 based in large part on the promise that the state would recover territorial control and ensure security throughout Colombia. Through his 'Democratic Security Policy,' Uribe sought to strengthen the military forces and to promote collaboration amongst the civilian population as a means to 'win the war against terrorism'. As a component of the Democratic Security Policy, the peace policy offers socio-economic and legal benefits to combatants who agree to turn in their weapons and reintegrate into civilian life.

At the height of their 'career', and animated by the promise that the government would secure the territories 'liberated' from the Marxist threat by the paramilitary fronts, several paramilitary commanders accepted the government's offer to engage in a demobilisation process.[14] In July 2003, government representatives and AUC paramilitary leaders signed the 'San José de Ralito' Accord. Both parties cited 'national peace' as the overall objective to the Accord, a goal that should be achieved

> through the strengthening of democratic governance and the re-establishment of the monopoly of force in the hands of the State.[15]

Under the Accord, the paramilitary leadership agreed to demobilise its troops by 31 December 2005 and the government committed to reintegrate the demobilised combatants into civilian life. Between November 2003 and April 2006, 30,431 paramilitary combatants were demobilised in 31 public

Department of State, 'Country Reports on Human Rights Practices-Colombia' (8 March 2006); Human Rights Watch, 'The "Sixth Division" (n 3 above); 'Human Rights Watch, 'The Ties That Bind: Colombia and Military-Paramilitary Links' (1 February 2000), available online at http://hrw.org/reports/2000/colombia/ ; and Human Rights Watch, 'Colombia's Killer Networks: The Military-Paramilitary Partnership and the United States' (1 November, 1996), available online at http://hrw.org/reports/1996/killertoc.htm.

[13] *Case of the 19 Tradesmen v Colombia* (n 9 above); *Case of the "Mapiripán Massacre" v Colombia*, Inter-American Court of Human Rights Series C No 134 (15 September 2005); *Case of the Pueblo Bello Massacre v Colombia*, Inter-American Court of Human Rights Series C No 140 (31 January 2006); *Case of the Ituango Massacres v Colombia*, Inter-American Court of Human Rights Series C No 148 (1 July 2006).

[14] See Rangel, *El Poder Paramilitar* (n 11 above).

[15] *Acuerdo de Santa Fe de Ralito*, available online at http://www.altocomisionadoparalapaz.gov.co/acuerdos/acuerdos_t/jul_15_03.htm (visited May 2005).

ceremonies throughout the country.[16] Out of the total number of demobilised combatants 86 per cent were male, 14 per cent female and 19 per cent of this total were children.[17] In addition, between August 2002 and September 2007, 9,800 guerrillas have voluntarily deserted their organisations, risking death, to enter into the demobilisation programme.[18]

The paramilitary demobilisation process, however, does not reflect a more comprehensive peace process involving other armed actors. Peace talks between the FARC and the government are not foreseeable in the near future. Despite efforts made by official delegations of foreign governments (particularly European) and Catholic Church representatives, both parties have even rejected several proposals for the liberation of hostages in exchange for the release of FARC combatants currently serving prison sentences. In December 2005, the less powerful ELN entered into a series of exploratory dialogues with government representatives in Cuba, but a cease-fire or unilateral cessation of hostilities remains uncertain.[19]

While the national government, political elites aligned with the government and the paramilitary leadership have not consistently employed terms such as 'transition' or 'transitional justice',[20] they consistently refer to the right to truth, justice and reparations. The national government claims that as the paramilitary demobilisation process presents a 'peace process', the establishment of peace as a key priority necessitates exceptional measures, namely the suspension of ordinary criminal justice.[21] For its part, the paramilitary leadership affirms that the reintegration of ex-combatants would respect 'universal principles of truth, justice and reparations ... within the framework of peace, equity, development and reconciliation'.[22]

[16] Colombia, Alto Comisionado para la Paz, 'Desmovilisaciones colectivas de las autodefensas-estado de la reintegración' (visited 20 October 2006) at 2.

[17] *Ibid.*

[18] República de Colombia, Ministerio de Defensa, 'Logros de la Política de Consolidación de la Seguridad Democrática' (September 2007) at 38. Available online at http://www.mindefensa.gov.co/descargas2/anexos/2649 _Logros_y_Retos_de_la_Politica_de-_Consolidacion_de_Defensa_y_Seguridad_Democratica.pdf?PHPSESSID=051b92497c82520eb239e47e6321c706.

[19] República de Colombia, Alto Comisionado para la Paz, 'Fase Formal Exploratoria Gobierno-ELN: Conclusiones de la Cuarta Ronda de la Fase Formal Exploratoria entre el Gobierno Nacional y el ELN, La Habana, Cuba' (26 October 2006). Available online at http://www.altocomisionadoparalapaz.gov.co/noticias/2006/octubre/oct_26_06.htm.

[20] However, the term was extensively used by the *Procurador General de la Nación* (local mixture of Solicitor and Prosecutor General functions) in a comprehensive report on Demobilisation and Reintegration of ex-combatants and by the Constitutional Court in the decision regarding law 975/2005 (Sentencia C-370, May 2006). Procuraduría General de la Nación, *Seguimiento a Políticas Públicas en materia de Desmovilisación y Reinserción* (Bogotá, Procuraduría General de la Nación, June 2006).

[21] See Ministry of Interior and Justice, 'Exposición de Motivos al proyecto de ley estatutaria número 85 de 2003-Senado' (n 2 above).

[22] República de Colombia, 'Proceso de Paz con las Autodefensas—Informe Ejecutivo' (June 2006) 123. On file with author.

As a result, transitional justice discourse very soon became, to a certain extent, absorbed into the criminal justice language and was a key element of the public debate surrounding the need for and the length of prison sentences.

In July 2005, the Colombian Congress approved Law 975/2005 establishing a special criminal justice procedure directed at ex-combatants facing criminal charges or sentences (issued in absentia) for gross human rights violations. Widely referred to as the 'Peace and Justice Law', Law 975 was adopted after a two-year public debate in which the national government, the donor community, intergovernmental agencies, local political elites and various civil society actors debated the merits of comparative transitional justice experiences and their applicability in the Colombian context, in particular the applicability and content of the rights to truth, justice and reparations.

To date, this putative transition has not resulted in other institutional sites of political transformation, such as a constituent assembly, institutional reform ad hoc commissions (police, military, executive, human rights, women issues and land-tenure, among others) or new local or regional governance structures. Thus, while the national government, certain political elites, the paramilitary leadership, and certain donor countries point to a Colombian transition, certain academics, liberal and left-wing politicians, organised communities and NGOs consider the official 'transition' to amount, in reality, to the collective demobilisation of more than 30,000 paramilitary combatants.[23]

Moreover, debate persists as to the extent of the dismantling or transformation of the paramilitary structure. Reliable information does not exist on the security situation in many regions of Colombia that were or continue to be under effective paramilitary control. The Secretary-General of the Organisation of American States (OAS) has recognised the demobilisation process as a positive development in general, as illegal military structures have disappeared and the majority of ex-combatants have returned to their regions. However, the Report also notes that three types of illegal armed action involving ex-combatants remain. First, ex-combatants have regrouped in the form of criminal gangs that exercise control over certain communities and illegal economic activities. Secondly, factions of demobilised fronts remain active. Thirdly, the report points to the appearance of new armed actors and/or the strengthening of the ones

[23] See R Uprimny (ed), *¿Justicia Transicional sin Transición?* (Bogotá, Centro de Estudios de Derecho, Justicia y Sociedad—De Justicia, 2006) at 14 (claiming that even in the best case scenario, successful negotiations with paramilitary groups would only lead to the dismantling of paramilitary structures and not the end of the conflict as a whole).

already existing in areas left by demobilised fronts.[24] Thus, the OAS concluded that, with the exception of a few regions, 'the reintegration program faces a crisis and endangers the long term viability of the peace process'.[25] In addition, the International Crisis Group points out that

> despite government efforts to offer basic social behaviour modules and counselling, only 10 per cent (of the demobilised) have entered the workforce.[26]

These concerns have been supplemented by media and governmental reports of emerging criminality linked to demobilised paramilitaries. An official intelligence document leaked to the media in May 2005 reports the emergence of a 'third generation of paramilitaries'. The report documents 22 new illegal armed groups that are occupying certain former paramilitary territories and strategic areas in the big cities. There is also evidence of the creation of an armed structure formed by ex-combatants in a marginal borough of Bogotá, and allegations that 25 community leaders have been forcibly 'disappeared' and a further five killed by this new structure.

Thus, in Colombia, official rhetoric has reduced the complex and open-ended concept of political transition to a flawed process of paramilitary disarmament and engagement with a governmental reintegration programme. Although formally linking 'national peace' with the 'strengthening of democratic governance', the paramilitary 'peace process' has arguably not been about the widening, deepening or strengthening of democracy in the country. Political and security institutions remain largely unchanged and there is little evidence of genuinely transformative process of legislative or social reform. It remains uncertain whether the criminal justice arena upon which all attention to date has been focused has the potential to itself become a catalyst for such a broader process of transformation. In the next section, I will explore in more detail the disjuncture between the stories coming 'from above' (ie state sources) and those coming 'from below' (the communities affected by the paramilitaries).

III FROM DE FACTO TO DE JURE CONTROL: COLOMBIA'S CRITICAL VOICES 'FROM BELOW'

The political and economic agendas of community and civil society sectors were little considered in the political negotiation. As a result, crucial issues

[24] Organisation of American States, 'Permanent Council, Sixth Quarterly Report of the Secretary General to the Permanent Council on the Mission to Support the Peace Process in Colombia (MAPP-OEA)' (16 February 2006) OEA/Ser.G CP/doc4148/06.

[25] *Ibid.*

[26] International Crisis Group, 'Colombia: Towards Peace and Justice?' (14 March 2006).

for such actors including restitution, redistribution of land and paramilitary interference in local community development and governance bodies have not been addressed by institutionalised transitional mechanisms. This omission has been referred to specifically by the *Movimiento Nacional de Víctimas de Crímenes de Estado* (MOVICE),[27] a broad coalition of more than 200 victims' associations and social organisations that have been specifically targeted by paramilitary groups and state actors. They have argued that a 'genuine transitional justice arrangement' should address the

> recognition of victims of State crime and the participation of the State in the creation of the paramilitary project; a holistic approach to reparations including not only financial compensation but the reconstruction of political projects, collective organisational structures and world-views, the return of property and territories, and environmental damage to African-Colombian and Indigenous communities; adequate punishment to the planners of such activities and to those who benefited from paramilitary violence; and the benefits of property illegally acquired by the paramilitaries, their friends and families.[28]

In short, the Colombian experience exemplifies how contemporary transitional justice could be progressively abandoning goals of real political transformation and rather serves as an instrumental variant of 'conflict resolution' which favours the interests of the powerful.[29]

National human rights NGOs and their networks, social organisations and national victims' organisations have claimed specifically that the paramilitary demobilisation does not reflect a peace process and is not oriented towards dismantling the paramilitary project, but rather to its legitimisation. For example, MOVICE directly questions the idea that Colombia is experiencing a transition and as a result, contests the consequent application of the transitional justice framework, in particular the 'Justice and Peace Law'.[30] It claims that, 'in order for transitional justice to exist, a transition is needed', defining transition as 'a political transformation requiring that those who brandished weapons decisively contribute to peace, democracy and reconciliation'.[31] MOVICE's view aligns with that of many other community and civil society organisations

[27] Translated as 'National Movement of Victims of State Crime'. It symbolises the extermination campaign conducted by paramilitary groups in conjunction with official military, police, and intelligence units particularly against left-wing political forces, trade-unions, grassroots cooperatives and other communal associations. The MOVICE has become the widest victims' network in the country.

[28] Movimiento Nacional de Víctimas de Crímenes de Estado, 'Carta a Guillermo Hoyos y a los demás organizadores del seminario *Verdad y reparación desde la perspectiva de las víctimas*' (8 May 2006), available online at http://www.movimientodevictimas.org/node/76 (visited 30 November 2006).

[29] R Teitel, 'Law and Politics of Contemporary Transitional Justice' (2005) 38 *Cornell International Law Journal* 837 at 839 (expressing similar concerns).

[30] MOVICE (n 27 above).

[31] MOVICE (n 27 above).

claiming that Colombia is in fact witnessing the consolidation of a de facto authority exercised by the paramilitary leaders and their organisations. As a human rights leader of one of the cities in the country most affected by paramilitary violence (Barrancabermeja) puts it, the paramilitary groups have established in the territories under their control 'para-institutional governance systems', replacing the authority of the state with de facto regimes.[32] The paramilitary demobilisation thus risks institutionalising those de facto regimes into de jure regimes.[33]

In fact, according to American anthropologist, Kimberley Theidon, the great majority of ex-combatants she interviewed in paramilitary areas were very sceptical about the collective demobilisation process. With few exceptions, the ex-combatants refer to the process as a 'shame' and a 'mockery'. For example, a former paramilitary combatant commented that, 'the negotiations are not changing anything. They are just transforming the illegal into legal'.[34] Similar concerns have been raised by the Women and Armed Conflict Working Group,[35] a national research and coordination initiative constituted by more than 20 women's groups, community and grassroots organisations and human rights NGOs. In its fifth Annual Report (covering the period between June 2004 and June 2005), in the section dealing with the demobilisation process and the consolidation of paramilitary power in the Magdalena river valley,[36] the Report explains that the paramilitary project was developed there—as in many other regions of the country—in three consecutive phases: incursion, consolidation and legitimisation.[37] As such, the Report implies that the legitimisation phase is perfectly compatible with the demobilisation process. As a woman who was present in a meeting convened by the paramilitary front controlling her town, reported:

> they [the paramilitaries] say '[d]emobilisation does not mean the end of the organisation, but precisely the legitimisation of our struggle'.[38]

The Report further notes that

[32] JC Meza, 'Situación de los Derechos Humanos y propuestas para la incidencia en políticas públicas en verdad, justicia y reparación frente a la paz en Barrancabermeja' in *Píldoras para la Memoria* (Bogotá, Instituto Popular de Capacitación de la Corporación de Promoción Popular, 2006) 139.

[33] SM Hincapié Jiménez, 'Propuestas de políticas públicas para la verdad, la justicia y la reparación' in *Píldoras para la Memoria* (n 32 above) at 93.

[34] K Theidon and PA Betancourt, 'Transiciones Conflictivas: Combatientes Desmovilisados en Colombia' (2006) 58 *Revista Análisis Político* 92.

[35] http://www.mujeryconflictoarmado.org/

[36] A vast strategic region of the country, which was for three decades under the control of the guerrillas of the ELN and was, during the last decade, taken over by the paramilitaries.

[37] Mesa de Mujer y Conflicto Armado, 'Quinto Informe sobre violencia socio política contra mujeres, jóvenes y niños en Colombia', November 2005. Available online at http://www.mujeryconflictoarmado.org/media/Informes/QuintoInformeEsp.pdf.

[38] *Ibid.*

> in the legitimisation phase the paramilitaries penetrate local economies and local power structures supporting the expansion of capitalism and the liberal-conservative two party system. In this phase paramilitary resources are generated by legally bought businesses. Paramilitaries create foundations and cooperatives in order to promote productive projects; they participate in community-based initiatives, particularly in poor areas; and they try to control political and electoral processes at regional and national levels. As the paramilitaries strengthen their control and neutralise their opponents, some human rights violations decrease, but they maintain the control over the lives of inhabitants of the communities.[39]

The paramilitaries of the Central Bolivar Bloc (Bloque Central Bolivar, BCB), for example, have created a 'social department' within their organisation. The 'social department' is a group in charge of organising communities around the paramilitary project. The 'social department' leads various initiatives such as the creation of groups for developing economic productive projects and the promotion of certain candidates running for local and regional public positions.

The *Asociación Nacional de Mujeres Campesinas e Indígenas de Colombia* (ANMUCIC)[40] confirms the implementation of the paramilitary legitimisation strategy.[41] The Association tells the story of the 'appropriation' of the communities' organisations and civil society spheres by the paramilitary groups. Organised ex-combatants seek legitimisation in the municipal councils, the villages' mayoral offices and administrative contracting proceedings.

IV TRANSITIONAL JUSTICE AS 'BOTTOM-UP' RESISTANCE: THE POTENTIAL OF THE TRUTH, JUSTICE AND RIGHT TO REPARATIONS DISCOURSE

While I would contend that the government, paramilitaries and other elites have adapted the language and discourses of transitional justice for their own political ends, it would be wrong to leave the impression that they have done so without challenge. Indeed, community and civil society organisations have themselves increasingly deployed legal and 'transitional' terminology in pursuit of their objectives on at least two levels. First, they have prominently engaged in the public debate on the legal framework for the demobilisation and reintegration process and the drafting of the Justice and Peace Law. Colombian players from below (backed by international human rights NGOs, inter-governmental agencies and certain European governmental cooperation agencies) have contested the official discourse of

[39] Mesa de Mujer y Conflicto Armado (n 37 above).
[40] National Association of Indigenous and Peasant Women of Colombia.
[41] N 37, above.

transitional justice as an evasion of retributive justice through the manipulation of the right to truth, justice and reparation. Secondly, players from below are increasingly employing the rights to truth, justice and reparations language within workshops, research projects, publications and campaigns themselves.

For example, victims' mutual support groups and local reconciliation committees in East Antioquia have elaborated on the specific meaning that the ideals of truth, justice and reparations should entail.[42] The African-Colombian Conference is conducting a field research project with grassroots initiatives and organised communities to collectively formulate a proposal on truth, justice and reparations for African-Colombian communities.[43] A leading development and human rights NGO in Barrancabermeja published a book describing the paramilitary siege of the city and the contribution of truth, justice and reparations processes in its recovery.[44] Finally, the MOVICE offers to its affiliates a diploma, which includes a truth, justice and reparations module. As is detailed below, the practical and legal outworkings of transitional justice discourses in Colombia have become the terrain upon which these very differing meanings are contested from below and above.

A Background to the Justice and Peace Law: The Alternative Penal draft legislation

Supported by international actors, civil society and community organisations successfully entered into the public debate on the drafting process of the 'Justice and Peace' Law. They used international legal materials to lobby the Colombian and influential foreign governments. They gave input to the various Congressional debates and they played a significant role in influencing national and international public opinion. All of this mobilisation proved key to securing substantive modifications to early versions of the Justice and Peace Law in favour of victims' rights.

The first version of the Justice and Peace Law was called the 'Alternative Penal Draft Legislation' and was conceived by the legal team of the Office of the High Commissioner for Peace on the direct instructions of the

[42] Conciudadanía, Asociación Regional de Mujeres del Oriente Antioqueño, Programa por la Paz de la Compañía de Jesús, 'Primer Encuentro Regional de "Víctimas a ciudadanas-os": para que otras voces se escuchen y el dolor sea propuesta' (November 2005). On file with author.

[43] E Cuesta Pino, 'Construcción Colectiva de una Propuesta Marco para el Ejercicio de los Derechos a la Verdad, Justicia y Reparación desde las Comunidades Afrocolombianas' in *Píldoras para la Memoria* (n 32 above).

[44] Corporación Nación, 'Agendas Civilistas de Verdad, Justicia y Reparación en Barrancabermeja' (March 2006.)

President of the Republic.[45] The President's aim was to avoid using politically contentious amnesty language by offering demobilised combatants judicial pardons within the context of the criminal justice system. The 'Alternative Penal Draft Legislation' was crafted using certain language drawn from the theory and practice of restorative justice without a clear official understanding of the meaning, requirements and applicability of that framework, particularly in a context within which massive human rights violations had been committed. The Minister of Interior and Justice explained that in order to overcome the war bold alternatives to criminal justice were necessary in order to harmonise peace and justice and, as such, had to go beyond the notion of justice as punishment. Rather, justice should be understood as a means of fostering co-existence.[46] Even though at that stage the phrase transitional justice was not explicitly used, the draft legislation did make some references to the right to truth and reparations for victims.

Under the 'Alternative Penal Draft Legislation', the President of the Republic was empowered with the discretion to request judges to suspend the execution of prison sentences on the condition that the demobilised combatants committed to the cessation of hostilities and any further commission of crimes under international law. Article 2 of the Draft Legislation provided that the judge should impose on the demobilised an 'alternative sanction' to the prison sentence[47] from a list contained in the draft legislation, ranging from 'geographical restriction of freedom' to 'disqualification for public duty'.[48] The judge was also vested with the discretion to impose certain reparatory obligations from a list, including community service, the hand-over of property to the state or to institutions devoted to victims' services, and effectively contributing to the clarification of crimes that occurred during the armed conflict. Those 'reparatory acts' were not obligatory, but a matter of discretion of the judge. After a probation period of between one and five years in which the demobilised

[45] Interview with Roberto Mora, Human Rights expert Lawyer at the Office of the High Commissioner for Peace (May 22 2006.) The Colombian President happened to be studying at Oxford University when the Good Friday Agreement was signed in Northern Ireland. He personally instructed the High Commissioner for Peace to create a legal mechanism inspired by the early release provisions of that Accord. For a discussion on the provisions of those mechanism see K McEvoy, 'The Agreement, Prisoner Release and the Political Character of the Conflict' (1999) 26 *Fordham International Law Journal* 145.

[46] See Ministry of Interior and Justice, 'Exposición de Motivos al proyecto de ley estatutaria número 85 de 2003-Senado' (n 2 above) at 5.

[47] República de Colombia, 'Proyecto de Ley Estatutaria No 85 de 2003', 436 *Gaceta del Congreso* (27 August 2003) Art 2.

[48] *Ibid* at Art 11.

combatant was supposed to comply with the obligations mentioned, the judge would then declare the prison sentence expunged.[49]

However, the 'Alternative Penal Draft Legislation' did not provide genuine mechanisms for reparation of victims. The draft legislation did not contemplate the creation of a properly resourced administrative reparations programme. Nor did it make the suspension of the prison sentence conditional upon the effective realisation of reparations. Both the Colombian and the international human rights community criticised the 'Alternative Penal Draft Legislation', with local human rights NGOs and other civil society actors mobilised against the legislative initiative. In conjunction with European and US-based human rights networks, the Colombian human rights community launched lobbying campaigns targeted at donor governments and inter-governmental organisations to put pressure on the Colombian government to substantially modify the draft legislation. Organised indigenous, African-Colombian and peasant communities, trade unions and women rights groups subscribed to NGOs lobby documents and press releases and also incorporated the critique of the 'Alternative Penal Draft Legislation' into their own agendas and advocacy strategies.

The critique of the draft legislation was framed in terms of the rights to truth, justice and reparations, and the violation of international law contained therein.[50] The rights rhetoric was successfully used to oppose official arguments based on the need to manipulate transitional justice standards in order to overcome the war. The international community also made clear that its political and financial support for the demobilisation process was conditional upon the adoption of a 'legal framework' compatible with international truth, justice and reparations standards.[51] The UN High Commissioner for Human Rights, the European Union and the donor community all expressed their concerns about the marginalisation of victims' rights within the demobilisation process.[52]

B Civil Society Effecting Change: The Justice and Peace Law

Due in great part to international pressure, the government was forced to revise the 'Alternative Penal Draft Legislation' and to discuss modifications to it with certain groups in Parliament who had both criticised the initiative and indeed had drafted an alternative text. A version of the new

[49] República de Colombia, 'Proyecto de Ley Estatutaria No 85 de 2003' (n 47 above) at Art 5.

[50] See eg the series of press releases and advocacy documents by the Comisión Colombiana de Juristas (Colombian Commission of Jurists). Available online at http://www.coljuristas.org/inicio.htm.

[51] International Crisis Group, 'Colombia: Towards Peace and Justice?' (n 26 above).

[52] International Crisis Group, 'Colombia: Towards Peace and Justice?' (n 26 above).

draft which was known as the 'Justice and Peace Law' was approved in Congress in July 2005 and signed by the President of the Republic.

The Justice and Peace Law maintained the same structure, organising principles and procedural mechanisms as the Alternative Penal Draft Legislation. However, it incorporated two key new sections: one establishing the general rights of victims to truth, justice and reparations; and the second dealing with specific reparations for victims. According to the 'Justice and Peace Law', ongoing investigations, prosecutions and trials against demobilised paramilitaries involving serious crimes will continue. However, the alternative forms of punishment, such as alternatives to a prison sentence were removed and replaced with a reduced prison sentence of between five and eight years.[53] The 'Justice and Peace' Law did not, however, condition the benefit on a full disclosure of the facts of the crimes. Neither did the law establish any special non-judicial truth-telling mechanism. Rather it assigned the task of producing a report about 'the causes of the emergence and development of the illegal armed groups', to a National Reparations and Reconciliation Commission (CNRR).[54] CNRR is also in charge of the preparation of a national plan for collective reparations and the formulation of criteria directed to the 'Justice and Peace' magistrates to be considered for the reparations orders, which the tribunals have to include in their final decisions.

Despite recognising that ex-combatants who have been declared responsible for serious crimes have a 'general duty to repair', Law 975/2005 did not make sentence reduction conditional upon an effective contribution to the reparation of victims, despite the financial wealth of paramilitary commanders and mid-ranking cadres. Rather, the law only exhorted ex-combatants participating in the special criminal 'Justice and Peace' process to return illegally acquired assets to the state. Law 975/2005 also failed to establish a clear state obligation to provide individual economic compensation, but provided only for limited restitution and rehabilitation from a newly created trust fund.

[53] Ley 975 de 2005, Art 29. However, according to Art 30 of Law 975/2005, the government had the power to determine the facilities where the prison sentences should be served. Based on this provision, the paramilitary leadership claimed that prison sentences can be served on private ranches or 'peace villages'. Consejo Editorial Ex Comandantes AUC, 'Situación actual de las autodefensas: de la crisis a las propuestas' (10 September 2006). Art 30 was declared constitutional by the Constitutional Court on the understanding that the detention centres should met security and austerity standards similar to those applicable to prisons administered by the official prison administration.

[54] *Ibid* at Art 51.2.

C Constitutional Court Challenge

Several local human rights NGOs actively supported by grassroots and community-based organisations, challenged the 'Justice and Peace Law' before the Constitutional Court. In May 2006 the Court decided to uphold the law, but struck down several provisions and declared that the validity of others was conditional upon certain constitutional interpretations. The Constitutional Court admitted that Law 975 was approved as an instrument to assist in resolving the internal armed conflict, and as such, its various mechanisms—that restrict the rights of victims—should be considered in light of constitutional principles and the right to peace.[55]

The Court examined the institution of alternative punishment ('*alternatividad*'—in practice, reduced prison sentences), strictly balancing the constitutional interest in peace with the rights of victims to truth, justice, and reparations.[56] The Court found the concept of alternative punishment to be in accordance with the Constitution and ruled that it did not entail a disproportionate compromise of the constitutional principle of justice. It found this on the basis that the Justice and Peace magistrates would impose an ordinary sentence, according to the rules of the Criminal Code, which would still be enforced if the person sentenced failed to comply with the conditions on which the benefit of sentence-reduction was based. However, the Court found that making the alternative punishment conditional upon a general collaboration with justice, as required in Article 3, was not specific enough to guarantee the right of victims to truth, justice, reparations and non-repetition.[57] Consequently, the Court declared the constitutionality of Article 3 to be conditional upon the interpretation that 'collaboration with justice' should be directed to guaranteeing the rights of victims to truth, justice, reparation, and non-repetition.

The Constitutional Court declared that the criminal procedure established by Law 975/2005 did not 'effectively promote full disclosure of the truth'. The Constitutional Court also clearly stated that the concession of substantive benefits of sentence-reduction without requiring full (complete and genuine) disclosure of the facts of all the crimes in which the ex-combatant may have participated constituted a violation of the right to truth.[58] Following previous constitutional jurisprudence[59] and consolidated jurisprudence of the Inter-American Human Rights Court, the Constitutional Court declared that the right to truth formed part of the Bill of Rights incorporated into the Colombian Constitution.

[55] Corte Constitucional de Colombia, Sentencia No C-370/2006, s 5.
[56] *Ibid* at ss 6.2.2, 6.2.1.3 and 6.2.1.4.
[57] Corte Constitucional de Colombia, Sentencia No C-370/2006, s 6.2.1.5.
[58] Corte Constitucional de Colombia, Sentencia No. C-370/2006, s 6.2.2.1.7.5.
[59] Corte Constitucional de Colombia, Sentencias C-228/2002 and C-578/2006.

According to the Court, the special criminal procedure established by Law 975/2005 did not attribute any real consequences to the deliberate obfuscation of grave breaches by the ex-combatant; neither did it encourage full disclosure of the truth about such crimes.[60] The Constitutional Court explained that the procedure created by the Law did not punish false or incomplete versions of events and that the sentence-reduction was unaffected despite later evidence suggesting that the complete truth was not revealed. Consequently, the Court struck down the relevant provisions that permitted sentence-reduction where crimes were not fully acknowledged in the first instance.

The Constitutional Court stated that ex-combatants who benefitted from the provisions of Law 975/2005 should contribute from their personal estates, including legally acquired property, to the financial compensation of victims. In consequence, the Court struck down several sections of Law 975/2005 that limited the duty of the ex-combatant to the return of illegally acquired assets 'when possible'. The Court affirmed that the state was not authorised to exempt those responsible for gross crimes from civil responsibility.[61] The Court explained that under Colombian and international law, economic compensation is one element of the right to reparations of victims and a condition to promote the fight against impunity.[62] The Constitutional Court also struck down the limitation of economic compensation ordered by a judge within the 'Justice and Peace' criminal procedure to official budgetary restrictions.[63] Moreover, the Court declared that all the members of a certain demobilised illegal armed front, bloc or structure should respond collectively to the harm caused by the criminal action of individual ex-combatants.[64]

The national and international human rights communities lauded this strong decision by the Constitutional Court. The paramilitary leadership responded by depicting the decision as a 'mortal blow to peace'. Indeed, some expressed their concerns about the reparations aspects of the decision—apparently they had expected to keep significant portions of their fortunes safe.

Now, the key question is whether or not these technical criminal justice processes contained in the 'Peace and Justice' law have the potential for the transformation of long-standing power structures. It remains to be seen whether prosecutions, trials and reparations under this Law have the collective capacity to break up the hegemonic influence that paramilitary structures have exercised in significant elements of Colombian public life at

[60] *Ibid* at s 6.2.2.1.7.15.
[61] *Ibid* at s 6.2.4.1.11.
[62] *Ibid* at s 6.2.4.1.12.
[63] *Ibid* at s 6.2.4.3.1.3.
[64] *Ibid* at s 6.2.4.4.7.

the national level. In addition, on the ground, according to many who live and work in the communities in which they operate, paramilitary violence has particularly targeted the communal governance and participation structures. At leadership and middle-level structures of local governance, researchers and activists report systemic infiltration and attempts to control such bodies, in effect maintaining paramilitary hegemony through political and lawful means. Can a small number of criminal processes against the paramilitary leadership and some mid-ranking cadres under the 'Justice and Peace' law really impact upon such control strategies in local communities? Finally, in Colombia the paramilitary 'project' of dominance has involved local and regional land-owners, rich merchants, businessmen and politicians. Their activities would not have been possible without such political, financial and logistical support. The narrow focus of the Justice and Peace Law upon demobilised paramilitaries in effect obfuscates that broader architecture of support and complicity amongst some the country's most powerful actors.

V TRANSITIONAL JUSTICE FROM BELOW: LOCALISED EMERGING SITES OF TRANSITION

The previous two sections have addressed the engagement of national human rights NGOs, organised communities and grassroots initiatives in public debate on transitional justice. These sections sought to demonstrate the ways in which players from below contested the images of an official transition and use rights rhetoric in particular to resist state-directed hegemonic understandings of what is occurring.

Using two examples, I will argue in this section that players from below are also creating localised sites of transition beyond the national 'Peace and Justice' legal framework. Forced to confront transforming local power dynamics, players from below are deploying their own variants of transitional justice discourses to deal with concrete issues associated with ex-combatants and recipient communities. Although not part of the mainstream transitional justice framework, these scenarios indicate the possibilities for transforming violent and oppressive dynamics within communities, and can be perceived as emerging sites of transition. As Santos and Rodríguez- Garavito affirm, discussing the approach of 'Subaltern cosmopolitan legality', the idea is precisely to 'render visible and credible the potential that lies implicit or remains embryonic' in these experiences.[65] I am seeking here to interpret these kind of embryonic experiences in a spirit that has been described by Santos as the 'sociology of emergence':

> This approach allows us to identify and explore emerging themes or activities that might otherwise be dismissed as idealistic, hopeless or past-oriented.[66]

A Recognition of Victims, Truth-Telling and Property Restitution: the Experience of the Government of the City of Medellín[67]

The city of Medellín has been one of the key areas of urban conflict in the Colombian conflict. Inhabitants of Medellín's peripheral boroughs have experienced successive wars involving Marxist militias, counterinsurgent paramilitary fronts, drug cartels, criminal gangs operating at the service of all of them, and official military and police forces. In addition, Medellín is one of the most important urban reception centres for ex-combatants in the country: by March 2006 the city was receiving 14 per cent of the total number of demobilised and 3,859 ex-combatants were living in the city.[68]

Within the framework of its Security and Co-Existence Policy, the city administration decided to establish the Peace and Reconciliation Programme to offer ex-combatants additional reintegration benefits beyond those offered by the national government, including the opportunity to participate in the design of 'co-existence initiatives'. The Peace and Reconciliation Programme has become one of the city's flagship programmes with an annual budget close to US$1million .

Despite a very low budget and little political visibility, the Secretary of Interior of the city also launched the 'Victims of Armed Conflict' project ('the Victims' Project') in 2004. This project aims to dignify and rehabilitate direct and indirect victims of the armed conflict. The local administrative division that established the project advocated making victims' issues visible in order to give them a 'social dimension' by organising academic, artistic and educational activities to sensitise mass media and the public around the existence, stories and actual problems of the victims of the

[65] B de Sousa Santos and CA Rodríguez-Garavito, 'Law, Politics and the Subaltern in Counter-Hegemonic Globalisation' in B de Sousa Santos and CA Rodríguez-Garavito (eds), *Law and Globalisation from Below: Towards a Cosmopolitan Legality* (Cambridge, Cambridge University Press, 2005) at 18.

[66] *Ibid.*

[67] The discussions advanced is this section draw upon formal and informal interviews and visits between August 2005 and June 2006.

[68] G Villegas (Director del Programa de Paz y Convivencia de la Alcaldía de Medellín), 'Modelo de Regreso a la Legalidad' in *Reinserción, Reconciliación y Ciudades* (Bogotá, Fundación Ideas para la Paz/ Konrad Adenauer Stiftung/ Alcaldía Mayor de Bogotá/ Alcaldía de Medellín/ Foros Semana, 2006) 37.

armed conflict.[69] The city plans to open a space for collective catharsis that could contribute to the social recovery and reconciliation and intends to support victims in accessing ordinary public education, health and training services and to provide psycho-social and legal assistance to victims.

As such, both the 'Peace and Reconciliation' and the Victims' Project have opened localised sites of transition within communities which have been previously immersed in local wars. The city has established direct contact with victims, ex-combatants and recipient communities. With detailed knowledge of power dynamics within communities, the administration has intervened to try to contribute to the resolution of concrete problems within the community. The local administration states that they appeal to explicitly expressed community values (such as the reconstruction of damaged familial relationships) in its interaction with ex-combatants and victims.

The direct intervention of the local administration has decisively contributed to the return of urban property illegally taken by paramilitary ex-combatants. They have also worked on clarifying the circumstances surrounding the deaths and disappearances of certain members of the community. Through psycho-social support workshops, the Victims' Project received complaints from victims who claim that ex-combatants forced them to abandon their properties and in many cases their neighbourhoods. Paramilitary militias and criminal gangs associated with them used their houses as barracks, rented or sold the properties to finance the armed group or gave the properties to their own family members or friends. The Victims' Project identified and contacted the heads of the gangs, militias or paramilitary fronts (demobilised combatants participating in the Reintegration programme or combatants serving prison sentences) to persuade them to return the properties back to their legitimate owners. In cases in which houses had been sold or rented to third persons, the Victims' Project insisted that the ex-combatants return the price to the buyer or terminate the lease, so that the houses could be returned to their original owners. By July 2006, 194 urban properties had been returned.

The projects have also contributed to the initiation of discussions at the community level about what happened during the war and the motives and consequences of violence. During the psycho-social support process, ex-combatants participating in the Reintegration into Civilian Life Programme have expressed their need to tell their own stories of victimisation and to explain to the families of their victims why they did what they did.

[69] While discussing different alternatives, the team has started to take and house testimonies of victims. They have organised writing workshops to encourage victims to tell their stories. 20 of those stories are being compiled in a book for publication. Alcaldía de Medellín, 'Proyecto Víctimas del Conflicto Armado'. Available online at http://www.medellin.gov.co/victimasconflicto/quehacemos.jsp.

In a few cases, ex-combatants who participated in forced disappearances, executions, sexual assaults, threats and forced displacements have confronted the family members of the victims and have explained to them their versions of events. Perpetrators acknowledge the crime but at the same time want their own suffering heard and recognised. In the majority of cases in which the ex-combatant comes forward to acknowledge his own wrongdoing, he also presents and perceives himself as a victim. Crimes are often explained and justified as: 'I killed your son because he killed my brother' or 'I killed your brother to vengeance the tainted honor of my sister'.

B Transforming Victims into Citizens: Grassroots Reconciliation Initiatives in Eastern Antioquia Province[70]

Medellín is the capital city of Antioquia, a region which has been an epicentre of the Colombian armed conflict. The eastern region of the province has been disputed territory between the Marxist insurgency and the right-wing paramilitary forces allied with official military forces. East Antioquia had during the 1980s one of the most active social movements in the country around the distribution of economic benefits derived from the construction of several hydro-electric and communication projects.[71] During the 1980s and 1990s the region was one of the major strongholds of the two main guerrilla groups, but in 1997 the paramilitaries entered the region implementing and deploying a proven 'terror strategy' against the population. As the paramilitary fronts did in other regions of the country where trade-unions, civic and grassroots organisations were particularly strong, they conducted several selective killings and massacres, targeting peasant leaders and their communities, accusing them of being guerrilla supporters. In the late 1990s and early 2000, the region suffered a serious humanitarian crisis, including the forced displacement of more than 30,000 people.[72]

In spite of the acute military confrontation and the terror strategy implemented by the paramilitary fronts in the region, the tradition of social organisation and active participation in public matters persists. During the worst years of the humanitarian crisis (from 2000 onwards) a strong peace

[70] The discussions advanced in this section are based on the author's participation in several workshops with victims, multiple conversations with community leaders and those in charge of the project at the two local NGOs involved and several visits conducted from 2003 to 2007.

[71] SM Hincapié Jiménez, 'Contexto de los Crímenes de Lesa Humanidad—Valle de Aburrá y Oriente Antioqueño 2000–2004' in Instituto Popular de Capacitación de la Corporación de Promoción Popular, *Píldoras para la Memoria* (n 32 above) at 31.

[72] *Ibid.*

movement developed in the region, gaining national and international recognition. Local mayors, in association with civic and grassroots organisations, promoted local humanitarian agreements among all armed actors in order to protect the civil population and democratically-elected authorities. Organised communities, social organisations and grassroots initiatives continued to actively take part in democratic participatory scenarios and exercises. Participatory planning, budgeting and controlling mechanisms flourished in the region.

In particular, the women's rights movement has played a key role in the empowerment of victims and in setting the reconciliation agenda in the region.[73] The *Asociación de Mujeres del Oriente Antioqueño* (AMOR),[74] a grassroots organisation which traditionally worked on women's political and civic participation, decided in 2003 that it needed to develop focused activities to support and empower victims who had been most affected by the armed conflict. With the support of a well-known NGO based in Medellín, Conciudadanía, and the 'Peace Programme' of the Jesuit Community, members of AMOR were trained as 'Promoters of Life and Mental Health' and were encouraged to form victim's mutual support groups in their villages.

More than 70 'Promoters of Life and Mental Health' have now completed their training with each leading a victim's mutual support group. More than 850 victims take part in the groups. According to a 'Promoter of Life and Mental Health' leading the work with victims in the municipality of Alejandría, 'the work with victims of the war has permeated many things'[75] in her town. The victims have started to rediscover their voice, to gain agency and to reconstruct their life projects. In different municipalities women victims participating in the support groups have stopped serving food to their disappeared sons and husbands and have started to participate in community organising activities. The women have also become less aggressive and have worked on enhancing their parenting skills.

AMOR activists, youth organisations and civic leaders of the municipalities—encouraged by Conciudadanía and the 'Peace Programme' of the Jesuit Community—are now forming local 'Reconciliation Committees' in a number of villages of East Antioquia with a view to empowering victims. According to their leaders, these Reconciliation Committees should be able to advocate for and encourage victims to exercise their

[73] SM Hincapié Jiménez, 'Contexto de los Crímenes de Lesa Humanidad—Valle de Aburrá y Oriente Antioqueño 2000–2004' in Instituto Popular de Capacitación de la Corporación de Promoción Popular, *Píldoras para la Memoria* (n 32 above).

[74] Translated as 'Association of Women of East Antioquia'.

[75] Interview with Enith González, Promoter of Life and Mental Health of the Village of Alejandría, East Antioquia (July 2006).

rights and play a role in the reconstruction of the local social fabric. With the support of local NGOs, the 'Peace Programme' of the Jesuit Community and, in some cases, local administrations, the Reconciliation Committees have organised different actions for the recovery of the memory and dignity of victims. They constantly organise peaceful demonstrations and public gatherings showing pictures of the dead and disappeared; they have started to compile names, dates and brief descriptions of circumstances of the death and disappearance of members of their communities; and more recently they have engaged in the 'justice and peace' debate articulating what they consider as reparations.

In November 2005, AMOR, Conciudadanía and the 'Peace Programme' of the Jesuit Community called for the first regional forum of victims of the armed conflict. Under the banner of *Transforming Victims into Citizens*, they argued, 'we want other voices to be heard and to transform our pain into proposing capacity'. The forum aimed to open the space for reflection among victims in order to encourage them to adopt their own agenda to advocate for their rights to truth, justice and reparations; to encourage the peace movement in the region to acknowledge the victims and to show its solidarity with them; and to strengthen local women's organisations and AMOR networks. Four hundred persons of all the 23 municipalities of the region participated.

At the end of the forum, different working-groups presented their conclusions. The victims did not promote the incarceration of perpetrators, but were more concerned with truth-telling and the recovery of their daily social and economic life. The working-groups agreed that truth presents a crucial component to any reconciliation effort. The participants understood 'truth' in various ways: that the testimonies and stories of victims should be publicly heard in order to recover the dignity of the dead and the disappeared; that information about the fate of the disappeared is disclosed; that offenders could tell their stories, considering that many of them are also victims who decided to take revenge. The groups even mentioned the desirability of establishing a truth commission in the future.

Various discussions emerged concerning the relationship between victims and government authorities. Participants stressed the need for state acknowledgement of the existence of victims and the implementation of programmes for guaranteeing their rights to housing, nourishment, health, education and access to jobs. Various groups identified the 'Promoters of Life and Mental Health' as a significant human resource among their communities and they asked the local administrations to incorporate or articulate the work of those women into the official health and community development services.

With regard to reparations, the participants reached consensus on the need for 'holistic reparations' and stressed that the state must comply with its obligation to grant economic reparations. In the case of the forcibly displaced population, the participants argued that the state should restitute the land and other property that had been stolen by armed actors. Symbolic reparation was also seen as important, but could not replace economic reparation.

With the paramilitary demobilisation process the municipalities of East Antioquia have become ex-combatant reception centres. A certain percentage of ex-combatants (not yet to be determined by official or non-governmental agencies) have decided to return to the villages where they were born and grew up and where they still have family members.[76] Grassroots initiatives are inviting ex-combatants to take part in democratic participatory initiatives as a way to start including them in reconciliation discussions and—in the future—reconciliation actions. In a few cases, ex-combatants have approached AMOR activists to ask for psycho-social support and as an entry point to community life.

Community leaders, among them the 'Promoter of Life and Metal Health', in the town of Alejandría established a series of closed meetings with the six ex-combatants living in the village.[77] The ultimate purpose of the process, as conceived by the 'Promoter of Life and Mental Health', is to open the door for reconciliation. Reflecting on reconciliation, she asks herself:

> How are we supposed to reconcile? The victims alone cannot reconcile, neither can the victims and civil society; we need them (the ex-combatants).[78]

The 'Promoter of Life and Mental Health' perceives the sessions with the ex-combatants as an opportunity for some victims to embark on a mourning process. According to her, the process could lead to the recognition by the ex-combatants of the existence of the victims and the harm they have caused. She insists that:

[76] *Ibid.*

[77] All of the ex-combatants were born, grew up and started their productive life in the village (Alejandría). However, the area of military operations to which they were assigned did not include Alejandría but neighbouring villages. Five of the ex-combatants have very basic literacy level and only one completed secondary school. With economic support of the National Reintegration into Civil Life Programme, four of the ex-combatants established a pork-raising productive project in the outskirts of the village. The other two are working on the fields in the rural area of the municipality. They want to stay in the village because they feel safe there. The ex-combatant who completed secondary school is de facto acting as a leader of the others. He has stated that he wishes to be respected and esteemed, and not stigmatised, by the community—so far the ex-combatants are looked at with certain suspicion by their neighbours. The ex-combatants argue that the war was legitimised and financed by others—they were just the 'trigger operators', but behind them there is a long chain of merchants, ranchers and businessmen who gave the orders and paid for the operations. Unlike them, they claim, these people are not coming forward—they are invisible. Ex-combatants also claim that being in the front was in fact the only job opportunity available to them. Interview with E González (n 76 above).

[78] Interview with E González (n 76 above).

> victims and ex-combatants will end up facing each other. The victims are demanding certain things from them—to know where the disappeared are, for example—and the ex-combatants want to know about the victims.

In fact, in the second closed session with the two psychologists and the 'Promoter of Life and Mental Health', the ex-combatants expressed their curiosity about the public activities of the victims' movement in the village and in the region. The 'Promoter of Life and Mental Health' explains that the encounter between the victims with whom she has been working in the village and the ex-combatants could probably happen easily because the front to which they belonged did not attack the village and its community. She believes that probably, once the ex-combatants understand the pain and the needs of their fellow community members (the victims living in Alejandría), they will want to approach the victims of the villages in which they caused harm.

Such encounter between victims and ex-combatants of Alejandría might soon become true. With the financial support of the 'Peace Laboratories' strategy of the European Union, the Association of Municipalities of East Antioquia in January 2007 began implementing a development project in the urban area of Alejandría (economic production, housing improvement and technical training). Community leaders proposed to the local administration that the project should involve ex-combatants and victims and their families. The victims and ex-combatants consulted eventually accepted the proposal.

Anthropologist Kimberley Theidon, conducting field research on Disarmament Demobilization and Reintegration (DDR) in Colombia, affirms that demobilisation processes implicate 'multiple transitions'[79]. In her view, DDR programmes implicate transitions for ex-combatants turning in their weapons, for governments seeking a way out of conflict, and for communities receiving the demobilised. According to Theidon, at each level the transition is a complex, conflicting and dynamic equation involving truth, justice, reparations and reconciliation. In the Colombian case, she argues, this equation is even more complicated, since the multiple transitions have to be addressed in a 'pre-post conflict' context.

VI CONCLUSION

The Colombian context vividly illustrates that contemporary transitional justice should not be viewed as synonymous with political transition from oppressive regimes to democratic ones or with negotiated ends to armed conflict. Rather, contemporary transitional justice may form part of a

[79] Theidon and Betancourt, 'Transiciones Conflictivas: Combatientes Desmovilisados en Colombia' (n 34 above).

partial, messy and uneven process of state-sponsored transformation directed at one element of the conflict. There is little sense that the country is geared up for ending its 40-year internal armed conflict with the guerrilla groups and FARC in particular. Colombia is certainly not experiencing a transition in the sense of a radical political transformation at the national or institutional level—there is no deepening or widening of democracy.

What the National Government and the paramilitary leadership present as the *transition,* is perceived and experienced in a completely different way by players from below. While the former present the paramilitary demobilisation process as a 'peace process' that is enabling the state to recover control over the territory of the country, many of those on the ground in various regions of the country are experiencing the paramilitary demobilisation as paramilitary 'legitimisation' processes—ex-combatants becoming organised in participating in community governance structures and local economic, political and administrative life. At one level this is often precisely the goal of demobilisation processes—ensuring that ex-combatants are given the opportunity to retake their role in civic and political life. However, such a perspective pre-supposes a change in mindset and strategies amongst the ex-combatants. Despite the rhetoric and powerful symbolism of the televised demobilisation ceremonies, many in Colombian civil society are deeply cynical as to whether paramilitaries have in reality abandoned their oppressive techniques for the exercise of power in the local communities where they are strong.

However the Colombian experience also illustrates more positive examples of the capacity of transitional justice. At a practical level, the two examples discussed show that a capacity for positive communal transformation is emerging. The Medellín example shows how a local administration can play an active role with regard to victims' acknowledgement and truth-telling exercises. Medellín is also a good example of certain positive synergies between reintegration policies and those directed to victims' recovery. The experience of the 'Reconciliation Committees' in East Antioquia suggests that tremendous energy exists at grassroots-level victims' mutual support groups and shows how community leaders can play a significant role in reconstructing non-violent relationships between ex-combatants and recipient communities.

At a political level, the Colombian experience also suggests that transitional justice discourses may be used as a strategy of resistance by civil society and communities affected by violence. In particular the deployment of the truth, justice and reparations rights discourse has proved a powerful tool for such 'players from below' in their struggle against impunity. Building alliances with international human rights networks and deploying these discourses, such actors have successfully shaped the terms of the debate at the national level. They provided an antidote to official formulas that advocated the sacrificing of the interests of victims and communities in the name of this 'new concept of justice' which was used to justify the accommodation with the paramilitaries. 'Transitional justice from below' gave such actors a language and framework to challenge a state-sponsored attempt to use transitional justice as a cover for a much more base political accommodation.

10

Burden or Benefit? Paradoxes of Penal Transition in Russia

LAURA PIACENTINI*

I INTRODUCTION

AS THE WORLD becomes more internationalist and transactions between states cross all boundaries, it is becoming gradually more common to explore how the dimensions of transition and globalisation are felt on the ground, or 'from below'. In environments the world over political structures have collapsed and fallen away from national boundaries. Modes of governance (trade, transnational corporations, and developments in communication, transport and rule-making) have transcended the nation state. On the one hand, the effect is the integration of a range of hitherto demarcated activities across state borders. On the other hand, cross-border transactions depend on complex webs of dependency, relations and influence. In relating these developments to criminal justice, scholars have trained attention on a wide range of societies undergoing turbulent transition to democratic modes of governance. While transitional justice scholarship focuses on national and local transformation of domestic legal systems and criminal justice practices, in the wake of seismic global, political events, criminal justice institutions are also accountable to international norms enshrined in international bodies. Transitional justice, therefore, is subject to global and regional spheres of influence.

The collection of articles in this book trains attention specifically on the effects of transitional justice 'from below' and refers to the sites other than the state, in community, civil society or private sector locations. However, I want to argue that the focus should include an analysis of the outplaying of justice discourses in one state sub-system, albeit one which has traditionally been only marginally regulated by law: the prison. In particular, I am interested in exploring how a version of human rights discourse, inculcated

* I would like to thank Kieran McEvoy, Lorna McGregor and the reviewers of the chapter for their extremely helpful comments on earlier drafts.

as part of the supposed post-Soviet transition, has been interpreted and implemented 'on the ground' in the Russian prison system. Like other societies undergoing transition, the nature and scope of economic, political and social fragmentation and transformation in Russia have been monumental. Russia's legal, policy and ideological architecture has gone through a remarkable 'from above' re-theorisation from a Soviet one-party totalitarian model to a multi-party democracy.

The 'from below' perspective in this context is therefore one which analyses the way in which human rights discourses are implemented, co-opted or resisted during a transition from totalitarian rule. Such standards are classically viewed as 'other', 'foreign' or 'imposed' from above. The chapter argues that rather than lead to the indigenisation of criminal justice, Russia's penal transition might be indicative of a new era in global penal politics, whereby the forceful impetus of human rights discourses is becoming a forceful external mechanism for imbuing a sense of shame in institutions which were historically largely immune to such notions. The chapter will debate the burdens and benefits of these developments. The chapter begins by discussing transitional justice, prisons and global change. It then goes on to outline Russia's penal history, followed by empirical evidence gathered from five weeks spent in two Russian prison establishments in Siberia, where I interviewed personnel on aspects of Russia's penal transition.

II TRANSITIONAL JUSTICE, PRISONS AND GLOBAL CHANGE

Much of the theorisation that underpins transitional justice is constructed around addressing human rights crimes, establishing the rule of law, historical injustices, systemic abuse, and victims' and survivors' rights, though a variety of judicial and non-judicial mechanisms. In this respect, transitional justice reconciles conflict between widely disparate, often violent, groups with outcomes that become translated into new political entities and realities. Moreover, while transitional justice is designed to build local capacity in the emerging transition, promoting compliance with international obligations established in international law is also a core principle.

The parameters of transitional justice are discussed at length elsewhere and throughout this book and do not require detailed retelling here.[1] For current purposes, I am particularly interested in the notion of the symbolic

[1] See, eg C Campbell and F Ní Aoláin, 'Local meets Global: Transitional Justice in Northern Ireland' (2003) 26 *Fordham International Law Journal* 871; R Teitel, 'Transitional Justice in the New Era' (2003) 26 *Fordham International Law Journal* 893; and V Pupavac, 'Therapeutic Peace and Justice in Bosnia' (2004) 13 *Social and Legal Studies* 377.

importance of transitional justice as being emblematic of liberal transition.[2] I shall expand on this point further on but briefly here the post-Cold War period has been marked by transitions to market societies with the effect that transitional justice is constructed around 'liberalising' states.[3] Of key note is that Russia has reluctantly conceded that its colossal transition from a totalitarian one-party state to a multi-party democracy has been a legal failure, due in part to the failure of liberalisation and in part to the failure of examining law in the local environment that nurtures it, such that the rule of law is constructed as a 'negative myth'.[4]

When considered in the context of Russia there are two striking, if under-explored, aspects of transitional justice scholarship. The first is more general and relates to prisons as contested sites of transition. The second relates specifically to global transition. The decision to imprison a person, to remove from him or her the capacity to live and act in private society and to subject him or her to the supervision of the state is a fiercely contested political issue, particularly with regard to the acceptable limits to punishment and the legal and human rights of those held captive. Yet, despite the inexorable rise in international prison populations and a notable increase in prisoner complaints,[5] the prison remains the most recognisable symbol of a government's legal right to censure. If we consider this politically, the prison as a state sub-system operates as an exceptional site for mediating political, social, cultural and economic values in ordered and disordered societies.

Expanding on this point, the prison is sometimes referred to as a 'lawless agency' despite the density of prison rules, and that prisons 'exercise arbitrary power over prisoners' lives'.[6] This suggests a paradox, that prisons are rule-bound institutions, and also places where the rule of law is deficient. Such an argument is particularly pertinent for transitional societies where prisons have been used during conflict as an oppressive instrument, holding ordinary and political prisoners alike. In Northern Ireland, South Africa and Iraq, prisoners engaged with political struggle, and prisons were inhabited by captives who utilised imprisonment to become better schooled in political resistance.[7] With dissident voices

[2] Teitel, *ibid.*

[3] F Varese, *The Russian Mafia* (Oxford, Oxford University Press, 2001).

[4] DJ Galligan and M Kurkchiyan (eds), *Law and Informal Practices: The Post-Communist Experience* (Oxford, Oxford University Press, 2003) viii.

[5] S Livingstone, T Owen and A Macdonald, *Prison Law*, 3rd edn (Oxford, Oxford University Press, 2003).

[6] *Ibid* at 546.

[7] K McEvoy, *Paramilitary Imprisonment in Northern Ireland: Resistance Management and Release* (Oxford, Oxford University Press, 2001); FL Buntman, *Robben Island and Prisoner Resistance to Apartheid* (New York, Cambridge University Press, 2003); K McEvoy, K McConnachie and R Jamieson, 'Political Imprisonment and the War on Terror' in Y Jewkes (ed), *A Handbook on Imprisonment* (Cullompton, Willan Publishing, 2007).

speaking from the prison walls, keeping oppression and conflict in the international spotlight, the prison represents the struggle, demoralisation and isolation of prisoners, but also the locus of negotiated settlements. Thus, the prison itself is a site of transition. Indeed the recent prisoner abuse photographs from Abu Ghraib prison in Iraq released in 2006 serve as a reminder that prisons do much more than simply hold society's condemned. In the context of Iraq's transition the recent abuses at Abu Ghraib (which was also a notorious prison in the era of Saddam Hussein) and the ongoing operation of the Guantánamo Bay detainment camps in Cuba have re-ignited an anti-prison consciousness among large sections of the global community, particularly with regard to whether we have hit the limit of legality regarding humane punishment.

Where the rule of law is absent from prisons, this presents a challenge for transitional justice, particularly as prisoners are not a popular political cause generally, and are less likely to have their interests heard in the political arena. It is therefore recognised that for the transitional justice process to produce its desired effects in prisons in transition, international norms and international law are instrumental, as 'the fate of prisoners was a strong motivating factor in the creation of international human rights treaties'.[8] In this respect specialists in prison law and prison sociology use the phrase 'conventional wisdom' to refer to judicial reform of prisons in transition.[9] Conventional wisdom offers political stability and acceptability. Its 'evangelising instinct'[10] is transformed as the yardstick that transcends national borders such that: 'others are also hearing and are thereby in the process of being persuaded'.[11] Conventional wisdom can, therefore, lead to the homogenisation of ideas. The key universal statement that underpins conventional wisdom in the penal realm is that imprisonment *is* the punishment and is not *for* additional punishment. And it is tacitly assumed that states in transition incorporate this conventional wisdom into their national prison law.[12]

Turning attention to global transitions, transitional justice can also be interrogated beyond the local to the global level. The collapse of grand ideological narratives such as Soviet Communism, and the seismic political shifts in the Middle East such as the American-led movement to engage world governments in a democratic and ideological restructuring that commenced with the invasion of Afghanistan and Iraq, are evidence of global transition. Such shifts challenge transitional justice's localised focus

[8] See Livingstone, Owen and Macdonald, *Prison Law* (n 5 above) at 110.

[9] WA Pridemore (ed), *Ruling Russia: Crime, Law and Justice in a Changing Society* (Boulder CO, Rowman & Littlefield, 2005).

[10] JK Galbraith, *The Affluent Society* (Boston MA, Mariner Books, 1976) 10.

[11] *Ibid.*

[12] *See* Pridemore, *Ruling Russia: Crime, Law and Justice in a Changing Society* (n 9 above).

because nation-state restructuring is no longer the exclusive concern of national governments and is permeable to ideas and influences from international actors. Transitional justice scholars have recently focused on this arguing, that

> Local conceptions, while eliding the problems of extending abstract ideas of justice, run the risk of missing the broader power politics associated with the Post-Cold War globalising transformations.[13]

I see this as a two-stage process. First, by using the language of transition, dominant political actors are highlighting and reforming so-called 'failed societies'. Secondly, transitional justice ideas are being used internationally to link to legal, political and ideological re-structuring of a modernisation agenda, and this may cause difficulty in creating a dialogue about how to address state harms utilising existing national and local discourses.

The following section discusses Russia's century-long, oppressive penal system and is followed by a discussion of the research findings. I argue that Russia's post-Soviet transition has pulled its criminal justice system and criminal justice norms in different directions, particularly with regard to the integration of international standards in prisons that are felt as 'coercive', while local capacity for transitional justice is viewed as 'inferior'.

III RUSSIA'S TWENTIETH CENTURY PENAL ATROCITY

Russia has a brutal and atypical penal history that remains woefully neglected in the criminological and socio-legal scholarship. The Soviet Union was the world's biggest incarcerator for most of the 20th century, with as many as 12 million prisoners being held in places of confinement during Stalinism; a time when citizens were 'greedily consumed' by the state to work in forced labour camps.[14] Soviet penology was a complex mechanism. The exceptionality of the overly-powerful prison system was such that the carceral and the cultural met and meshed to create a unique penal configuration that fused political ideology with a supplanted legal discourse to create a camp-industrial complex. Crime and punishment were constructed around the utopian destiny of Marxism/Leninism: all crime was capitalist excess and punishment must therefore seek to politically correct deviants from being wreckers of Soviet harmony to become perfect proletarians. From a criminological perspective the myth-making was audacious. Prisoners would work on national economic projects,

[13] See Teitel, 'Transitional Justice in the New Era' (n 1 above) at 894.

[14] AI Solzhenitsyn, *The Gulag Archipelago* (London, Harper Collins, 1986) 214. See also \ Applebaum, *Gulag: A History* (New York, Random House, 2003).

elevating their status as builders of communism (and not as profaned convicts). The reality however was that millions of citizens were subjected to clandestine trials before being sent to prison camps all over the USSR and forced to work, often to death. If loyalty to the USSR was the ideological foundation of penal policy and criminal law then the Gulag (Central Administration of Camps) was one mechanism that operated political correction of the captive population.

Created in 1934 the Gulag was a giant industrial camp complex that operated way beyond crime control in the usual sense by providing state functions. Indeed, the Gulag penal system became the exaggerated microcosm of Soviet bureaucracy and social control. It has been stated that

> [l]ife does not develop normally in the USSR and in accordance with its inner laws but is created artificially in ways not to undermine the basic principles of the ideology.[15]

Thus, 20th century criminal justice in Russia was artificially manufactured to service the command economy; rather than respond to crime per se. By the time the Soviet Union imploded in 1991, human rights abuses, massive overcrowding, disease and torture were found to be common in the prison system. Tuberculosis was rife, prisoners died of overcrowding and malnutrition. Victims of AIDS joined the prison population. The problems remain, and are particularly acute, in the remand prisons (*SIZO*). Although Soviet imprisonment was notorious having been discredited and discarded for decades by dissidents and the international human rights community, the horrifying scale of the brutality was reported as follows by the United Nations Special Rapporteur on Torture:

> The Special Rapporteur would need the poetic skills of a Dante or the artistic skills of a Bosch adequately to describe the infernal conditions he found in these cells ... The conditions are cruel, inhuman and degrading; they are torturous.[16]

The relentless negative publicity continued throughout the early 1990s when there was acute turbulence in the criminal justice system. Detention rates rose sharply in the period after the collapse, which, coupled with political and economic ineptitude, meant that few were clear about exactly which direction the penal system should take.

Although state violations and the monumental structural problems that created huge social and economic neglect were evident and deplored internationally, there was very little engagement with holding those

[15] S Bloch and P Reddaway, *Russia's Political Hospitals: The Abuse of Psychiatry in the Soviet Union* (London, Gollancz, 1997) at 14.

[16] N Rodley, 'Report of the Special Rapporteur, Mr. Nigel S Rodley, submitted pursuant to Commission on Human Rights resolution 1994/37, Addendum, Visit by the Special Rapporteur to the Russian Federation', UN Economic and Social Council (16 November 1994) E/CN.4/1995/32/Add.1.

accountable for state repression. This would mark a departure from the transitional justice project. Transitional justice demands a pragmatic and theoretical assessment of what is possible within societies that are deeply divided. As huge and dreadful as Russian criminal justice was, the human rights abuses in that country do not fit easily into the existing transitional justice orthodoxy of 'society at/in conflict' due to several factors. First, the USSR did not end following the particularly violent episode of Stalinism. Secondly, there were no violent politics upon which to establish peace and transform legal and non-legal judicial processes. Thirdly, as Russians often remark about their 20th century, there was a strong national identity and stability.[17] Individuals in Russia could have been held to account in the formal sense for penal atrocities such as unlawful sentencing, but exactly *who* is held to account over the collapse of Marxism/Leninism—an ideology that underpinned Soviet society for over 70 years—was a far more complex process. And with no indigenous sensibility that operated outside of the dominant repressive practices of the state, the Soviet case study presents a unique test case of administering transitional justice.

With regard to 'emerging' from a penal trauma, Russia therefore faces difficulties when the huge political events that have marked the late 20th and early 21st centuries are taken into account. Achieving the outcome of resolution and popular participation in the global transition context is extremely complex because traditional state structures have become more fluid and less demarcated. Thus, governments are looking to international law as the benchmark for galvanising accountability and it is now tacitly assumed that nations will integrate international norms into their national legislation.[18]

IV PENAL COSMOPOLITANISM AND TRANSITIONAL JUSTICE FROM ABOVE

Findings from prison research and analysis of official policy documents are presented. Prison research was conducted in two Siberian prison regions over five weeks in Omsk and in Kemerovo in 2003. I conducted semi-structured interviews with 27 senior prison personnel (12 in Omsk and 15 in Kemerovo, including the two Generals who manage each region). The research followed up a large-scale comparative study of four penal colonies in two geographically disparate regions (Omsk and Smolensk), that was

[17] A Meier, *Black Earth: A Journey Through Russia After the Fall* (New York, WW Norton & Company, 2003).

[18] D Galligan and D Sandler, 'Implementing Human Rights' in S Halliday and P Schmidt (eds), *Human Rights Brought Home: Socio-Legal Perspectives on Human Rights in the National Context* (Oxford, Hart Publishing, 2004).

conducted in 1999.[19] The research examined post-Soviet prison labour. Once the central tenet of the state, nowadays prisoners' work performs a myriad of confused and contradictory functions. The 2003 research aimed to return to the themes of the 1999 study and sought to interrogate the interface between indigenous and imported knowledges in the new penal landscape. How, for example, are new penal ideological frameworks formed? What is their point of origin? The research upon which this chapter is based found that contemporary Russian prisons are legally and ideologically shaped by international human rights discourses. I characterise this as a form of 'Penal Cosmopolitanism'; the inevitable outcome of tensions between transposing European ideas onto Russia and the insecure, politically illiberal government and the fractured social welfare infrastructure that worsened dramatically in the decade following the collapse of the USSR. How penal cosmopolitanism emerged is discussed below.

The collapse of the USSR led to a rethink not only of the political economy but also, and perhaps more importantly, Russia's sense of belonging, or not belonging, to the transnational world community.[20] Political scientists, writing on cosmopolitanism, argue that transnational connectivity was central to Russia's political positioning post-1991.[21] There is not the space here to elaborate in detail the cosmopolitan perspective except to say that it is associated with a normative politics and global democratic trend that view the individual as a citizen of the world or someone who wishes to transcend nationalistic outlooks.[22] It is invoked in this chapter because in the Soviet era, the demarcated ideological boundaries between global nation-states were seen increasingly as divisive, exclusionary and destructive. As there was a need to orient the political communities of the former Soviet Bloc towards integration, cosmopolitanism was the tradition that resolved philosophical and cultural differences. In the post-Soviet world, the global vernacular talked of 'advocacy networks', 'global social movements', 'humanity and citizenship'. The cosmopolitanism that Russia openly engaged with was grounded in the idea of world citizenship, with tangible benefits and pragmatic policy outcomes that included personhood rights, environmental responsibility and human rights.[23] Interestingly, in criminal justice, Russia stood in stark

[19] See L Piacentini, *Surviving Russian Prisons: Punishment, economy and politics in Transition* (Cullompton, Willan Publishing, 2004).

[20] See C Rumford, 'Cosmopolitanism and Europe: Towards a new EU studies agenda?' (2005) 18 *Innovation* 1.

[21] See G Delanty and C Rumford, *Rethinking Europe: Social Theory and the Implications of Europeanization* (London, Routledge, 2005).

[22] D Beetham, 'Human rights as a model for cosmopolitan democracy' in D Archibugi, D Held, and M Kohler (eds), *Re-imagining Political Community: Studies in Cosmopolitan Democracy* (Cambridge, Polity Press, 1998).

[23] B Rosamond, 'Discourses of globalisation and the social construction of European identities' (1999) 6 *Journal of European Public Policy* 652.

contrast to its high-prison society counterpart, America, with its preference for an incapacitative and retributivist criminal justice system. In Russia, a multiplicity of other identifications of universality emerged quick and fast in criminal justice and legal jurisdictions.

How a penal cosmopolitanism committed to human rights was imported into Russia during transition is due to three key events. First is the exposure of the inhumane prison conditions; second was the proposed accession of Russia to the Council of Europe (a process predicated on invigorating the notion of Russians as European citizens); and third was the ineptitude of the Yeltsin administration and its failure to develop a localised, indigenised penal framework. The momentous effect of these three key events was that criminal justice, criminal law and penal law came to mainstream 'European human rights values'. Constitutional re-structuring dominated the immediate post-Soviet era. In 1992 some very important changes were made to penal law in order to protect the rights of prisoners. In 1992, a new Corrective Labour Code was passed and this marked—officially at least—a process of change. The Russian Parliament adopted amendments to 41 Articles of the Corrective Labour Code. The changes reflected the provisions laid down in the United Nations Minimum Standard Rules for the Detention of Prisoners.

Alongside the corrective labour legislation that regulates the execution of criminal sentences, the Law of 21 July 1993 on establishments and organs executing custodial sentences, which is in fact a law on the prison system, also came into force in Russia. 'A Concept Paper for the Reorganisation of the Penal System of the Ministry of the Interior of Russia', published in 1995, aimed at ending the system of penal exile and defining a 'concept of human rights' that could be written into the criminal justice legislative organs and legislation. The concept paper also envisaged changes to custodial arrangements so that criminals could be sentenced and dealt with in the region where they lived. Bowring has listed many different changes and has assessed the effects of the establishment of a Constitutional Court in 1994, in particular the significant decisions of the Court to entitle prisoners with legal rights to complain about their treatment, to direct judges to acquit cases where there was insufficient evidence rather than send cases back for further investigation and, perhaps most significantly, to declare the death penalty unconstitutional).[24]

[24] B Bowring, *Recent Developments in the Russian Justice System. Department for International Development*, Roundtable Discussion on Russian Prison Reform, 28 November 2002.

A Emergence of External Drivers 1996–99

The main impetus for penal reform during Russia's transition was the proposed accession of Russia into the Council of Europe. In preparation for this the Council of Europe's policy in the early 1990s was to actively review Russia's compliance with Council standards in preparation for rendering a decision on admitting Russia as a member state. The Council of Europe Delegations from 1992 onwards made human rights their centre-piece issue. The Council sent teams of independent experts and Parliamentary Assembly representatives to gather information and conduct interrogations including conducting first-hand prison visits and meeting with government officials and human rights groups. The Council of Europe in 1995 reported:

> [t]he criminal-procedure legislation does not yet entirely comply with international legal instruments concerning the protection of human and civil rights. In particular, it is still necessary to introduce into Russian legislation a system of judicial control over basic investigatory actions.[25]

Although Russian authorities embraced compliance with external bodies relatively quickly, the transition to liberalise criminal justice was slow to take effect on the ground. Until 1996 the Special Rapporteur's reports stated that the presence of UN monitors had no noticeable effect on inhumane conditions in Russia's overcrowded pre-trial detention facilities.[26] At a Novokuznetsk penal facility, 11 people died and dozens of others required hospital treatment for oxygen deprivation—by far the worst result of negligence. Human Rights Watch reported that suspects spent on average 10 months in detention during the investigatory period, and 16 per cent of all pre-trial inmates languished for months or even years awaiting trial. Interestingly, non-governmental organisations (NGOs) reported at that time that the Yeltsin government welcomed human rights delegations with rapacious speed but that

> [p]olitical pressure to grant Russia membership in order to win political and economic compliance jeopardised broad and sufficiently serious consideration of the experts' concerns.[27]

[25] The Council of Europe, 'Russia's request for membership of the Council of Europe', Doc 7443 Addendum II, 2 January 1996 (appendix to the Russian message to the Parliamentary Assembly on the improvement of the Russian legislation and law enforcement practice in accordance with the Council of Europe's standards), available online at: http://assembly.coe.int/Documents/WorkingDocs/doc96/EDOC7443ADII.htm .

[26] See N Rodley, *The Treatment Of Prisoners Under International Law* (New York, Oxford University Press, 2000).

[27] Human Rights Watch, 'Developments in the Russian Federation (1996)', (World Report 1997), available online at http://www.hrw.org/reports/1997/WR97/HELSINKI-13.htm#P530_158817 (visited 19 July 2006) 2.

By 1997, Russia had joined the Council of Europe and new criminal procedure and criminal correctional codes based on the standards and principles of the Council of Europe were introduced. Russia had also ratified key international conventions that included: the European Convention for the Prevention of Torture and Inhuman or Degrading Treatment or Punishment; the Convention on the Protection of Human Rights and Basic Freedoms; and the Convention on Legal Aid and Legal Relations. Indeed, since Russia's accession into the Council of Europe, there has been a legislative avalanche, with over 2000 legislative acts or amendments, including laws on the Status of Judges, the Agencies of the Judicial Community, the work of Defence Lawyers and the Bar, and Freedom of Conscience and Religious Association.

B Tensions between Local Actions and External Drivers 1999–2003

As Woodiwiss notes, reforms coupled with social and cultural relations, political ties and the prospect of greater economic cross-border growth are some of the features of 'good states'.[28] Although Russia had passed the test of political credibility through accession to the Council of Europe, it was clear that the direction in which Russia was heading under Yeltsin jeopardised its burgeoning international standing. Yet amid all the chaos and turbulence of the Yeltsin years, there were some interesting developments in the prison realm.

Previous research into the post-Soviet penal transition has found that for a period in the mid-late 1990s the incompetence of the Yeltsin administration in all spheres weakened the central government's control of the penal system with the effect that penal regions managed and administered their own budgets and practices (although prison establishments remained subject to the Penal Code). An amalgam of confusing and contradictory interventions emerged.[29] This was a particularly interesting period because there was policy transfer but also partial historical continuity, particularly to the East, which retained some Soviet penal ideology (the importance of work in the social context) but within a new community justice vision. This is not to say that human rights did not feature. Rather, central government was weak and the regions were left to fend for themselves.

International pressure subsequently mounted on Russian authorities and the problem of the rapidly deteriorating penal system was deemed to require international solutions. Thus, the significant end of Yelstin's era in

[28] A Woodiwiss, 'Human Rights and the Challenge of Cosmopolitanism' (2002) 19 *Theory, Culture & Society* 139

[29] See Piacentini, *Surviving Russian Prisons* (n 19 above).

1999 and the early years of President Putin marked (in the criminal justice realm at least) the improved the status of human rights.

Prompted by a new internationally popular President and with no clear, unifying indigenous discourse emerging, the move to 'conventional human rights wisdom' was inevitable, particularly as the human rights movement found a particularly receptive environment. Looking at the situation from above, the Council of Europe's experts intensified interrogating and monitoring human rights. The government was committed to penal reform and with good intentions reduced the prison population noticeably through amnesties. Other reforms included a moratorium on the death penalty (although there is a poverty of data with regard to which prisoners serving life imprisonment had been previously sentenced to death), access to the various EU bulletins for prisoners, improved visiting rights and a new Penal Code.

C Becoming a 'Good State'

Russia now possessed some of the characteristics of a 'good state'. In accordance with the Russian Federation's commitment to the protection of human rights of prisoners, the most recent legislative changes to affect prisoners and prison conditions are Orders 1652-k and 1650-k of 25 October 2001 and 675-k of 7 May 2002, when the Ministry of Justice created the Human Rights Division within the Prison Directorate for Pre-trial Centres and Prisons. Under these provisions 84 Assistants for Human Rights Protection in the penal system (*Pomoshchnik Prava Cheloveka*) operate in each of the *oblasts* (regions) under the supervision of a new Division for Human Rights. The year 2004 marked another key moment of penal transition: Russia's penal system changed its name. The Chief Administration for the Implementation of Sentences (GUIN) became the Federal Service for the Implementation of Sentences (FSIN). Headed by Yuri Kalinin, a long-time advocate for penal reform, FSIN is responsible for the penal institutions and the Criminal Inspectorate, which works with offenders serving non-custodial sentences, offenders on parole and released prisoners.

Moreover, true human rights commitment demanded a rejection of the Soviet past, thus strengthening Russia's position as a 'good state'. Yet, this came in the form of increased centralisation of the penal system amid greater regulation of all public spheres, rather than in a process of reconciliation and addressing past harms. Human rights were, therefore, associated with standardising the penal system to international norms. Thus, penal cosmopolitanism has provided for a ready-made mode of 'acceptable' penal governance and emerged just when Russia was seeking closer relations with the international community. While it was necessary for Russia to embark on a course of transition committed to improving human rights, there were some limitations, namely the indigenous modes of penalty that fell into obscurity in the late 1990s. The remainder of the chapter presents a thematic discussion of the effects of Russia's criminal justice transition as understood by senior prison personnel who are responsible for delivering Russia's new penal priorities 'from below'.

V FAILED PENAL SOCIETIES AND TRANSITIONAL JUSTICE FROM BELOW

While there is a presumption that human rights should exist, how it is organised and how it is understood by those administering it has yet to be empirically researched in-depth. The purpose of presenting the data here is not to challenge the philosophical basis of human rights, or to negatively critique the remarkably positive steps Russia has taken to address its poor human rights record. Indeed, regardless of the society in question, there will always be opposition on the part of some towards human rights. While these findings may not be typical, they certainly suggest that human rights could be construed as a double bind; that to obtain greater political status in the transnational environment, the local 'from below' perspective is at risk of becoming subverted and to a degree silenced. It is hoped that what follows will re-animate a discussion of transition but within the context of how 'failed' states become 'good' states through enforceable regimes of knowledge that are Western in origin.

A Human Rights as a Code to Follow

The first theme that emerged concerns how human rights came to be objectified as a code of conduct; utilised to measure complaints rather than as a set of prisoner entitlements or a philosophical approach. That human rights have become Russia's new penal narrative was further evidenced in the responses to a series of questions about how the terms 'human rights' and 'prisoner rights' were understood. It became immediately clear that the language of policy no longer conveys Soviet discourse and instead speaks to the 'norms of international law'.[30] This marked a paradigmatic shift regarding what constitutes good prison performance: '[w]e ensure that no faults with practice were found'.[31] It was explained to me that European as opposed to Russian modes of professional values have been introduced.

[30] *Ugolovnii Kodeks Rossiskoi Federatsii*, 'Rossiskaya Federatsiya Zakoni' (Moskva, Ministerstvo Yustitsii, 2006).

[31] Interview with Officer A.

When probed as to what constituted European values, they were expressed as targets to meet, performance goals to reach and bureaucracy: '[d]evised to manage the extra paperwork generated from the human rights monitoring missions'.[32]

For some respondents, human rights talk reached faith-like proportions, constructed around an assumption that *successful prisons* were found in nations that believed in human rights. And with Russia now in ratification of a number of international human rights treaties, there was an implicit assumption that the penal system was acceptable and modern. Yet, in response to an author question: what does it mean to believe in human rights in Russian prisons? the following themes emerged.

Some respondents understood human rights as having a normative orientation of welfare and protection. Undertaking assessments of conditions underpinned the positive custody of prisoners:

> [w]hen we get told that progress is being made, I feel good ... we are getting somewhere.[33]

> Human rights are important because they are about promoting care and humanity for inmates. Yet we are seeing more control ... we have to be seen to meet norms.[34]

Prison personnel understood that adherence to human rights signified progress and something to feel positive about. Nevertheless, we also see emerging here human rights as a means of control and governance through international values, which forms the third theme.

B Human Rights as International Accountability

One of the most remarkable aspects of transitional justice is that it gives promise of new democratic responses to crime, while seeking to indigenise new ideas about punishment. Earlier, the chapter stated that there was a period in the late 1990s of partial indigenisation of penal knowledge in Russia. In the 2003 study, many respondents viewed human rights as a form-filling exercise to be pushed along desks rather than to be experienced in the cells:

> It is about the maintenance of standards. It's about ensuring we meet norms. We get sent EU bulletins now in Russian. We know the outcome that needs to be achieved.[35]

> My job is to check the bulletins to see how many of our prisoners complain.

[32] Interview with Officer A.
[33] Interview with Officer C.
[34] Interview with Officer C.
[35] Interview with Officer F.

> I am the Human Rights Assistant. My job is to fill in the necessary forms.[36]

There was some resentment expressed that human rights were not created by Russian prison authorities for Russian prisoners, and that distinctiveness was neglected in favour of human rights compliance. This forms the fourth theme, whereby the increasing influence of Western NGOs and the practical knowledge and Western expert views written into training manuals and texts on improving penal management led not to engagement but to some anti-Western attitudes.[37] This raises the question of human rights as a form of cultural imperialism.

C Human Rights as Western Decadence

Western penal systems have been critiqued for developing a 'punitive turn' that has led to punitive mentalities emerging in the penal sphere and to the evaporation of rehabilitation and care narratives. In this study, a punitive turn was not in evidence. Instead the transition was directly associated with external moves to Europeanise Russian society, which was viewed from below with disdain and frustration:

> The Westerners come here to tell us how bad our system is and then leave.[38]

> What does Europe know? Why should we listen to you? We are in Siberia; we have our own Siberian human rights [laughs].[39]

> I am annoyed that these are not our changes. We cannot possibly be like Europe, but I feel the pressure.[40]

One senior official added:

> Why do our prisoners need the EU? If you look at EU bulletins, it's Britain, France and other countries where more prisoners are reporting grievances. Hardly any prisoners from Russia are mentioned. Our prisoners are fine. I can't stand NGOs. They just say all the negative stuff. They are righteous. They base their reports on an entirely aggressive and negative approach.[41]

Interviewees made clear that for a modern penal system to be properly so-called in Russia, then the penal system must legalise human rights and translate European values into policy. It is also ironic that the view of human rights as bureaucracy was not entirely lost on personnel who, for

[36] Interview with Officer K.
[37] A Coyle, *A Human Right's Approach to Prison Management: A Handbook for Prison Staff* (King's College London, International Centre for Prison Studies, 2001).
[38] Interview with Officer H.
[39] Interview with Officer H.
[40] Interview with Officer K.
[41] Interview with Officer M.

the most part, had trained under the Soviet system. The irony here is that the Soviet system was underpinned by an exceptionally powerful 'Russian' ideology. Nowadays, the human rights bureaucracy is administered efficiently, but with those administering it feeling culturally adrift. Cynical responses also dominated as respondents found it difficult to explain their understanding of human rights. Paradoxically, these occurred alongside expressions of ambivalence and a growing acceptance:

> When I think of human rights, I think of the rights of the prisoners. But I must admit I don't really know what that means because we never focused on prisoners' rights in our society. Now we have to listen.[42]

> I have forms to fill in every day. Do they have enough water? 'Yes'. Do they have minimum standards? 'Yes'. I cannot answer 'no' to any questions or we are in trouble with the regional chiefs. I see human rights as a list of criteria to meet.[43]

The responses moved from cynicism to detachment, and exposed a paradox that the penal system must meet Western standards (regardless of whether the 'turn' is towards punishment or rehabilitation) if it is to define itself as 'modern' penal system:

> You ask us about how we understand punishment in the new post-Soviet society. I never ask myself these questions. I get depressed. We have failed in our punishment. We got it completely wrong and we now have a big mess, a terrible system.[44]

> We used to have a principle of imprisonment. It was work and education. We've gone through great change. They tell us that human rights are the most important thing to concentrate on. When we talk or read about prisons we discuss the human rights issues and not much else.[45]

From detachment came acceptance. Although human rights norms were difficult to understand, the consequences of human rights violations were clearly understood: 'Ideas? ... they're not important. We must deliver human rights'.[46]

D Human Rights and Defiance about the Past

We have seen how human rights discourse is viewed by some as a commodity. For others, guarding their old identities was of primary importance to minimise what appeared as an inferiority complex. A defiant nostalgia was evident in the remote prisons:

[42] Interview with Officer R.
[43] Interview with Officer N.
[44] Interview with Officer N.
[45] Interview with Officer M.
[46] Interview with Officer C.

> It wasn't all that bad in the past [laughs]. We did have some good work practices. Work was so important for prisoners.[47]

The following striking comment was made:

> I was born in the Gulag, my father was a prison guard as was his father. I feel that human rights are good for the West but not here. What do you Europeans know about us? We are not European. I can't define human rights because it is not something that we created. The Gulag was ... great. I am a patriot for that penitentiary system.[48]

In summary, there appears to be a significant contradiction in how the transition in criminal justice in Russia is understood from below. On the one hand is Russia's commitment to 'enforcement'. On the other hand are the prison personnel who simply do not understand what human rights mean. Without the bearers of the message believing or understanding the message and its social and philosophical dimensions, how can true penal transition occur? Not only has human rights conventional wisdom come to be viewed in the abstract, but also other former Soviet satellites are hearing the message and being shamed into improving practices. The human rights import—as a mode of interrogation—might be evidence of a *symbolic identity penal politics* that has weakened avenues for bottom-up approaches to inform the international implementation process.

VI CARCERAL DISGRACE AND THE IMPORTANCE OF SHAME

There are clearly tensions between enforcement of human rights norms and providing for better human rights understanding. Yet, human rights do appear to be winning. The benefits of embarking on a course of transition that is committed to human rights are clear. Human rights standards have exposed degrading conditions and abuses when otherwise there would be silence. The government has been held to account over appalling conditions and prisoners' rights are judicially recognised. Often, national jurisdictions operate prisons at their own discretion, so to impose a system of regulation provides standards against which national laws can be scrutinised, as testified to by the 2006 US Supreme Court ruling that the US government must recognise the Geneva Conventions in relation to those held under US control in Guantánamo Bay.[49] In Russian prisons, there is a positive prospect that an active engagement with extending human rights standards to human rights understanding will follow the positive evocation for human rights. Moreover, as we have seen from the *Kalashnikov* case,

[47] Interview with Officer F.
[48] Interview with Officer F.
[49] *In re Hamdan* 126 S Ct 2981 (Mem) US, 2006.

human rights have created a new actor in the form of the Russian prisoner whose position has changed now that s/he is armed with international rights.[50] So, too, might prison officers change their view of themselves as members of an internationally recognised profession of guarding.

I do caution, however, that the harmful effects of globalisation within criminal justice should not be overlooked. The international legal community has made it more difficult for countries in transition to grasp ratification of treaties as something much more than simply a proxy or implementation . I concur here with transitional justice scholars that the domestic effects of fitting technicist, universal standards into local measures are counter to transitional justice.[51] And I conclude that in the face of the evidence, human rights as the principle mode of transitional justice offers limited possibilities for understanding the economic, cultural, social and political contexts surrounding imprisonment in Russia.

It could further be said that failure to meet international norms leads to *carceral disgrace* the basis of which is an acute sense of a prison's failure in its duty of care to its charges that can escalate into international discreditation and shaming. While no society in the world can be said to have a perfect penal system, in those societies which have been discredited for having 'failing' systems, their prisons operate against international human rights standards. 'Russia's disgrace', said Officer A, was its prison system. Carceral disgrace produced different levels of emotionality in respondents. Shame, defensiveness and confusion led to apology, fused with a need to engage with manuals for best practice, performance indictors and targets. There was an engagement with penal propriety as though human rights offered some sort of carceral respectability in the global political community, which in turn could re-align political order and diminish global differences. Indeed, it is the burden of carceral disgrace that looms large for all penal systems in transition.

One explanation why the 'from below' transitional justice perspective is so perplexing in this case study is that the Russian context suggests that transitional justice from below requires a focus not just beyond the state, but also in the state sub-systems on the ground. Penality in Russia developed from a subverted and supplanted legal discourse on crime. There was penal artifice that evolved into penal fantasy where loyalty, honour and glory replaced demonisation of the offender. Prisons represented social and cultural progress and through their economic role, were in some sense ingrained into a mental and cultural psyche that placed the highest value on collectivism, a common purpose and an optimistic future. Hence the

[50] European Court of Human Rights, *Chamber Judgment in the Case of Kalashnikov v Russia.* Press release issued by the Registrar, 15 July 2002, available online at http://www.echr.coe.int/eng/Press/2002/july/Kalashnikovjudepress.htm (visited 4 April 2006).

[51] See Teitel, 'Transitional Justice in the New Era' (n 1 above).

social memory of society was held back by 'interpretive denial' where the state argues: 'this is not what you think, this is different from what it looks like'.[52] Given that the penal system was a mechanism that galvanised culture to crime, how has it become attached or detached from individual and social memory in Russia? The normative question of dealing with past atrocities through social commemoration is vitally important to ensure that societies move forward and not backward.[53] However, the globalising politics of human rights has meant that transitional justice in Russia has moved away from bringing in all the actors who experience imprisonment. While there has been NGO and academic activity aimed at social remembering at various periods in the last 30 years, Russia's social remembering has not fully formed. Instead, with human rights committees having authority to adjudicate violations that are brought before them, a society such as Russia can be first shamed and secondly controlled in ways that were not possible in the 20th century. And if we factor in that human rights are tied to very idea of individual rights, its application raises many more questions for Russians who grew up in a society constructed not around the self but around the collective.

VII CONCLUSION

Although Russia's penal transition has improved conditions and raised standards, it has also served to blur rather than to clarify the most pervading questions that should be asked of prisons in transition: Why do we punish? And what do modern, democratic prisons look like? It would appear that prisons in transition come to be engaged with a symbolic penal politics predicated on a linear progression from national to universal concepts of penal punishment; a penality of homogeneity rather than a penality of difference. Ironically, Russia's transitional justice has created weak 'narrativising spaces' for social reflection and has also left structural frameworks intact because transitional justice is a normalising standard of conduct that forms the basis for the expansion of global civil society.

The standards of civilised societies share a common position with the standards of transitional justice—each seeks to improve society through an authentication of institutions and norms. But political, economic and social advancement reached through authentication has a problematic application in penal systems because it is those states that operate in positions of political dominance that process the authentication of less powerful states

[52] S Cohen, *States of Denial: Knowing about Atrocities and Suffering* (London, Polity Press, 2001).

[53] J Braithwaite, *Restorative Justice and Responsive Regulation* (Oxford, Oxford University Press, 2002).

and their criminal justice systems. It is succumbing to the process of authentication (styled as 'working together') as much as it is the outcome that is the salient prerequisite for better transnational relations. While it is intended to reduce difference, human rights enhances subordinate status because it is based on liberal power, and on the regulation of economic, political and social practices. If those administering human rights—those from below—fail to meet norms, the political legitimacy of a country is targeted as failing (Turkey's delayed accession into the European Union is one example of how political discreditation arises in part from carceral disgrace). And for prisons during transition, change is all the more problematic because the relations of political power in these unseen and unfelt institutions shift constantly.

Over the last 50 years, human rights regimes have expanded, but the design and promotion of human rights weigh heavily on states in transition. I do agree that the international community must be extra vigilant with regard to the implementation of transitional justice. Those first steps following transition are critical in establishing the future trajectory of societies. As a way of internalising norms and developing a democracy that establishes clearly what is acceptable, human rights can engage all sides with noticeable benefits. However, in making decisions to develop human rights in a society like Russia, the design and promotion of human rights could be improved so that their effects are not simply presupposed. The international community should seek to carefully and cautiously consider the ways in which Russia's obligations to effect a humane penal transition are felt on the ground. That way, human rights can improve the lives of those it is meant to help.

Index